It was a pleasure for me to re
GUARD, especially since, to .
ample of leadership at its best, and I have used him and his leadership qualities in lessons on the subject in seminars I have held. Don's extensive research on him and his context in both Persia and Jerusalem is evident throughout.

Using Nehemiah, the bodyguard, as a model, he bolsters his material with examples from the lives of great historical leaders, many from the Bible, including Jesus. He also includes supporting citations from current respected leaders and authors who have written widely on the subject. He packs the book with illustrations from his own ministry, frequently "confessing" with transparency some of his own positive and negative actions that have proven corrective in his leadership journey.

Throughout, however, the character, thinking, agonizing, planning, decision-making, and actions of Nehemiah constitute the glue that holds all the material together, the thread that runs through the leadership "tactics" that furnish the framework for the book. Inserted at key points are the "Food for Thought" sections that encourage readers to ask and answer pertinent questions concerning the qualities of leadership that have just been discussed with an implied nudge that they might apply to their situations.

What impresses me most about the work is its shire breadth. I have never seen so many facets of leadership treated in one work. Don hardly leaves a stone unturned in covering the principles, best practices, likely pitfalls, and both good and bad roads to success and failure. I have no hesitancy to recommend LEAD LIKE A BODYGUARD to both novice and seasoned leaders, convinced that all of us can profit from its reading and the application of Nehemiah's leadership tactics.

By the way, I am proud to claim Don as an alumnus of Johnson University under my presidency.

— **Dr. David Eubanks**, *Former President of Johnson University in Knoxville, Tennessee*

In *Lead Like a Bodyguard: The Bold Leadership of Nehemiah*, Dr. Don Mark Hamilton completes two feats in one – he presents the rich history of the Israelites in a compelling, engaging manner while also calling attention to the timeless leadership principles demonstrated by Nehemiah. However, Dr. Hamilton does not stop there. He then breaks these principles down, using examples from his own life to show how readers can apply these principles to increase their influence and accomplish goals. Anyone interested in being the type of leader God can use to advance His kingdom should read this book.

— **Dave Ferguson**, *Lead Visionary for NewThing and Author of Hero Maker & B.L.E.S.S.*

"*Lead Like a Bodyguard* captivated me from start to finish. Dr. Hamilton's vivid storytelling brings Nehemiah's journey to life while skillfully translating ancient lessons into relevant leadership takeaways. This book delivers an inspirational blueprint for leading change with courage, overcoming adversity, and achieving the impossible. A motivating must-read!"

— **Joseph R. Myers**, *Lead Narratologist, Consultant | Speaker | Best – Selling Author*

During my nearly 50 years of ministry, I have come to appreciate leadership tools written by those whose wisdom has been fine-tuned and tested by decades of service on the front lines of the kingdom. Gimmicks and trends come and go, but the combination of scriptural principles contextualized by a real-life leader never fails. My good friend Don Hamilton has been there and done that, and his book *Lead Like a Bodyguard* reflects 40 years of quality leadership using Nehemiah as his biblical foundation. His inspiring, personal, and practical lessons will serve any leader group within the church, non-profit organization, or corporate setting well. Well done, Don, well done.

— **Dr. Tom Jones**, *New Thing Network Church Planting*

LEAD
LIKE A
BODYGUARD

FIFTY TWO TIMELESS
LEADERSHIP LESSONS

Dr. Don Mark
Hamilton

Lead Like A Bodyguard
Copyright © 2023 by Don Mark Hamilton. All rights reserved.
5016 Shetland Court
Mechanicsburg, Pennsylvania 17050
Phone: 717-439-9608

No part of this book may be used or reproduced in any manner whatsoever without written permission, except in the case of brief quotations embodied in critical articles and reviews. For more information, e-mail all inquiries to info@mindstirmedia.com.

Published by MindStir Media, LLC
45 Lafayette Rd | Suite 181| North Hampton, NH 03862 | USA
1.800.767.0531 | www.mindstirmedia.com

Printed in the United States of America.
ISBN-Paperback: 978-1-961532-86-1
ISBN-Hardcover: 978-1-961532-87-8

Table of Contents

Preface xiii
Acknowledgments. xv
Foreword. xix
Introduction xxi

Part One: The Bodyguard's Story

Chapter One: Living The Life 3
Chapter Two: A Lesson From History 9
Chapter Three: Nehma's Story Begins 15
Chapter Four: The Tragedy Unfolds 19
Chapter Five: A Challenge Accepted 29
Chapter Six: A City In Ruin 33
Chapter Seven: A Midnight Ride And A Crucial Meeting . . 37
Chapter Eight: The Walls Go Up 41
Chapter Nine: No Good Work Goes Without Opposition . . 43
Chapter Ten: Project Complete, Time For A Party 53
Chapter Eleven: Long-Term Results. 55

Part Two: Lead Like a Bodyguard

Bodyguard Tactic One: Choosing the Unlikely Candidate . . 61
Bodyguard Tactic Two: Those Who Answer the Call . . . 67
Bodyguard Tactic Three: There's a Job for Everyone . . . 73
Bodyguard Tactic Four: Never Say Never 79
Bodyguard Tactic Five: Leaders Take the Heat 85
Bodyguard Tactic Six: Beware The Success Syndrome . . . 91
Bodyguard Tactic Seven:
If It Were Easy, Everybody Would Do It 99
Bodyguard Tactic Eight: Hearing The Hard Thing . . . 105
Bodyguard Tactic Nine: The People Who Got You There . . 111
Bodyguard Tactic Ten: Celebrate Early And Often . . . 117
Bodyguard Tactic Eleven: A View For The Long Haul . . 121
Bodyguard Tactic Twelve:
Communicate Thoroughly And Often 125
Bodyguard Tactic Thirteen:
Don't Forget To Honor Your Team 131
Bodyguard Tactic Fourteen: Tell Me The Story 135
Bodyguard Tactic Fifteen: Servant Leadership 141
Bodyguard Tactic Sixteen: The Fear Factor 145
Bodyguard Tactic Seventeen: Create Your Team. 151
Bodyguard Tactic Eighteen: Be A Good Follower . . . 157
Bodyguard Tactic Nineteen:
Leadership Teachers Are Everywhere 163
Bodyguard Tactic Twenty: Resource Your Team. 167
Bodyguard Tactic Twenty-One: Find a Need and Fill It . . 173

Bodyguard Tactic Twenty-Two: Nothing Is Ever Easy . . . 181
Bodyguard Tactic Twenty-Three: Timing Is Everything . . 185
Bodyguard Tactic Twenty-Four: Take a Chance 189
Bodyguard Tactic Twenty-Five: Deep Roots 195
Bodyguard Tactic Twenty-Six: Make Informed Decisions . 199
Bodyguard Tactic Twenty-Seven: Assembly Required . . . 205
Bodyguard Tactic Twenty-Eight: Homework Required . . 209
Bodyguard Tactic Twenty-Nine: Concentric Circles . . . 213
Bodyguard Tactic Thirty: Go For The Heart 217
Bodyguard Tactic Thirty-One: Be A Catalyst 223
Bodyguard Tactic Thirty-Two: Washington's Secret . . . 227
Bodyguard Tactic Thirty-Three: Start a Movement 233
Bodyguard Tactic Thirty-Four: Give Them Tools 237
Bodyguard Tactic Thirty-Five: Always A Foe 241
Bodyguard Tactic Thirty-Six: Don't Lose Your Cool . . . 247
Bodyguard Tactic Thirty-Seven: Decisive Action 253
Bodyguard Tactic Thirty-Eight: Define Your Enemy . . . 257
Bodyguard Tactic Thirty-Nine: They Want To Know Why . 263
Bodyguard Tactic Forty: Step Up! 269
Bodyguard Tactic Forty-One:
Keep The Main Thing The Main Thing 275
Bodyguard Tactic Forty-Two: Trouble Within 281
Bodyguard Tactic Forty-Three: Watch Yourself 287
Bodyguard Tactic Forty-Four:
Servant Leadership Revisited 291
Bodyguard Tactic Forty-Five: Why We Do What We Do . . 299

Bodyguard Tactic Forty-Six: Give It A Rest! 305

Bodyguard Tactic Forty-Seven: A Lesson From Archery . . 313

Bodyguard Tactic Forty-Eight:
Tackling The Change Monster. 319

Bodyguard Tactic Forty-Nine: Making It Last 327

Bodyguard Tactic Fifty: Close The Loop 333

Bodyguard Tactic Fifty-One: Movin' On 339

Bodyguard Tactic Fifty-Two:
Looking Back And Moving Forward 343

For Gail

We all want to leave a legacy. GAIL DID TOO. Before Gail Hamilton went to live with Jesus on October 18, 2018, she spent the final years of her life empowering women who were starting churches in South Asia. By partnering with *Enhance** and *Stadia,* Gail's family continues to work as catalysts to provide funds that **resource, equip, and empower women** to start thriving churches in South Asia. They would love to invite you to make an impact in this way!

Ten percent of the proceeds of every book will be donated to www.gailsgirls.org, an organization that supports under-resourced female leaders, providing them with vocational and biblical training and necessary items to help transform impoverished towns and villages in South Asia.

Thank you for your support.
The Hamilton Family

Preface

My first master's degree class was on leadership. The professor gave us a reading assignment including the Bible book of Nehemiah and a book study on the same character. The experience was enlightening to a young pastor still wet behind the ears, making Nehemiah one of my leadership heroes. I embraced the lessons gleaned from this ancient master and, over the years, made them my own.

A few years later, I developed a strategic planning model based upon Nehemiah, which I followed throughout my entire ministry of forty years. I still use this model in both my professional and personal life, and it has served me well. I always thought the material would make a helpful leadership book along with many other lessons from Nehemiah.

Nearly two years ago, a local publisher asked me to produce a "pocket" mini-book on Nehemiah. When I started the book, I realized I would rather write a full version using stories from my life and that of fellow comrades in leadership positions across the world. *Lead Like a Bodyguard* is the result of that endeavor.

The ancient bodyguard has guided me well through the years, and I hope you might discover the same assistance within the pages of this book. Thank you for taking time to read it.

This work contains many personal stories of my experiences in life and leadership. I realize the passing of time sometimes clouds our memories and that each of us experiences life through different lenses. It is my intention to relay these stories as accurately as possible. If I have missed important information or misinterpreted a situation, please accept my apologies ahead of time. I have done my best to share experiences of myself and others in such a manner that others can gain wisdom and insight. Thank you for giving me a touch of grace.

Acknowledgments

Any work of this magnitude is the result of thousands of influential people contributing to the author, far more than one can recall. I am indebted and thankful to all of you. In this document, I'm able to acknowledge only a few, so if I missed you, please forgive me.

To my wife, Gail, who passed five years ago. Thank you for putting up with my dark sides while enjoying our adventure together. As much as any other person, you made me who I am. You were an amazing woman, and a precious wife and mother who loved your God.

To my parents, Ralph and Genell. Dad, I'll never forget our conversation when you told me, "Don, you can accomplish many great things if you are willing to work hard and long enough, learning all along the way." You were so right! I learned vision from you. Mom, you held your hand on my head many adolescent nights while I vomited after consuming way too much alcohol, yet you never condemned me. I learned grace from you, which ultimately made my life pleasant and filled with friends. Neither of you ever seemed to doubt that I might turn out okay. I hope I've made you proud.

To my children, Andrea, Lauren, Kristin, and Rachel. You are the joy of my life and my greatest cheerleaders. I learn from you every day as you keep telling me, "You can do this, Dad!" Your mother would be so proud of you. Thank you.

To my sisters, who are life mentors, Pat Roberts and Hamilton Koebrugge. We've somehow put up with each other all these years and remained close through it all. Thanks for saving my bacon so many times and giving me such wise counsel time and again. Oh, the good times! I am immensely proud to call you my sisters.

To my friend, business partner, and most ardent supporter, Lori. For nearly forty years, we served, learned, laughed, and cried. Thank you. This book would never have been written were it not for your constant encouragement and kicks in the seat of the pants. We have made a good team, and we're still growing.

To my good friend and Lori's husband, Rick. You have given me wise advice and constant support through thick and thin. You believed in me to complete this work when I did not believe in myself. Go Blue!

To my nephew and dearest friend Joseph. My fellow Peregrino, we have enjoyed much, learned much, and laughed precipitously our entire lives. You are my faithful friend and fellow traveler. We're still figuring it all out while having a little fun along the way. May we never stop growing.

To my close friends and comrades, Tom, Brent, John, and Bert. Bourbon and cigars on me. We have experienced much life together and perhaps made some difference for the Kingdom. What an honor to serve alongside you. Thank you for being my friends.

To Paige and Lynne, precious friends since college, which is way too long ago. You have stood by me through thick and thin. We have enjoyed so many wonderful experiences and I always know where I can go for solace and advice. Let's take a road trip! Thank you.

To Cabot and Darcy. You continue to show me what it means to be an authentic Christian. Cabot, those late-night discussions in the gravel parking lot on Good Hope Road came to fruition, my friend. It's been a good ride.

To the elders of Vibrant - a Christian Church. What an interesting and exciting journey we experienced together. Thank you for being there for me, holding my feet to the fire, listening to my crazy ideas, and teaching me godly shepherding. You've had much influence in my life, and together we made a difference in people's lives.

To Jim and Jim. You both got me started on this journey. I hope I've done you proud.

Foreword

by Kevin Harrington

Original Shark from ABC's hit TV show *Shark Tank* and Bestselling Author

As a public figure in the entrepreneurial space, I have worked with some of the most powerful business leaders in the world. They are admired for their leadership characteristics recognized by most people, including strength, communication, strategy, and the ability to seize opportunities. But beyond those traits, true and effective leadership also demands depth of character, a commitment to service, and the courage to protect and uplift others. This is why *Lead Like a Bodyguard* by Dr. Don Mark Hamilton hits home. As someone who has spent decades building businesses and evaluating countless leaders on *Shark Tank*, I respect the profound insights and practical wisdom that Don brings to these thought-provoking pages.

Lead Like a Bodyguard is not just a book about leadership; it is a masterclass on how to lead with the heart of a protector and the mind of a strategist. Drawing inspiration from the Book of Nehemiah, the bodyguard-turned-leader from ancient Biblical times, Don offers a rich tapestry of lessons that are as relevant today as they were centuries ago. Nehemiah's story is a compelling example of how an ordinary individual can rise to extraordinary challenges, a theme that resonates deeply with my own life experiences.

Like many self-made entrepreneurs who built their success from scratch, breaking barriers and overcoming obstacles required a certain leadership mindset not possessed by many.

Don Hamilton's extensive research and personal anecdotes weave together a narrative that is both enlightening and engaging. His ability to draw parallels between ancient leadership principles and modern-day applications is nothing short of brilliant. Whether you are a seasoned leader or just starting your journey, this book will equip you with the tools to lead with integrity, resilience, and compassion.

One of the key takeaways from *Lead Like a Bodyguard* is the emphasis on servant leadership. In the competitive world of commerce, it's easy to forget that true leadership is about serving others and creating an environment where everyone can thrive. Don's insights remind us that the most effective leaders are those who prioritize the well-being of their teams, inspire trust, and lead by example. This is the type of win-win scenario I strive for with my team and in any business relationships I cultivate.

Moreover, the book's practical approach, with its "Food for Thought" sections encourages readers to reflect on their leadership style and consider how they can apply Nehemiah's tactics to their own lives. This interactive element makes the book not just a read, but a valuable tool for personal and professional growth.

As the inventor of the infomercial and a lifelong entrepreneur, I understand the value of clear, actionable advice. *Lead Like a Bodyguard* delivers just that. It is a guidebook for anyone looking to make a significant impact, whether in the boardroom, the community, or their personal life.

I am honored to pen the foreword for this remarkable book and to support Don Hamilton in sharing these timeless leadership lessons. May readers find inspiration, courage, and wisdom within these pages, and may you lead with the boldness and dedication of a bodyguard.

Lead Like a Bodyguard
The Bold Leadership of Nehemiah

Introduction

It was 1963 on a warm Dallas day when the motorcade rolled through the city. The presidential limousine led the procession, followed by an open limousine carrying the governor of Texas with his wife in one seat and President Kennedy and the first lady in the rear. The motorcade was headed to the Dallas Trade Mart for a luncheon.

Suddenly, the sound of gunfire pierced the air, and in a matter of a few seconds the right rear side of the president's head was splattered all over the car and Jacqueline. As Mrs. Kennedy, in shock, reached down to retrieve her husband's skull pieces, a Secret Service agent leaped over the trunk of the car, pushed her down, and covered both the president and first lady with his body. Unfortunately, the agent was two seconds too late. The thirty-fifth president of the United States was dead.

Clint Hill was the bodyguard who placed himself between the president and harm's way. Clint was a second-generation Norwegian who grew up with adoptive parents, loved sports, joined the Army, and became a counterintelligence agent. After serving in the military, Hill joined the Secret Service and ultimately became one of the president's bodyguards. He protected five U.S. presidents and was Jacqueline Kennedy's personal guardian for many years. Soon after Kennedy's funeral, Hill was honored at the White House for his courageous acts on the fateful day of President Kennedy's death.

Being a bodyguard is all about life and death; the stakes are high, especially with influential political leaders. Anyone who chooses this line of work has a profound sense of protection. Their whole world revolves around two matters: keeping someone safe and upholding the honor of the protected. From monarchs to political leaders, bodyguards have always played a significant role in their lives.

In the fifth century B.C., there was another famous bodyguard whose sense of protection and honor moved him to become a high-profile, accomplished leader. His name was Nehemiah.

Nehemiah was a Jewish exile living in Persia who advanced through the ranks to become the chief bodyguard for the most powerful leader in the world, King Artaxerxes. The Persian Empire enveloped much of the known world and a large portion of its population. Nehemiah's specific position was cupbearer to the king.

Cupbearers were bodyguards responsible for the purity of food and wine brought to the king's table. Since poisoning was a common method of eliminating a political foe, this kind of protection was critical to a monarch's survival. The position also involved staying on top of possible threats and preventing them before they happened.

Like Clint Hall, Nehemiah's life revolved around protecting the king and his honor. Bodyguards knew secrets of the kingdom and guarded the honor of their employer. They must be willing to place their own lives in danger to perform their job, something Nehemiah enjoyed. Every time the cupbearers sipped the king's wine or tasted his food, they laid their own life on the line.

Cupbearers were also bodyguards who often became well-acquainted with their boss to the point of friendship and mutual respect. Nehemiah was one such servant. His relationship with Artaxerxes and his wife was more than that of an employer and employee; he and the king were friends.

Though living in exile from one's homeland was not ideal, a few, like our bodyguard, held important positions of influence. Nehemiah had the ear of the king and led a large team of servants responsible for the king's table.

However, one may adapt to new circumstances thrust upon them, but many never lose sight of their homes. Such was the case with this man. Nehemiah loved his homeland and his people no matter how comfortable his life was in Susa, Persia.

One day, Nehemiah received news from the motherland that its most important and sacred city was in ruins, unprotected and shamed. His people were harassed, helpless, and living in disgrace. The walls of the great city of Jerusalem had been destroyed long ago by Babylonian King Nebuchadnezzar, who overran the people and destroyed its defenses and the mighty walls that protected its citizens.

The report devastated the cupbearer. His people had a proud heritage dating back centuries when they were called out to be God's chosen people. But they turned against their Creator and suffered dire consequences. Nehemiah wept for days, pondering the fate of his beloved Jewish nation. His entire life revolved around protection and honor, and now his people received neither.

The terrible news set a fire inside the Jewish bodyguard's soul. Something must be done. The walls must be restored, and his people's integrity renewed, and he was to be the man to lead the effort.

Thus began the story of the bodyguard who became the restoration vessel for his people, a savior of sorts. A marvelous tale unfolded of superlative leadership from an unlikely source—Nehemiah, the bodyguard to the king.

Nehemiah returned to his home and orchestrated the rebuilding of Jerusalem's walls in only fifty-two days, a historical accomplishment. The account of the bodyguard turned leader is inspiring and instructional for anyone called to lead others. Nehemiah became a master leader from whom we can learn many critical leadership lessons.

Join me in the following pages to learn ancient leadership wisdom from the bodyguard who restored integrity to his people. Every bodyguard must learn special tactics to properly execute their job. In the following pages we'll recount the story of Nehemiah and explore fifty-two bodyguard leadership tactics.

Part One

The Bodyguard's Story

Chapter One

LIVING THE LIFE

The old priest, Eli, and his friend, Nehemiah, sat in the large portico looking out onto the plaza where a mass of Jerusalem's citizens were celebrating their monumental accomplishment. The once dilapidated walls and charred gates protecting the city once again stood proudly guarding the city of David. The two men sipped wine and treated themselves to fresh dates and almonds as they discussed the past year of their lives.

"You sure know how to throw a party," said the old priest Eli to his distinguished host. "The Holy City hasn't seen this much excitement since Solomon dedicated the temple way back in 957. Thank you for making this possible. You've delivered something to these people they haven't possessed in years. You brought hope back to a hopeless city. Bodyguard, you have become a formidable leader and I have learned many wise lessons as I watched you orchestrate this project. Your name has proven true, Nehma. God has indeed comforted this city through you."

"Well," said Nehma, "when you live in the court of King Artaxerxes and pour the royal wine, you see a lot of partying. Persians love to party, and my boss looks for every chance to throw a good soirée. I'm glad you are enjoying it.

"But you know, Eli, I am beyond amazed that we are experiencing this moment. The whole year has been beyond the scope of my imagination. I have been a servant to a powerful man for years. Though I managed a large staff, I never even considered a role like this. My job was as high as it gets in the Persian Empire, aside from the monarchy. But God had something else in store for me. Now, I've led an historical accomplishment and restored not only the wall of the Holy City, but dignity to our people. I learned that an unlikely person can be used in profound ways by God. I learned many valuable leadership principles throughout my life, more than I realized, and now all those experiences have produced fruit. Sometimes leadership is deeply fulfilling.

Eli, I learned how to lead a movement. God can use anyone to do amazing feats if they are open to his leading. The disgrace and travails of my people back here in Judah rarely entered my mind. I was far too busy running the king's kitchen, attending to his needs, and scanning every possibility of intrigue. I've witnessed crazy stuff you wouldn't believe. It seems like someone always wants to take a shot at the throne. But rebuilding this wall in a mere fifty-two days tops anything I've ever seen. Honestly, I never thought this moment would happen. When I started, I felt totally inadequate. Who was I to think I could lead such a massive effort? Our God seems to choose some unlikely people to accomplish his purposes, and I'm one of them.

OUR GOD SEEMS TO CHOOSE UNLIKELY PEOPLE TO ACCOMPLISH HIS PURPOSES.

I've experienced more scary moments in the past year than all the rest of my life combined. Indeed, this celebration is nothing short of a miracle to me, Eli."

The priest nodded with a smile, for he too had witnessed much of the exhausting process. He had watched an unknown leader with big ideas roll into town, stand down every detractor, every enemy, and every challenging moment while accomplishing something generations could not muster. Eli thought, *This was a daunting project, and Nehma is the one who could make it happen.*

Nehma continued his story. "I also savored the good life living in the court of a wealthy family, enjoying the services of many servants and slaves."

Nehma paused for a moment, gazing into the distance and contemplating his home in Susa.

"What's your favorite food, Eli?"

The holy man stroked his beard and replied with a dreamy look in his eyes, "I love a good mutton sandwich made with fresh-baked wheat bread and some strong mustard sauce. Add a couple of glasses of good red wine, and you've really got something. You're making me hungry, Nehma!"

"Eli, where I come from, there are fields of grazing sheep as far as you can see. We have every spice you can imagine from all over the world and storage rooms stacked to the ceiling with every kind of cheese there is. And it's all served on gold and silver platters spread on the finest linen tablecloths. My master owns thousands of skins of wine from every region in his vast kingdom. It's a far cry from the place you call home.

"Every Sabbath, I walk among the astounding royal gardens considering my lot in life and thanking my heavenly Father for blessings I could never have imagined. I recline on my satin sofa, sipping fine wine and enjoying juicy dates as I read scrolls from the king's vast library. Back in the royal city, the cupbearer is a highly respected and influential man, and I am lucky to hold that position."

Eli nodded in agreement. "We're lucky you came here."

Nehma smiled and nodded in agreement.

The two leaders gazed over the party taking place below them as they continued to ruminate about the events of the past three months. Eli gently massaged his tired hands. The high priest hadn't done that much physical labor in years. His ordinarily soft, smooth hands were now a little beat up from hauling and stacking the large stones needed to rebuild the Sheep Gate on the northeastern side of the city. His thumbnail was black after the not-so-skilled builder hammered it while trying to reattach a hinge to the massive wooden door.

The wealthy old clergyman lived in an expansive home by Jerusalem standards, and it stood between the work of fellow priestly leaders, Baruch and Meremoth. Like in any town, large ornate homes represented wealth and social status. Eli was a well-known fixture in the ancient city, a man of status.

Nearly everyone in town was worn out and sore as the project progressed. "Argh" was a frequent exclamation as people like Eli, who rarely wielded a hammer, missed the intended destination and landed on a finger. More than one foot bore bruises from a stray stone landing on it, and blisters were a fact of life for nearly three months. Several inexperienced builders spent much of the time laid up from falling off a ladder or exhaustion. It isn't easy hauling seventy-pound rocks up a rickety ladder, and there were thousands of stones to be toted. For these folks, this was an undertaking of epic proportions, which was why no one before Nehma had the chutzpah to tackle the problem. Their new leader from the king's court was indeed a unique person. In proportion to the entirety of a society, only a few dared to step forward when the call to leadership sounded. Nehma was one of the few.

ONLY A FEW STEP FORWARD TO THE CALL OF LEADERSHIP.

The wall rebuilding had worked its way counterclockwise around the perimeter of the old city until the tradesmen adjoined the fortress near the high priest's home. Men and women of all social strata applied their elbow grease to this project, a testament to the bodyguard's leadership acumen. An effective leader finds jobs for those with various competencies and time commitment levels. The entire event was a site to behold.

AN EFFECTIVE LEADER FINDS JOBS FOR THOSE WITH DIVERSE COMPETENCIES AND TIME COMMITMENT LEVELS.

Chapter Two

A Lesson From History

Nearly 160 years earlier, King Nebuchadnezzar of the Babylonians declared war on Israel, and his powerful forces swept down from the north and almost flattened the entire country, including the most important location, Zion, the city of Jerusalem. Nebuchadnezzar was one of the most famous monarchs of history, the first northern king to soundly defeat the Egyptians at Carchemish, which was a battle of epic proportions. Every Jew in Palestine heard stories of his march across Judah down to the old Philistine city, Ashkelon, one of Israel's nemeses during the reign of revered King David. Just as their young King David defeated the giant Goliath, the Philistine kingdom now bowed to Babylon. The whole world bowed to Babylon.

From the Babylonian king's perspective, their armies were under the direction of Marduk, god of the heavens and earth. The King of Babylon was the deity's agent of expansion, destined to control all the kingdoms of the world. Nebuchadnezzar, an inspired builder, saw to the construction of the impressive Ésagila temple complex containing the massive ziggurat, which was built and rebuilt by successive Babylonian kings. His city included the famous, or infamous, Tower of Babel and the magnificent Hanging Gardens the ruler built for his wife, Amytis. It was said she missed the greenery of her home far to the north in Media. Their marriage sealed a peace pact between the Median and Babylonian Empires. This metropolis was the pinnacle of ancient religion. Nebuchadnezzar ruled the largest kingdom in the known world, wielding influence from Egypt to the Far East and Greece. Everyone would eventually bow to Marduk.

Ancient writers testified that King Nebuchadnezzar was not only a triumphant conqueror but was a master builder. He was tolerant of other religions and was a devout person. Hebrew writers paint a different picture of a stubborn, hard-hearted monarch set on ruling the world, even if by force. It makes sense that if a foreign conqueror destroyed all you knew and loved, you would not give him glowing reviews.

From the Jewish point of view, it appeared that Marduk's plan was working. Babylon was one of the most famous cities in the world, and every Palestinian quivered at the mention of Marduk's conqueror, Nebuchadnezzar.

Along the Babylonian king's path of destruction lay Zion, the city of David, surrounded by walls nearly forty feet high and eight feet wide. The Jewish capital existed long before Abraham, the father of their culture, settled a few miles south and west of the Holy City in a place called Hebron. In those days, a Canaanite tribe occupied the area known as Jebus until King David of Israel conquered the city and made it his own. The home of Judaism was one of the oldest cities on earth and was fraught with a backdrop of wars and unrest.

Nebuchadnezzar assaulted the city twice, and the second time his siege lasted almost a year and squeezed the population until they were powerless to defend themselves. Many citizens ran as fast as they could to numerous nearby lands, while those left in the city nearly starved to death, including the king. Once the inhabitants were decimated, Nebuchadnezzar sent his army to destroy the city and eventually the temple of the Jews built by their ancestor, King Solomon.

How could anyone ever undo the deeds of King Nebuchadnezzar? But God specialized in the impossible.

GOD SPECIALIZES IN THE IMPOSSIBLE.

Solomon's Temple was conceived by a man after God's own heart, David, but completed by the warrior king's son, who was said to be the wisest man ever to live. He was immensely wealthy, and the entire Western world came to his doorstep for advice and wisdom. Solomon's Temple represented the zenith of his wealth and power and the success of this tiny nation on the world scene.

An entire culture was nearly wiped out because of their foolishness. Nehma and his compatriots could now see the panoramic history of their people, and it wasn't a pretty sight. They had been freed from enslavement by Moses, conquered their territory through Joshua, and solidified by the greatest ruler in their history, David. Like the history of many prosperous countries, their success and wealth made them soft and vulnerable. The pagan people of the region were no longer enemies; they were an integral part of their society. Young men and women freely intermarried with Canaanites, and Jewish business owners broke Sabbath laws by buying and selling goods on their holy day. Success and wealth have a way of polluting even the noblest of causes, and hindsight is often wiser than foresight.

But a few faithful God-followers still existed, and Nehma was one of them. The entire portrait of his people disturbed him to the core. *What idiots we have been!* he thought. *We had our chance and blew it. Our people are at God's and this pagan king's mercy.* Good leaders owned not only their own shortcomings but those of their followers as well.

QUALITY LEADERS TAKE RESPONSIBIITY FOR SHORTCOMINGS.

The Jewish ordeal was precipitated by young King Jehoiachin, who became monarch at eighteen years old. Like too many fledgling leaders, the Jewish king was full of himself and decided he did not need to bow to the most powerful man on earth, Nebuchadnezzar. Big mistake! He refused to pay tribute to the guy who ruled the world and was taught a painful lesson. Don't mess with Nebuchadnezzar.

Ultimately, the entire fortification and the holy temple were dismantled stone by stone. Vicious Babylonian soldiers destroyed the fortress and burned every gate in the city to the ground. Nebuchadnezzar left the city in utter ruin and disgrace. The once proud "children of God" were now the scorn and laughingstock of the world.

Prophets like revered Moses predicted the fate of Israel hundreds of years before it happened. He told them that although God would treat them kindly, with grace and infinite patience, the fickle nation would inevitably betray their deity and suffer the consequences. Those who studied history knew this to be the fate of so many kingdoms and powerful leaders. As they say, "Power corrupts, and total power corrupts totally." It was not those who aspired to worthy causes but those who enjoyed the fruit of success and its excesses who tumbled down the mountain of success into the valley of despair.

BEWARE OF THE SUCCESS SYNDROME.

Meanwhile, the brilliant Babylonian general force-marched the prominent citizens, including teenage King Jehoiachin, 900 miles back to the ancient city of Babylon. The defenseless Israelites were left to the mercy of numerous regional enemies who relished subjugating God's people. Many generations ago, the Jewish nation entered Canaan, routed the local tribes, and took control of their "Promised Land." Old grudges died hard, passed from generation to generation, and if the opportunity for revenge presented itself, enemies were pleased to oblige.

Chapter Three

Nehma's Story Begins

Eli spoke up. "Nehma, you have done so well. You are an extremely competent leader. Who would have dreamed that the walls of our beloved city would ever stand again? God works in marvelous ways. Please, tell me how this all came to be. Share some of your leadership secrets. So many of our citizens grew from your example, knowledge, and training in the art of making things happen. Your leadership wisdom is valuable."

"Very well," said the exile-turned-hero. "I will recall for you how the Master Builder used a simple, quiet person like me to marshal a broken people and accomplish the Lord's will. I am surprised and honored to be in this position, but it wasn't easy, and I've learned many lessons the hard way through this process."

Eli thought to himself, *A humble leader is a beloved leader that many people will follow. And Nehma is one of those people.*

PEOPLE LOVE A TRULY HUMBLE LEADER.

Nehma began. "As you know, by Divine Providence, I rose through the ranks of King Artaxerxes' household to become his cupbearer. Neither food nor drink touches my Lord's lips without first touching mine because, as you know, poison is a favorite murder weapon used to extinguish monarchs. Art's father learned that lesson the hard way. Nothing even enters the kitchen or storage rooms without my inspection and consent. I oversee a staff of about one hundred and fifty servants and work closely with farmers and tradespeople throughout the region. Being a cupbearer is a high-stress position, considering the king's life depends on my job performance. One screwup and you are as dead as the king who drank the fatal elixir.

"I'm not sure why God chose me for this position since I don't consider myself particularly outstanding among men. At the same time, I felt humbled and honored but shaking in my sandals. Leading this undertaking was the scariest thing I'd ever tried, but it seems that anytime someone steps in front of the crowd there is a fear factor. Leaders willingly place themselves in full view of others, making them easy targets for all kinds of arrows. Sometimes shots come from those you thought to be allies; others pierce you from a secret, hidden source. Either type is painful.

LEADERSHIP IS A SCARY PROPOSITION.

"I endeavor to maintain high standards of integrity and conduct, and the office I occupy in Persia is built solely upon trust, and in that manner, I have the king's ear. Many emperors have suffered treachery by gathering unsavory characters and foolish advisors around them. I'm sure you remember well what started all this mess in the first place, Eli. Our foolish ancestor, King Rehoboam, refused the counsel of wise advisors and turned to his band of stupid young drinking buddies for advice. Our nation's unity was destroyed, and the slippery slide to the ruination of our people began. A successful leader gathers a group of experienced friends and supporters who will give them advice, and they should take care who they choose for this role. If their counselors are honest, their guidance may not always be what the leader wants to hear.

"I've watched many so-called leaders come and go. Some tried to do everything themselves and micromanage their workers. Those leaders only possessed a small handful of high proficiencies, of which one or two stood out. The rest of their abilities were normal to slightly above average at best. When they spread themselves too thin, they burnt out and fell by the wayside. Those pseudo-leaders failed to recognize that it was those who supported their cause that would determine its success. They wasted the valuable talents of those below them. The more quickly leaders discovered and practiced this principle, the more rapidly they climbed the ladder of success."

Nehma continued, "My lord is a wise and benevolent sovereign. He does not require his subjects to bow to his gods but allows people like us to worship and conduct our religious faith as we wish. His open-minded attitude unlocked the door for his majesty to choose me, a Jew, for this critical position, not to mention his stepmother, Esther, still has considerable influence in the kingdom. Though the king's power is absolute, he recognizes and appreciates the cultural diversity in his realm.

"Eli, you know, I think God orchestrates every aspect of his will for our people, and it is remarkable to watch."

Nehma contemplated his story a few moments as he furrowed his eyebrows in thought. "My position allows me to observe how the king and his advisors navigate many consequential situations and policies. I've watched him navigate wars, internal conflicts, intrigue, diplomacy, and magnificent building projects. Artaxerxes is my leadership mentor. Influential people don't get that way by doing one stupid thing after another, and there is plenty to learn from anyone practicing quality leadership. How humorous of our God to create a partnership between a pagan king and his Jewish cupbearer. It is not necessary for one to be a follower of God to be a proficient leader. Without Artaxerxes, this place would still be a pile of rubble. Though many will credit me with this feat, the King of Persia stood in the background and made it happen. I've learned that faithful supporters quietly make a leader shine."

Nehma's attitude toward his boss revealed a critical leadership principle. The bodyguard's deference to the king fostered loyalty from the one positioned to provide assistance for his work.

> **GENUINE DEFERENCE FOSTERS LOYALTY FROM THOSE WHO CAN HELP A LEADER'S CAUSE.**

Nehma turned serious as he continued to explain the origin of his divine mission. "It was in December, our 'month of dreams,' my friend, when my brother and his friends from Jerusalem conveyed a disturbing report about our Holy City."

Chapter Four

THE TRAGEDY UNFOLDS

Hanani and Nehma had been close friends their entire lives. Under the guidance of Uncle Mordecai, both were men of integrity and high morals. They were fine-looking gentlemen who possessed natural athleticism and got along well with both their Persian counterparts and their own people. It was no surprise to anyone that Hanani and his comrades were chosen to journey to the Holy City and return with a report of the condition of their people back in the homeland.

Nehma explained the situation to Eli. "When Hanani and his friends returned from their expedition to Jerusalem, we gathered for drinks and conversation. My brothers and I remained close friends after our parents were murdered when we were just boys, and Uncle Mordecai saw to it that our relatives raised us. Witnessing your father and mother killed by ruthless people is about as traumatic as it gets. Still, the Lord provided for us, and the royal family took notice of our intelligence and athletic abilities early in our boyhood. Looking back on our lives, Eli, I can see that Yahweh had plans for us all along. Some of that plan included you, my friend, when my brother filled me in about meeting you and all the information you shared about our people.

"We spent an hour or so catching up, and then I eagerly inquired about the homeland. Hanani's countenance immediately sank like a rock in a pond, and I could tell he was disturbed and anxious about sharing his findings."

Hanani explained the situation to his brother. He had visited the Holy City and was astounded at what he found. "Brother, the place is a mess! We safely traveled through dangerous territory only to arrive at the decayed ruins of our city on a hill. As we entered the region, the land became parched and barren, as were our Israelite brothers and sisters. We ran across a brother trying to draw water from a nearly dry well. His eyes were as hollow and barren as the parched land, and he moved slowly toward the last refreshment he might receive from the once sparkling source of life."

Hanani spoke to the old gentleman and inquired, "Greetings, my friend! How goes it today?"

The worn-out soul gazed toward the obviously wealthy entourage with disgust.

"Are you here to steal more taxes from a poor old man? I've already given the king every penny I have and sold off my daughters to serve that wretched, wealthy, so-called Jewish brother a few miles down the road from here. They are providing him with wine made from the fruit of my vineyard! Well, I can tell you, if you are looking for more money, you've come to the wrong place. There is nothing left to take, so you might as well move on to the next poor sap."

The Tragedy Unfolds

Hanani and his entourage were taken aback by the poor gentleman. The bodyguard's younger brother continued, "Nehma, I was shocked by the less-than-gracious greeting but quickly realized this was only a taste of what was to come. I dismounted my donkey and approached the poor soul with my waterskin in hand."

"Sir, I am not here to take your money. To the contrary, I am here to see how we might help you and other brothers and sisters left here in the homeland. Please, take a drink. I am not here to hurt you."

The beaten-down farmer eagerly received the kindness offered and asked where we came from and where we were going.

"I felt this was the first bit of goodwill he had experienced in a long time, and his condition touched me deeply, brother.

"We chatted with our new friend, inquiring about the locals and how they were faring. None of it was good news, Nehma. These people had suffered a long time, as far back as they could remember, with no end in sight. The weary man of the land explained, 'There is no longer abundant life in Israel, only hardship.'

"We remounted and pressed on to our beloved city. At least we were warned now about what was coming, but one could only see it to believe it."

Eli looked at his friend as he bore his soul. "Hanani continued to describe the conditions in the city while it took everything in my power to keep from breaking down in tears. How could it have been? The situation was disgraceful. I was angry and embarrassed at the same time. We are the people of the one true God, and we're making Him look impotent and distant. This tragedy is our fault, not His. My anger quickly turned into repentant, sorrowful prayer, Eli. Before long, the news would turn into a calling that would change my life forever.

"Eli, have you ever risen from bed one day looking forward to a fruitful day of labor, a bit of laughter, perhaps some good conversation with friends, and then it all went sour in a flash?"

The old priest nodded in agreement. He knew what was coming.

"I expected a happy reunion with my brother, but when his lips spoke of the Holy City the air went out of my sails. I soon learned that Yahweh orchestrated the entire turn of events to place a burden on me that only my faithful response could lighten. I am glad that I have good friends willing to tell it like it is. For the next four months, I called out to the Lord and begged forgiveness for myself and my people. It was a long winter, Eli, but with the promise of spring I sensed it was time to talk with the king."

LEADERS NEED FRIENDS WHO WILL TELL IT LIKE IT IS, EVEN IF IT HURTS.

"Eli, I honestly don't know why the news of Jerusalem disturbed me to the core. I grew up in wealth and privilege and lived in comfort. Most people didn't know anything about my heritage, and I didn't want to open any possibly dangerous doors by volunteering the information. There are still plenty of 'Hamans' in the Persian kingdom who would like nothing less than to usurp my position and bring another disaster to our people. Artaxerxes remembers well that his own father, Xerxes, was murdered by schemers trying to take the throne. Sometimes, being royalty is not what it's cracked up to be, Eli.

"Though there would always be a chasm between the king and his bodyguard, Art and I became friends. I grew up in the king's court, so he knew me from when I was just a boy. The king was tolerant and inquisitive about other cultures and religions, mine included. He also has a good sense of humor. The Persians are more lenient than the ruthless Babylonians who tried to wipe us out. He and I hit it off quickly and spent many hours discussing kingdom, family, culture, and scientific matters. Artaxerxes is very interested in Jewish history and religion. Remember, it was the Israelites who many years ago befuddled and escaped their Egyptian captors. Persians and Egyptians are archenemies, so their interest in Jewish history goes back a long time."

Nehma continued, "And speaking of family, Esther, Artaxerxes' stepmother, still resides as the Queen Mother after her husband, Xerxes, was poisoned. Eli, you recall how our Lord used Esther to save our people the first time, but she was about to help do it again. God does indeed work in mysterious ways and for such a time as this, my friend!"

The older priest sat enraptured by his friend's story as he stroked his long white beard. He sat with his legs crossed and his flowing long linen robe covering his entire body. His turban looked like a giant flower bud ready to bloom that covered snowy hair acquired from many years of service. Eli's face was craggy from dozens of seasons of hot, dry Palestinian sun, and his eyes revealed the wear and wisdom of gathered years. For the first time, the old priest heard an entirely different side of Jewish history about their Persian conquerors. Perhaps they were not as brutal as he grew up learning from his parents and the other priests.

"I could hardly bear the news of walls lying in rubble and charred gates blocking the entrance to the destitute city. My people were living impoverished and demoralized lives. I could picture bands of outlaws pillaging my innocent brothers and sisters. How could the Land of Promise and the city of our ancestors become a pathetic joke to our enemies?

"You know, it's kind of funny, Eli. I was living a luxurious life in the king's palace. Once you've tasted the good life, it's hard to give up. Though I was still an alien in Persia, I made the best of the hand that was dealt to me. No matter the circumstances, one either moves forward or wallows in the dream of a past that can never be recovered. It seemed my future would be spent serving the king, living in Susa. I moved on from dreams of a home in my native land, and God was blessing me. A person who lives in the past forfeits the present and future."

Eli pondered his friend's words. "Nehma, the Lord prepared you and your circumstances your entire life. He was assembling all the parts of His plan even though you were completely ignorant of His scheme. Sometimes many years of experience and preparation come to fruition at just the right moment in time. Our sister Esther heard those fateful words from her uncle, 'Perhaps you have come to your royal position for such a time as this?' Though your heart was always ready, Nehma, perhaps your leadership skills were not. I am sure you learned many leadership principles from such a powerful man as King Artaxerxes, not to mention his advisors and Esther. God uses who He wishes to mentor our development. You were wise to observe and learn."

Nehma responded, "I suppose you are correct, my friend. God called me to a mission well beyond my scope of perception. I spent most of my life preparing for this one thing. More accurately, *God* spent most of my life preparing me for my new job description. It is clear that God equips those He calls upon.

THOSE WHOM GOD CALLS, GOD EQUIPS.

"The history of our people is dotted with stories of God preparing leaders for consequential missions. Our revered leader, Moses, grew up in a household where leadership decisions were part of everyday life. After the 'running from Pharaoh' incident, God tutored him for forty more years while listening to a bunch of whiny sheep. I doubt the Shepherd of Israel harbored grandiose visions of glory while herding a flock of someone else's unruly sheep, yet tending sheep taught him many valuable lessons that would come into play while shepherding an entire nation. That's a long training program,

Eli! And our conqueror, Joshua, sat under Moses's tutelage for forty years. Many people have been unknowingly groomed for greatness. I don't consider myself anyone great, but I understand and appreciate that our heavenly Father had a specific purpose for me.

"Though I made a good life in the new empire, I could not erase the home of my heart. The disheartening news from the homeland was not simply the story of some distant culture about which I had no concern. These people are *my* people. This land is *my* land, and the Holy City is *my* hometown. Their need was *my* need. Leaders take it personally, and that makes all the difference.

"Perhaps this perspective is a critical factor that separates leaders from followers. Leaders see needs others disregard or overlook and want to act. Others may see needs but lack the motivation to do something about it. In any case, Eli, I had to do something, but not yet.

LEADERS SEE NEEDS OTHERS IGNORE OR OVERLOOK AND THEY WANT TO ACT.

"As God would have it, I sat in misery for four months. I couldn't rid my mind of the horrible picture of David's city lying in waste. The ruin of Jerusalem ruined me. So I prayed and fasted and fasted and prayed, and then I prayed and fasted again. I can see now that God was preparing what was to come, but the waiting was excruciating. Solutions to big problems usually consume more time than we like, don't they? Sometimes we act too soon and create more issues than we solve.

IT WILL TAKE MORE TIME, COST MORE, AND TAKE MORE WORK THAN YOU THOUGHT.

I thank our gracious Father for granting me the patience to wait for His timing. I have learned that a person's willingness to act is paramount, but timing is crucial and requires long suffering to discern. A leader must take *calculated* risks.

"Finally, the day came, and I implored God to show me grace by making the king favorably disposed toward my upcoming request. I prepared myself to make the leap of faith required of any leader who wants to make a difference. What happened next was astounding, Eli. The king is a perceptive man, and when I delivered wine to his table, he noticed my downcast countenance. This was not the first time I had come into his presence disheartened in the preceding few months. But on this day, the king reacted because his wife, Damaspia, noticed my change in demeanor long before her husband. I think they probably had some discussions about me, Eli.

TIMING IS EVERYTHING.

"Then God did His thing. The most powerful man in the world inquired about my health and welfare. 'Why are you so downcast, Nehma? What is wrong? It is not like you to behave in such a manner.' I prayed through every step into the dining hall, right up to the moment I set the wine on the table. I was so afraid that my hands were shaking, and I feared I might spill the royal beverage. Red wine on the king's wife's white tunic would certainly not gain me any favor. But then I didn't have to broach the subject with the king. He initiated the conversation himself. What an answer to prayer! Now, I discovered that all I had to do was answer my king truthfully, and humbly ask for his assistance. God went ahead of me and made the way to fulfill His greater purpose. Artaxerxes immediately granted my request and permitted me to return to the homeland, along with all the necessary paperwork giving me the authority to rebuild the walls of Jerusalem. He even sent officers and cavalry to protect my entourage.

"This experience will always remind me that wise leaders pray, fast, meditate, and wait, expecting that God will answer their requests. The Almighty is pleased to oblige.

"Eli, let's have another glass of wine and toast again to the marvelous ways of our God!"

"By all means, Cupbearer of Israel!" proclaimed the grateful priest. "To Jehovah-Jireh, our Provider."

PRAY, FAST, MEDITATE AND EXPECT GOD TO SHOW UP.

The smiling pair then lifted their goblets once more. Eli proclaimed, "A toast to the king and the cupbearer, a partnership created in the heavens."

"Here, here!" affirmed Nehma.

Chapter Five

A CHALLENGE ACCEPTED

"For the next few months I prepared for the long journey to Jerusalem. There was much to do before my trek could begin. I needed to gather lumber, metals for hinges and latches, food and tools for the project. I recruited a team of builders and secured all the necessary paperwork to prove I was authorized by the king to make this journey. I traveled through hostile territory and across deserts and mountains with a large entourage of workers and soldiers. We would be four months en route to Zion and would encounter opposition along the way."

Nehma's prime opposition was a character named Sanballat, a Horonite governor of Samaria, Judah's archenemy. Jewish society had degraded so much that Sanballat's daughter was wed to Eli's grandson, making him a relative of the high priest, in direct dereliction of the Law of Moses. Not good! Sanballat, who was a Samaritan, consolidated a garrison of soldiers and built a temple on Mt. Gerizim, making his son-in-law a priest. The debate between Judaean and Samaritan Jews concerning where worship was to be conducted, Jerusalem or Gerizim, lasted for centuries.

Nehma continued his story to Eli, "My entourage stopped in Samaria for an audience with the wily, conniving blowhard of a governor. It appeared that the head honcho held all the strings, having numerous other tribal leaders in his pocket. He had no intention of allowing some upstart from Susa to claim part of his territory, and his partners in crime would back him whether they liked the old rascal or not. And that term is an understatement, my friend. Sanballat despises our people and savors nothing less than keeping us under his thumb. He was a formidable foe, but he lacked one resource, God!

"God never said it would be easy, did he, Eli? Easy it was not. But if it were easy, everyone would do it."

GOD NEVER SAID IT WOULD BE EASY.

Eli sat up and leaned forward as if offended by Nehma's comment, but the opposite proved true. He locked eyes with the cupbearer and stated, "You are right, my young friend. The task was certainly beyond my will and courage. I am one of a long line of so-called leaders who did nothing about our plight. Instead, I acquiesced to my fears. Even a pig gets used to living in the mud."

Nehma could see the pain in the old priest's eyes as he faced his truth. The new governor felt compassion as his elder bore his heart in the face of what could have been. "Eli, don't be too hard on yourself. Our fears and shortcomings get the best of all of us sometimes. It is not how we start but how we finish that counts. You are far from being swine. Sanballat already has a corner on that market." They both laughed, and Eli reclined and sipped his wine.

Nehma would get to know each of these regional leaders in not-so-pleasant ways. They tried intrigue, gossip, intimidation, and even brute force to stop him, but they never slowed the wall-builder down. This shrewd leader was on a mission from God, and no Horonite and his cronies were going to stop him!

Every Jewish child heard stories of the destruction of God's city and knew their grandparents' blatant disobedience precipitated their downfall. They also learned to despise local Canaanites due to their mistreatment of the Jewish community.

Chapter Six

A City In Ruin

Eli's life had been far removed from the luxury of Persian palaces. He and Nehma came from very different places and lifestyles. Though the cleric was born of a long line of priests, this position was not held in the same esteem as when the Davidic kingdom was at its pinnacle, yet the sometimes-wavering representative of Yahweh was an important man in the Holy City and wealthier than most.

Life in Jerusalem was tough for anyone. Food was always in short supply, as was water and nearly anything that made for a comfortable life. The entire region presently suffered a drought that took many lives and decimated many farmers' families while entire villages were dangerously close to starvation. Israelites had long since relinquished most of their pride as they walked with the daily reminder of their godless blunders that resulted in their living conditions. And there were always threats from the Horonites,

Ammonites, and Arabs of the region, whose racist views of Jews exacerbated their constant harassment of "God's people." Arrogant Canaanites relished making life difficult for the enemy who had once forcefully wrested the land from their hands.

"Where is your God now?" they taunted. "He must be on vacation, or perhaps He's deserted such a bunch of losers!"

"Everyone knows Gerizim is where you will find the *real* God, not this bleached carcass called Zion."

"Jerusalem is Marduk's toilet!" they jeered.

Growing up in Jerusalem was like living in a bombed-out, suppressed war zone with little hope of progress. Such difficult conditions ripened people to compromise their beliefs and social norms, and Eli's family was no different. His grandson married Sanballat's daughter, something strictly forbidden by the Law but easily set aside by generations who saw intermarriage as trivial and even advantageous. Eli may not have agreed with his grandson's decision but he knew the union might help his people. Many a Jew had succumbed to less-than-holy ways of living as the hard years of existence took their toll. Nehma would discover that the old priest made a few expedient choices with his enemies that might have lightened his load but were reprehensible to his God.

Sometimes Eli excused his actions. "We all make compromises, don't we, Nehma?" But the old fellow knew better. He had simply caved under pressure.

Nehma replied, "Yes, my friend, I suppose we do. In weak moments, many leaders compromise their values, but our mistakes do not have to define us."

Jerusalem residents lived a hardscrabble existence. It was hard enough just to get enough to eat, much less feed the family while taking time to build this wall. But there were standouts among them; one carried the name Baruch.

Baruch was an optimistic, energetic man who ardently applied himself to whatever he chose to accomplish. The vision and challenge of reconstructing part of the northern wall where so many armies had attacked the city was invigorating. He had no intention of anyone surpassing his handiwork on the portion of the Holy City with his signature on it. The confident priest attracted his gorgeous wife with his "can-do" attitude, and his kids often called their dad "the man of extremes." Baruch was your man if you wanted to get something done right.

Nehma discovered many citizens with the same attitude. The cupbearer turned construction manager considered the uncommon unity and willingness to work as a distinguishing mark of the Almighty's hand upon his efforts. He knew people like Baruch were critical to a restored wall rising from the rubble.

Restoring the walls around the ancient city was a monumental task, more Herculean than any mortal's puny efforts. It was just like Jehovah to recruit a novice leader in exile from a distant empire working for a pagan king. The king and cupbearer were fruitful allies for a God-sized project, not to mention contributions from the king's wife and from the Jewish hero queen, Esther.

Israel was an impotent nation compared to the colossal kingdoms that surrounded it. Egypt, Assyria, Babylon, Persia, Media, and the Greek city-states subdued significant portions of the world's population. The Jews were no competition for their military might and expansionist aspirations. In their heyday, the Persians ruled nearly a third of the world's population, but expansion ceased when the Greeks defeated Xerxes's army at Salamis. Earlier, Xerxes's massive military force defeated the Greeks, led by famous Spartan soldiers at the battle of Thermopylae, and then proceeded to Athens, where they burned the city to the ground.

Meanwhile, the Persian king foolishly decided to engage the much smaller but strategically superior Greek fleet at Salamis and was soundly defeated. Poor Xerxes returned to Persia with his tail between his legs, and after a few years of excessive spending and debased relationships, his council poisoned him. Such was one's fate growing up in the company of powerful, ruthless men. Artaxerxes's life behind closed doors was not as easy as it appeared to the average Persian citizen.

The new king took the throne with a great legacy of power, but now the kingdom was in decline and fraught with woes. Finding people he could trust, like Nehma and his stepmother, was like discovering diamonds in the backyard. Every leader needed a small band of trusted friends.

Chapter Seven

A Midnight Ride and a Crucial Meeting

As you know, Eli, in a few months, our paths crossed, and I would find myself entering the Holy City as the district governor and soon-to-be agent of restoration and honor to my people. The fortress walls of our city would rise from the rubble, the gates and ramparts reconstructed, and our people's disgrace would end.

"Eli, this celebration makes my heart soar like an eagle."

Tears flowed freely from Nehma's eyes and rolled down his tanned cheeks into a salt-and-pepper beard. Pure satisfaction encompassed his face, a far cry from the distress-filled look of anguish the king had witnessed many months before. Nehma was reminded of the song King David composed for the temple's dedication when he proclaimed that weeping lasts for a night, but joy comes in the morning. The christening of this wall was the dawning of a new chapter for the Jewish people.

But the project was not easy, and it took the skills of a master leader to make it a reality. It all began with a midnight ride.

"I rested for three days, during which I walked through the city and got a firsthand feel for the residents. I found my brethren going about their daily business, almost oblivious to the condition of their city. Generations had come and gone, and people succumbed to lethargy. Everywhere I looked, there were piles of rubble and charred wood. I thought, *How could they just let this mess sit here year after year? Where is their pride? Where is their honor? This situation is worse than I thought.* I began to formulate a strategy for this daunting project. No matter why this mess existed, I was determined it would not stay that way, and I would not leave this city until it changed.

"Late one night, I gathered a small group of men who had accompanied me from Susa, and we quietly rode around the city, frequently stopping to examine the condition of the walls and gates. We discussed what could be done, and I was advised several times that this was no small undertaking. My associates questioned if this ragtag population could or would rebuild their city. I quietly nodded, but I knew something they did not understand. The restoration was not my project or theirs; this would be the work of the Lord Almighty. He created the heavens and the earth; constructing a wall was not a major feat for him. My little miracle paled in comparison to the accomplishments of Moses or Gideon. One night just before I drifted off to sleep, I thought, *How amusing is this? Joshua tore down walls; I'm going to build one.*

"The next day I called a meeting of my influential brethren of Judah to reveal my mission and plans. I felt like Daniel about to enter the lion's den. The city was already buzzing with rumors about my arrival and the governorship of Judah. It was known that Ezra approved of my appointment, which bolstered my credibility. I knew not everyone would trust me, but I detected that all these folks needed was hope, a plan, and plenty of resources. I intended to provide all those ingredients while the Lord moved in the hearts of my countrymen.

"Nearly all the leading men of Judah attended my 'dream' session, some probably out of curiosity. I opened with a bit of my story and how I came to occupy this position. Many a wary eye and frowning face gazed on the newcomer with big plans, but I would not be deterred. I had already successfully stood before the most powerful man on earth. I explained how God used my brother to spark my calling and confirmed my passion and desire by making the king and his wife favorable to my cause. I appealed to our brethren's sense of pride and heritage and the welfare of their children and grandchildren. To my delight, the Lord again showed up in full glory, and my comrades' hearts were turned in my direction.

"They replied with one impressive voice, 'Let's rebuild these walls!'

"So began our fifty-two-day odyssey to restore this beloved city to its former glory. Long hours, back-breaking work, intimidation, and short tempers would be our lot until the final gate was hung."

Chapter Eight

THE WALLS GO UP

How appropriate that Israel's new leader chose this gate to start the restoration of the walls of Jerusalem. The high priest, whose name meant "God restores," would lead and become the first builder. Eli recognized the master builder's wisdom in choosing him and his fellow priests to start the project. He understood that the people would likely follow if the high priest and his peers were ready to build, and Eli was proud to lead the way.

Priests frequently used this entrance to the city. Through this passage, the holy men would guide the sheep they would sacrifice in the temple. The Sheep Gate was an important entrance, so it was wise that Nehma rebuilt this portal first. He intuitively understood that a big win and celebration early in a project is always a good thing.

CELEBRATE EARLY AND OFTEN.

Nehma was wise, knowing that it was effective to celebrate early but to keep the long view in mind. Centuries later, Jesus Christ, often called the Lamb of God, came and went through this gate near the Pool of Bethesda, where the Teacher performed one of His extraordinary miracles. Out of all the gates the Jews rebuilt, the Sheep Gate was the only one to have an official dedication ceremony. It was essential to recognize the first significant accomplishment of the restoration project publicly and continue communicating through the entire project.

KEEP THE LONG VIEW IN MIND.

Nehma learned to communicate thoroughly and often. Eli and his fellow leaders were proud to display their handiwork. Perhaps now, more people would get on board with this massive endeavor. People follow success, so it was an excellent strategy to make every win possible a "public" win. Nehma had observed the great Persian king hold an official celebration when the first of the 100 columns were completed on one of his signature structures. The Hall of 100 columns in Persepolis was a magnificent building.

COMMUNICATE THOROUGHLY AND OFTEN.

As with any large project, tempers occasionally flared, and Nehma was not immune. The project director was indeed a temperamental person. But he would persevere until the end.

Chapter Nine

No Good Work Goes Without Opposition

Within a few days, the ancient city resembled a giant anthill. A hive of workers from every community sector partnered to restore the walled city to its former glory. Nehma was indeed the catalyst, strategist, and equipper for this exciting restoration of such an asset. The exiled man with a plan not only enlivened and recruited people to his cause, the bodyguard made "his" cause into "their" cause—and he also laid out a strategy and provided the resources to get the job finished. Nehma had already secured something the people could not offer—physical resources. Timber and other construction materials were included in his original request to the king. He knew that people could not accomplish their job without resources only the leader could provide. These people had few assets at their disposal. Workers secured for a task and not given the necessary tools become disenchanted and demoralized. Nehma knew that you could not build a gate if you did not have the timber, hinges, and a good coach to make it happen.

A LEADER TURNS *HIS* CAUSE INTO *THEIR* CAUSE.

Nehma explained, "The process of equipping is often the step where leaders stumble."

A GOOD LEADER MUST EQUIP FOLLOWERS.

Eli laughed and said, "I haven't owned a mallet in years! You can look at my painful fingernail and see that."

Nehma prodded, "I think I'd keep your day job if I were you, Priest."

In a moment, Nehma's demeanor changed as their nemesis came to mind. One man caused more problems during this project than any other. Even when the needed resources and training were provided for the builders, the project was not without opposition and this person was the prime perpetrator.

Nehma now became more intense and shook his finger in disgust as he considered him. "It was then that the inevitable happened. Sam the Horonite, or Moronite, as I prefer to call him, and his crooked cronies started to oppose us aggressively. It seems to me that these dishonorable ingrates resisted us for two reasons.

First and foremost, they hate our people. All these tribes despise us Jews and do everything they can to oppress us. It has been this way ever since Joshua set foot on this soil. All these Canaanites hate us. Then those two idiots, Rehoboam and Jeroboam, exacerbated the problem and separated our people with their stupid, self-serving policies. If you ever want to learn how *not* to lead, check out those two miscreants! Of course, Sanballat is the beneficiary of their stupidity."

A flash of anger gripped Eli. "Yes, these godless pagans have suppressed our people for generations. And our feelings about them are no different than theirs toward us. We live in an uneasy truce, sometimes compromising our values to maintain peace. None of us were surprised when their leaders conspired against us. Sam and Tobias are treacherous men."

Nehma responded, "Yes, this is true, Eli, and there is a second reason they opposed us. A restored Jerusalem threatened their power and position. Tobiah's sweet deals with our merchants keep him well-fed and living the high life, as you can see from his enormous belly. Completing such a significant project would embolden our people, who had cowered under their rule for years. That is why we had to stand them down, and stand them down we did.

"Eli, you know as well as I that no significant project was ever completed without facing opposition. Outside opposition and discouragement within the ranks accompany grand plans. Therefore, I expected and planned for it, and these intimidators would not halt our project. The King of Persia never initiated a significant project without detractors. Though I do not possess his kind of power, the principle is the same.

NO SIGNIFICANT PROJECT GOES WITHOUT OPPOSITION.

"Besides, it wasn't truly *our* project; it was God's. So I called our people to pray, and the work continued until we completed the wall halfway. No malicious Ammonite or Arab was going to stop this work!

"Men like Tobias and Ammon are bullies. They boast and crow like roosters in the henhouse. People like Sam Horon intimidate and manipulate the weak to their advantage. But bullies and naysayers are afraid of steely determination and resolute opposition. We foiled their schemes when we posted guards and armed our citizens, and we sent those no-goods running with their tails between their legs.

"Then, as you remember, there was another kind of opposition. The combination of long hours of backbreaking work and external threats wore our people down. Fatigue and fear crept into the camp, and I realized that this could be a tipping point toward success or failure. There comes a time in any endeavor when progress slows, tempers get short, and morale wavers. King Artaxerxes calls this unsettling period the 'murky middle.' Emotions soar at the start of something big, and victory shouts accompany the end. But somewhere in the middle, fog envelops the scene, and people lose sight of the goal. My king talked about this phenomenon during nearly every significant initiative.

"Sometimes it starts with the leader himself. I was tired, frustrated, and ticked off when the commoner approached me with a disturbing but valid complaint that could derail the entire project. I complained to the Lord in no uncertain terms. 'Why did you call me to this godforsaken place with this bunch of hardheaded grumblers! I'm sick of this! I could be lounging on my portico with a bottle of wine, some delicious Egyptian cheese, pistachios, and a sweet, juicy orange served by my beautiful servants."

The wall-building leader had to manage his anger and frustration during this initiative. Otherwise, the person at the top could have been the one who derailed everything.

GET A GRIP ON YOUR ANGER.

Eli leaned back and put his feet on the seat next to him. "I must confess, Nehma, I did not think we would ever fully rebuild the walls. Our opposition seemed insurmountable. Many of our brothers and sisters were ready to throw in the towel. But you knew what to do. Kudos for that, my friend."

Nehma followed suit. "As I considered my course of action, I remembered when our people fled the Egyptians under our leader, Moses. They witnessed God's mighty hand wreak havoc upon their oppressors through the plagues. The people experienced deliverance from enslavement, but now the waters of the Red Sea stood between the new nation and freedom. It appeared all was lost. The recently freed slaves knew that the Egyptian army was pressing toward them. Fear seized their hearts and spread across the camp like a swarm of locusts. It was a pivotal moment when the Shepherd Leader stood before them and roused their courage. Do you remember what he said? 'Do not be afraid!' he proclaimed as he lifted his staff toward Heaven. 'Today, you will see the deliverance of the Lord. Be still.' The people listened, Moses raised his staff, and the waters parted.

"Moses showed me that when the tipping point that might lead to failure rears its head, the leader must act. So I called together the entire community and gave the same speech as the Master. I figured if it worked for him, maybe it would work for me.

LEADERS KNOW WHEN TO ACT.

"'Don't be afraid of them. Remember the Lord, who is great and awesome, and fight for your families, your sons and your daughters, your wives, and your homes.' I reminded them of their purpose, rallied the people to courage, and set them back to work. My hunch about Moses was correct. Recognition of a common enemy and a solid plan to defeat them is a powerful motivator. I also appealed to the workers as many of them had children. Parents will do just about anything when the welfare of their children is at stake.

A MOVEMENT NEEDS AN ENEMY.

An appeal to parenthood is a powerful motivator. I thought it also crucial to remind our workers why we were doing this. The *why* is always more potent than the *what*. Defending your family and your home is a powerful motivational force. So we solved the problem. From then on, half the people worked on the wall while the other half stood guard. Eli, the willingness and ability to pivot are critical for success. Nothing ever goes completely to plan, and if you cling to a plan when circumstances demand an adjustment you'll sink like the army of Pharaoh in the Red Sea."

THE WHY IS MORE POWERFUL THAN THE WHAT.

Eli retorted, "For a man who says he can't talk in front of a crowd, you sure proved yourself wrong! I'll remember that speech for the rest of my days."

"I suppose you're right. It was a pretty motivational speech," said the humble leader.

Then he returned to his story. "There would be more opposition to our quest, but I first turned to God for courage and wisdom each time and then went back to work. I did not let external forces deter me from my purpose. A leader must stay focused because when all is said and done a leader's gotta lead!"

Eli replied, "And lead you did, bodyguard! I remember those intimidating letters and the intrigue of our prophets who Sam

Horon and his conspirators paid off to have you killed or disgraced. But you remained steadfast and true. Moses would be proud of you, my friend. Please, go on."

A LEADER MUST STAY FOCUSED.

"When I was young, Uncle Mordecai taught me a valuable insight, and I've seen it play out many times. This axiom is tested and true and applies to Sanballat and his cronies. Uncle Mordi said, 'Nehma, always remember that a scared dog barks the loudest.'

"When you are under pressure and facing a formidable foe, you sometimes forget the powerful stance out of which you are operating. Sam Horonite can bark all he wants, but my authority runs up the line to the top. I held in my hands a sealed document from the absolute ruler of this territory, and he gave me credentials that trumped Sanballat's puny position. I had official documents, and soldiers under orders from my king stood behind me and my entourage. Sanballat is not a stupid man. He didn't lay claim to his power and wealth without making savvy plans and wise choices. Killing me would have brought the wrath of Artaxerxes down on his head, and I knew Artaxerxes could squash this chubby, conniving man like a Persian roach.

"But it doesn't end there, does it? My authority eclipsed even the ruler of the Persian Empire. He is the Lord Almighty, maker of the heavens and earth. This was his mission, not mine. Sanballat was intimidating, but I mustered courage the way I've always done it. Do you know what courage is, Eli?"

Eli thought for a moment, but before he could answer Nehma resolutely retorted, "Courage is fear that has said its prayers. It was prayer that cut the path for this meeting to happen, and it would be prayer that would pave the way to the next phase of the mission. I knew from whence and whom I came, and that story was rehearsed in my mind every time we faced opposition."

Nehma recalled another difficult moment. "But all our opposition was not from outside our camp. As you remember, our wealthy citizens were oppressing the poor and jeopardizing the entire work. I was surprised and disappointed that our brothers and sisters would exploit fellow countrymen to enrich themselves. And honestly, Eli, you weren't doing much to stem the tide of this travesty.

"I've learned that many a house has fallen due to forces from within. Just as I stood up to our enemies, I called our nobles and officials together and reamed them for their evil deeds. I called on them to return what they had stolen and extorted and then required them to take an oath upon it. Knowing the history of our people, I knew that internal intrigue is often the most discouraging kind of opposition. A strong leader must overcome the situation with patience, wisdom, and appropriate sternness. How many times did Moses's own people threaten their progress?

DON'T LET INTERNAL STRIFE BRING YOU DOWN.

"I recalled how one of Xerxes's trusted officials, Haman, plotted to disrupt the entire kingdom because of his hatred of our people. He devised a sly and ingenious plan to eradicate our entire race right under the king's nose, and Artaxerxes's dad fell for it. Haman was powerful and tricky, and he knew how to devise plans to feed his lust for more. When Uncle Mordecai learned of his scheme, he was beside himself. But my uncle was no pushover, and he wasn't stupid. His connections went all the way to the top—our beloved Esther. When he revealed the plot to our hero, she too was undone. But the two overcame their fear, anger, and insecurity enough to save the day. They gathered their thoughts and courage and implemented a genius plan, which worked! Eli, I couldn't help but think of my heroes, Esther and Uncle Mordecai, for wisdom and courage. The problem was solved.

"I've experienced that even good people will make compromises when their decisions that hurt others might line their pockets or fill their need for prestige. With our internal problems quelled, the work continued.

"Sometimes a leader can be his own worst enemy. Like our nobles, I too could have taken advantage of my position as governor. Being at the top affords one many fringe benefits, but it is not always wise to accept what is rightfully allotted to you." I decided I would make sacrifices like everyone else.

BE WISE ABOUT CLAIMING YOUR FRINGE BENEFITS.

Eli complimented his friend. "Yes, and for this, I admire you. I've witnessed many a noble or public official use their position to fill their coffers and live luxurious lifestyles off the backs of their people. Your integrity and willingness to stand shoulder to shoulder with your fellows endeared people to you. They love you, Nehma, and they are willing to follow you because of it. It was inspiring to see you carry stones and get your hands dirty, just like everyone else. I'll never forget the time you dropped that rock on your toe. Your consternation rang out through the whole town! You didn't ask us to do anything you wouldn't do yourself. You did not lord it over your followers because you are a servant leader. I think that is the best kind."

The self-deprecating man replied, "Thank you, Eli. It was God's project, and I was just along for the ride."

> **A GOOD LEADER DOESN'T ASK FOLLOWERS TO DO ANYTHING THEY WOULD NOT DO THEMSELVES.**

Eli countered, "Agreed, my friend. But nothing much happens if someone doesn't step forward to rally the people toward meeting a need. Good things get done because good people lead well. Nehma, you're the best one I've ever seen. You did not just build a wall. You built a community! You gave people hope when they were hopeless. You showed them the power of unity. You opened the doors that ushered them closer to God by seeing His marvelous work. You returned their self-respect and showed them justice. I think this was not really about a wall. It was about a people, your people and my people. May your story bring hope, guidance, and wisdom for generations."

Nehma responded, "A good leader sheds light on a problem and is skilled at motivating people to take action as part of a team. Leadership is ultimately always about people, not projects."

> **LEADERSHIP IS ABOUT PEOPLE, NOT PROJECTS.**

Chapter Ten

Project Complete, Time for a Party

In a mere fifty-two days, the untested Jewish leader-to-be had orchestrated an outstanding achievement in Jewish history. Jerusalem residents and dozens from surrounding regions were ready to celebrate. Nehma was wise enough to know that accomplishment without celebration was forgotten effort. He knew that his compatriots needed a date and a memorial that would become one of the Jewish victory stories told for generations. People needed stories of success to tell around the dinner table. The rebuilding of the walls would inspire Israel for millennia. The strong leader was right, and 3,000 years later the account guides people worldwide in how to rebuild their broken lives, organizations, and cultures, and Nehma became the stuff of legend.

STORIES OF SUCCESS LAST FOR GENERATIONS.

Eli sat down next to Nehma. The unlikely pair looked pleased, like parents watching their child receive an award.

Eli held up his glass of wine and proudly said, "To the city of our ancestors!"

Nehma followed suit and proclaimed, "Here, here, to the city of our ancestors!"

The two comrades listened to Ezra read the words of the Law. They heard a resounding "Amen, amen!" drift toward the heavens. Choirs sang, trumpets blasted, and joyful praise and thanksgiving filled the air like the roar of a lion. Finally, Nehma implored the jubilant partygoers to eat, drink, and be merry. Today would be the celebration of the century. Restoration of their dignity was one of the best gifts these people could ever receive. Great leaders were gift givers of the most critical kind.

Chapter Eleven

LONG-TERM RESULTS

It had been twelve years since the wall-builder was appointed governor by his gracious and helpful king. Now it was time to return to his work for the king, Artaxerxes. It was then that he learned a principle of the change process. As soon as the pressure was off, some people would return to their old ways. Nehemiah discovered change was a slow-moving boat headed upstream. The ship would drift back to sea if the captain did not stay diligent, providing inspiration, direction, and resources. Rebuilding walls was easy, but instituting lasting growth and development was another matter.

> **CHANGE IS A SLOW MOVING BOAT HEADED UPSTREAM.**

Long-term maintenance could wear down even the most decisive leader. If the person in charge did not address the root causes for the initial disintegration of the walls, the people sometimes ended up worse than before their restoration.

Sometime later, Nehma once again beseeched his king to return to the Holy City, and once again their partnership made his return visit possible. Artaxerxes was good to his friend and his people, and the Lord used this unlikely partnership between the king and his bodyguard to His good will and purpose.

When the governor arrived, he found the city once again a mess. He thought, *What is wrong with these people? Will they never learn?* Even his old friend, Eli, had drifted back into his former ways. It seemed that his job would never be finished.

He called out the old priest and, in no uncertain terms, said, "Eli, how could you let that pathetic Ammonite, Tobias, use the storeroom in the temple? Yahweh made it clear that no treacherous Ammonite or Moabite would ever enter the temple. I thought you were the High Priest of God and the leader of these people. Have you lost your mind? I advise that you get that unholy mess out of there now! Better yet, I'll do it myself. Now, let's get this place cleaned up." He made the priests and Levites gather all the supplies that allowed the temple to operate and neatly arranged them in the storehouse. The sad story was that the temple was once again not being used. Nehma was a forceful man and not one to mince words.

When the cat was away, the mice would play, and in the absence of Nehma, Jewish leaders returned to their old ways. Levites who were supposed to serve at the temple were forced to return to their properties and start farming again. They were not being allotted their portion of sacrifices and offerings, the temple showed signs of neglect, and every kind of commerce was being conducted in the city on the Sabbath.

When Nehma returned to the city, he quickly recognized the drift backward. His face-to-face chat with Eli set the old high priest straight. He vigorously rebuked the city officials. Finally, the bodyguard learned that many Israeli men married foreign women who led them astray from devotion to the one true God. This infraction put Nehma over the edge! He called this unholy crew to account, cursing them and beating a few. He yanked out their hair and made them take an oath to stop this godless practice. Sometimes, a leader must set things straight in no uncertain terms.

Some of Nehma's final acts as governor of Judah were defining moments in his leadership journey. The old cupbearer restored and updated many reforms and established systems to keep them intact. Nehma understood that he must systematically catalyze new growth or his people would end up worse off than before his intervention.

Then it was time to retire.

Nehma's job was full of ups and downs, highs and lows, and twists and turns. At its worst, it meant frustration, sleepless nights, and weariness. At its best, the work was ecstasy. Lives were changed, projects were completed, and lasting change was implemented. In the end, only the bodyguard could determine if it was worth the cost. But if he someday heard the words, "Well done," from the Only One who really counts, he felt it was worth the price.

Finally, Nehma ended the story where it began, on his knees. He once again beseeched his God, "Remember this in my favor, O, my God."

Like Nehma, may our leadership journey lead to nothing more nor less than the favor of our Lord, the Master Builder.

Every bodyguard must learn tactical proficiencies to properly execute their job. As we have read, Nehemiah's story reveals many of those strategies. Now it is time to explore fifty-two bodyguard tactics gleaned from the ancient wall-builder and bodyguard to the king.

Part Two

LEAD LIKE A BODYGUARD

Bodyguard Tactic One

Choosing the Unlikely Candidate

"Who was I to think I could lead such a massive exploit? Our God seems to choose some unlikely people to accomplish his purposes, and I'm one of them." —Nehemiah the bodyguard

The story of Nehemiah presents two unlikely characters who became influential leaders God used for His purposes. The first person presents a quandary for those who believe God only uses those who actively follow Him.

Artaxerxes, the King of the Persian Empire, 465-425 B.C., was responsible for restoring Jerusalem's temple and city walls, which was no minor job. It is sometimes characteristic of Christians to believe God only uses those who swear allegiance to Him, but history would differ. The Almighty did and does use all kinds of people for His goals, and many are credited as leaders.

Pharaoh is often cited as the first example of a prominent nonbelieving leader bidding God's work. The monarch in charge of Egypt's relationship with Moses and the Jewish race played a significant role in Jewish history. He was placed in juxtaposition with Moses when God repeatedly "hardened" his heart to reveal His power to both nations. God manipulated Pharaoh's natural will to make him act illogically in the face of culture-destroying plagues. The stubborn king's actions magnified his already prideful, pagan heart. In his mind, *he* was on God's throne, so the *real* Deity could easily stretch his already pride-filled soul to reject even the most convincing evidence that he was making foolish decisions. God often uses unwise, nonbelieving individuals to get the job done, and He is not particularly discriminatory.

However, the Orchestrator of history is not above using nonbelievers who wield *positive* impact to accomplish His will among us. Such was the case with King Artaxerxes of Persia.

I started my first ministry on Labor Day 1982 at a small church in Enola, Pennsylvania. Around three months after I arrived, I was asked to officiate a wedding for a friend of a friend at their home. I was excited and a little nervous since I would only know one person at the service, but was I ever in for a surprise! I arrived at the tiny home in the middle of town to find the yard filled with Harleys and bikers. I had no idea the couple getting married belonged to a local biker gang. Since I had recently returned from a few years as a prodigal and ran with unseemly characters, I wasn't too bothered.

I was introduced to the couple, and before long we were standing in the tiny living room packed with leather-clad, tattooed roughies. It was quite a sight. However, everyone was friendly and treated me with due respect. I thoroughly enjoyed the afternoon. After the wedding, my friend introduced me to another friend, and we hit it off quickly. We set a date for breakfast and started a forty-year friendship. At the time, my friend was not a follower of Christ.

Within a few weeks, in our small auditorium, I noticed my new friend sitting with a young lady in the back row. After the service, Bump introduced his daughter, Lori, who had been searching for a new church home. After the wedding, he called his daughter and told her he was picking her up Sunday to attend this cool new pastor's church, which he was confident she would enjoy. There was a non-Christ follower bringing his believing daughter to church. Bump never became a regular attendee of our church, but his daughter ended up on our staff for years. Meanwhile, he, his wife, and the entire family have remained good friends to this day. The Lord uses who He pleases to do His work!

THE LORD USES WHO HE PLEASES TO DO HIS WORK

Numerous others can be found throughout the pages of Scripture.

"This is what King Cyrus of Persia says: 'The LORD, the God of heaven, has given me all the kingdoms of the earth. He has appointed me to build him a Temple at Jerusalem, which is in Judah'" (Ezra 1:2 NIV).

Rahab was a pagan prostitute who saved several Israelite spies and ended up in the lineage of Jesus.

King Hiram of Tyre paid homage to Melqart, not Yahweh, but he was obliged to provide Solomon with wood, skilled labor, artisans, and advice on how to build the temple in Jerusalem. David and Hiram had been business partners and friends, and Hiram helped the Jewish king build his mansion.

King Herod was a ruthless murderer, yet God used his brilliant building skills to build the temple mount.

Even Jesus's close friend, at least everyone thought, turned out to be a spineless betrayer, yet his dastardly deed led to the Lamb of God being sacrificed for us all.

The other unlikely leadership candidate in our story is a Jewish captive who worked closely with the world's most powerful man. God showered Nehemiah with favor from his youth, though he was not in a prominent leadership role. Still, his position and standing were critical to the monarch. For many years, God nurtured a friendship and respectful relationship between the king and his bodyguard, knowing that he would make beautiful music through these two unlikely wall-builders.

Around ten years ago, our church started a second campus about fourteen miles from the original site. Our then youth pastor took the role of campus pastor and established the congregation in a small community south of Harrisburg, Pennsylvania. One of his first tasks was to make himself and the new congregation known in the community. Mike skillfully joined a local business association, befriended a local school principal and teachers, and attended community events, including football games and festivals. Mike and his new church quickly became a welcome addition to the region, often invited to speak and even handle the local school's movie night each month.

Many of these folks were not Christians, but they respected this young pastor and at times partnered with him for community-enhancing projects. Mike garnered the friendship of numerous "Hirams" who enhanced the mission of our church.

A local church is, in one genuine respect, simply another entity in the community, another organization among many. Nonbelievers often view these nonprofit, non-tax-paying entities with a wary eye. But the wise leader who gives other community leaders reason to admire his work will find partners in unlikely places.

Food for Thought

Would anyone in the community notice if your church went out of existence tomorrow? Why? Why not? (Be ruthlessly honest.)

Can you name numerous nonbelieving friends and business associates in your region? Where, if possible, do you draw them into your mission as candidates God might want to use to further your cause?

Read 1 Kings 5, which tells the story of David, Hiram, and Solomon.

Bodyguard Tactic Two

THOSE WHO ANSWER THE CALL

"Leaders are the rare breed who step forward to take charge when the call sounds."

In the twentieth century, there was a leader named Nelson Mandela. He was born in South Africa in 1918, when the country was deeply divided by racism and discrimination.

Mandela grew up in a small village and was educated in local schools. He later went on to study law and became an attorney. But he could not ignore the injustices he saw around him and became an active member of the anti-apartheid movement.

As the African National Congress leader, Mandela fought for the rights of black South Africans for many years. He was arrested and sent to prison in 1962, where he spent twenty-seven years behind bars.

Despite the difficult circumstances, Mandela never lost hope. He continued to lead the struggle for freedom and equality from prison, inspiring others to fight for justice.

In 1990, the government finally released Mandela from prison. The world watched as he stepped forward to lead the country toward a new future. He worked tirelessly to promote reconciliation and unity, becoming the country's first black president in 1994.

Under Mandela's leadership, South Africa abolished apartheid, and the country began to heal and rebuild. He worked to improve the lives of all South Africans, regardless of race, and his leadership helped to bring peace and stability to the country.

Mandela's legacy continues to inspire people around the world to this day. He showed that one person's leadership could significantly impact the planet, and he stepped forward to lead and changed the course of history.

The story of Nelson Mandela reveals a simple axiom of leadership: Somebody's gotta do it! A leader steps forward, even if sometimes by mistake. Take our friend Jane for instance.

There was a young woman named Jane who was timid and shy. Jane always preferred to blend into the background and avoid attention. She did not consider that she might have leadership potential but was content to provide support to other leaders.

Jane was at a company meeting one day, and the team leader asked for volunteers to step up and lead a new project. In a moment of confusion and hesitation, Jane stepped forward without really thinking about it. As soon as she realized her mistake, she immediately regretted it and wanted to take it back, but it was too late. She had been chosen to lead the project.

At first, Jane was convinced she was in over her head and would fail. But as she started working on the project, she found she was a natural leader. Her team respected her, and the fledgling leader was able to bring out the best in them. She organized them effectively and motivated them to work together to achieve their goals.

The project was a huge success, and the company was impressed with Jane's leadership skills. She received accolades and praise from her colleagues and superiors.

After that experience, Jane realized that sometimes taking a leap of faith and stepping out of your comfort zone can lead to unexpected opportunities and successes. She became more confident in herself and her abilities and stepped up for leadership roles in the future with more ease and enthusiasm.

Many years ago, I attended training sessions for certification to administer the DISC profile. About forty or fifty people participated in the class, most of them sent there by their companies. My friend Paige and I wanted to learn how to assess staff members and potential church planters. Leaders with specific personality profiles are more successful at initiating a new congregation than others. After several hours of teaching and class discussion, the facilitator divided attendees into several smaller groups of ten to twelve people.

He presented each group with discussion questions that my team enjoyed, though we were all strangers. After a while, the presenter told us each group must select a leader. Since none of us knew each other, I wondered how the exercise would work. After only a few minutes of discussion, one person said, "I think Don is the obvious choice for the leader of our group." To my surprise, everyone on the team agreed, and before I had time to consider the position I became the skipper of our little ship. I knew Paige could have done an admirable leadership job with this project as well.

Though I have led numerous endeavors throughout my life, I am not one to seek the position, yet many people recognize the leadership qualities of my personality more than I do. Interestingly, it took only a few short minutes and group discussions for me to emerge as the group leader by their choice. I was willing to step up and do whatever the facilitator called upon group leaders to do.

Often a leadership position is filled by an unlikely candidate, at least in *their* mind. Some assume that leaders are born, not made, thusly they automatically pursue opportunities to take charge. But often this is not the case. Leaders can emerge because others see the trait they do not. Other times, a problem or issue arises, and no one volunteers to take the helm until finally a future leader decides to do something about it.

This was the story of Nehemiah the bodyguard. Nehma held a responsible position in the Persian kingdom, but not one that required the skills and perseverance to embark upon a project of such magnitude as reconstructing the walls of a city 900 miles away. Yet Nehma received the call from his brother, who delivered disturbing news about his hometown. There is no indication the bodyguard ever had any inclination to return to the Holy City, nor can it be assumed that Hanani expected his brother to initiate plans for such a project. He was simply the bearer of bad news that had existed for over a hundred years. But Nehma sensed that surely somebody needed to do something, and it might as well be him. That is what a leader does.

The Battle of Gettysburg was one of the most significant battles of the American Civil War, fought between July 1 and 3, 1863. The Union Army, led by General George Meade, was able to defeat the Confederate Army, led by General Robert E. Lee.

One of the critical moments of the battle was the defense of Little Round Top by the Union's 20th Maine Volunteer Infantry Regiment, led by Colonel Joshua Lawrence Chamberlain. On July 2, the Confederate Army launched an attack on the Union's left flank, and the 20th Maine was ordered to hold the line at Little Round Top.

Colonel Chamberlain and his men were vastly outnumbered and outgunned, but they were determined to defend their position. They fought bravely, using the terrain to their advantage and conserving their ammunition.

As the Confederate Army pushed forward, Chamberlain's men were running out of ammunition. He ordered his men to fix bayonets and charge down the hill. The Confederate soldiers, expecting the Union soldiers to retreat, were taken aback, surprised by this bold move. The charge created chaos and confusion in the Confederate ranks, and they started to withdraw, leading to the victory of the Union Army on that flank.

The defense of Little Round Top was a turning point in the battle, and it is considered one of the most heroic actions of the Civil War. Colonel Chamberlain and his men's bravery and determination helped secure a Union victory at Gettysburg, which is still celebrated as one of the most outstanding examples of leadership and valor in American military history.

Chamberlain was another great leader who was born of necessity. By the way, like Moses, Chamberlain spoke with a stutter and had little military training. However, his leadership was rooted in solid character and deep convictions. General Grant also tapped his services to accept the Confederate surrender at Appomattox, where he famously instructed his troops to stand at attention and salute the Confederate soldiers as they passed in defeat. After the war, he became a four-time governor of Maine and president of his alma mater, Bowdoin College. Not bad for a guy who didn't set out to lead anything.

ALL LEADERS HAVE ONE THING IN COMMON: WHEN THE NEED ARISES, SO DO THEY.

Leaders emerge through a vast array of opportunities, but all possess one common characteristic: When the need arises, so do they.

Food for Thought

Do you believe leaders are made or born? Why and by what evidence do you hold your opinion? Are you willing to "go out on a limb" to respond to a need? What made you step into a leadership position?

The Apostle Peter was initially a leader who failed numerous times, yet Jesus saw something in the "Rock" that he did not see in himself, especially after the rooster incident. Read John 21 and consider leadership lessons from Jesus's and Peter's perspectives.

Bodyguard Tactic Three

There's a Job for Everyone

"An effective leader finds tasks appropriate for those with a wide range of various competencies and time commitment levels."

When I started leading a new church in 1982, I was on fire! A few years previous, I returned to the church after a few prodigal years, spent a year or so getting my act together, then off to Bible college. I left everything to make this move because I was on fire for God and ready to do whatever it took to get into ministry.

After five years, which included completing my bachelor's degree, a new marriage, and a brand-new church, I was ready to rock and roll. I landed in the Harrisburg, Pennsylvania area after my opportunity to serve in New York City fell through, but I was excited and convinced central PA was the place God wanted my new wife and me. Indeed, it was!

The church I served was small but committed to growth. In my naïveté, I assumed everyone was as devoted to the church as I was. Big mistake! Over the next ten years or so, I learned that people possess varying levels of commitment to anything in life, including the church.

Instead of analyzing each person's devotion, availability, and skill level, I thought all volunteers should give many hours and total dedication to every project, position, and financial endeavor of our church. When they did not, I became frustrated and sometimes angry. News flash: Welcome to the real world! As time elapsed, I learned my expectations were, well, selfish and unreasonable.

> **AS TIME ELAPSED, I LEARNED MY EXPECTATIONS WERE UNREASONABLE.**

Nearly every project or program a leader embarks on involves various levels of commitment, skill, and time constraints. A wise leader considers all those factors with each team member, paid or volunteer, and appropriates labor accordingly.

Leaders sometimes make false assumptions and use positional power to accomplish *their* goals rather than empower and resource those serving under their watch. The leader hopes for success, accolades, and advancement. Meanwhile, volunteers and lower-level employees can become pawns in a success game they want no part of.

A competent leader assigns tasks for all competency and time commitment levels in both volunteer and for-profit organizations to ensure that all members can contribute and feel valued.

A quality leader also recognizes that people's lives change, as does their availability. This factor is especially critical to realize in a volunteer organization. For instance, a mother with three children decides to start working full-time outside her home. Now her entire schedule has changed, and twenty to thirty hours are spent at work. She finds that she needs to reduce her volunteer hours to keep everything running well on the home front. The last thing she needs is to be placed on a guilt trip by an overzealous pastor. She needs understanding and support.

As a pastor, I enjoyed volunteering for organizations outside of my church. I served on committees to plan and implement conventions and conferences. I was asked to lead a state student ministry foundation and served on various oversight boards. Then I chose to start work on a master's degree while still pastoring full-time. It wasn't long before I was exhausted, so I had to make some difficult choices. I allowed myself to be spread too thin, and my predicament began to erode the time spent with my family and my work at church. I decided to continue my schooling, so I had to drop out of several other volunteer commitments.

People must make this kind of choice regularly, which means that one year they give perhaps ten hours a week to volunteer at church, but then something changes, and they can only give two hours. It is wise for leaders to recognize these transitions and adjust accordingly. It is unwise to make someone feel guilty because their schedule has changed.

The Situational Leadership Model, designed by Ken Blanchard and Dr. Paul Hersey, continues to be one of the most effective management tools to assist a leader in serving employees and volunteers well.

Situational leadership enables leaders to create a more inclusive and diverse organization and can also help to ensure that all tasks and responsibilities are handled effectively. Additionally, providing a range of job opportunities can help to engage volunteers at different levels of commitment, which can help to increase retention and overall satisfaction among volunteers. When the Situational Leadership Model combines with employee/volunteer availability level, the leader, organization, and the led are partnering for the optimal probability of success. It is worth any leader's time to invest in learning this model.

Nehma used situational leadership effectively in his role as governor of Judah. When he first arrived in Jerusalem, he found the city in disrepair and the walls broken down, leaving the residents vulnerable to attack. In this situation, the wise leader used a directing leadership style, taking charge and organizing the rebuilding of the walls. He set clear goals and expectations and provided the necessary resources and support to the workers. He also organized the people into teams, assigning leaders to each group to ensure the work was done efficiently.

> **NEHMA USED SITUATIONAL LEADERSHIP EFFECTIVELY AND IT WORKED.**

As the rebuilding of the walls progressed, Nehemiah switched to a coaching leadership style, providing guidance and support to the leaders of the teams. He also encouraged the people to take ownership of the project and to take pride in their work. He recognized the talents and strengths of each individual and used them in the best way possible to achieve the goal. Nehemiah successfully rebuilt Jerusalem's walls and improved the city's safety and security by effectively adjusting his leadership style to meet the situation's needs.

A quality leader usually invests more time, energy, and money into the organization they serve than their followers do. They also benefit from seeing the big picture, understanding how each person and task contributes to the goal more effectively than the worker who is "down in the weeds." This knowledge can tempt a leader or manager to overestimate a follower's passion and skills. This kind of oversight can cause unnecessary frustration for both the leader and the follower. This miscue is especially true in a volunteer organization where people serve without financial incentive. They are there working because they *want* to be present.

Church pastors sometimes make this mistake when they fail to consider that they are thinking about the mission and associated tasks full-time. Volunteers are usually employed and must think about other matters forty hours a week. I regularly reminded myself and staff members that their volunteers had already worked a full day *before* they showed up to help with a program or project. This fact alone shows a high level of commitment and should be regularly recognized by leaders.

Recognizing the passion, commitment, skill level, and availability of team members and adjusting expectations are critical features of quality leadership.

For Further Thought

1. What are the current needs and goals of the team or organization?
2. What are the existing skills and abilities of the individuals on the team?
3. What is the current level of development of the team or organization?
4. What is the current status of the motivation and commitment of the team or organization?
5. How can I adapt my leadership style to best support the team or organization in achieving its goals?

6. How can I provide the right amount of guidance and support to the team or organization in its current stage of development?

7. How can I best empower and motivate the team or organization to take ownership of its work and progress?

8. What are the potential obstacles or challenges that the team or organization may face, and how can my leadership style address them?

9. How can I evaluate the effectiveness of my leadership style and adjust as needed?

10. How can I ensure that my leadership style aligns with the company's culture and vision?

11. Google "Situational Leadership" and read up on the effectiveness of this management style.

Bodyguard Tactic Four

NEVER SAY NEVER

"God specializes in the impossible."

Have you ever encountered the impossible?

In the 1990s, our little 5,000-square-foot facility was maxed out. Our church had grown from around forty people to nearly three hundred, and we held three worship services to accommodate everyone. Our children's ministry areas were brimming with children, and the building had been remodeled several times as we sought to maximize the use of our space. Since the church only owned two acres, there was nowhere to expand our building, so we began searching for land to purchase. So we searched and searched and searched some more, to no avail.

Not only could we not locate land to purchase, but we also couldn't afford the rising property prices in our area. We were in a catch twenty-two. Finally, our neighbor across the busy street offered her six acres for $275,000. We had hoped for more than six acres but ultimately decided to purchase the property if something else did not come up quickly.

A few years previous, a local realtor friend approached me about purchasing fifty-three acres less than a mile from our current location for 1.2 million dollars. I chuckled for two reasons. The cost might as well have been a billion dollars, and what would we do with such a large tract of land? I turned the offer down quickly.

When my realtor friend once again called, we were about to set a closing date for the land across the street. She told me that the fifty-three acres were still for sale, and the price had dropped dramatically because much of the property would not meet percolation standards for sewer treatment and could not be developed. The owner was not keen on the land becoming another housing development anyway and would gladly sell her property to a church. The price was now $275,000! I was nearly floored, as were my leaders. But what about sewer treatment?

One of our elders was familiar with self-contained sewer treatment plants, and after some brief research we learned that we could install a waste-treatment facility. That was the last hurdle, and we took the offer. We were now about to purchase a 1.2-million-dollar property for less than a quarter of the price and about the price of an average home in our area. The fifty-three acres cost precisely what we were going to pay for six. The loan was approved, and we conducted a capital campaign to finance the purchase.

A few years later, our entire church family marched two miles from the old building to the new property where we held our first service that day. It was quite a spectacle. And what would we do with such a large parcel? A few months later, we decided to build a community park since community involvement was part of our DNA. Through the years, we kept developing new amenities for the park, including a two-acre special-needs-accessible playground, pavilion, and restrooms. The entire community rallied to construct Adventure Zone Playground, and thousands of people, including those with disabilities, used it. I will never forget watching the first child in a wheelchair roll into the play area without obstruction.

We believed that God was serious about his promise to Abraham that his descendants would bless the world, and we wanted to be part of the fulfillment of that guarantee in our little piece of the world. God honored our desire, and now the park boasts a disc-golf course, soccer fields, a snow-tubing hill, a prayer garden, two pavilions (one with special-needs fitness equipment), and an indoor special-needs playground.

ABRAHAM'S DECENDENTS SHOULD BLESS THEIR WORLD.

In our opinion, the church on Lambs Gap Road is a bona fide miracle!

God specializes in the impossible.

However, when you are on the precipice of the impossible, it is usually not a comfortable place. Impossible means we have exhausted all our human resources. Impossible makes us say, "I just don't get it. I don't know what we're going to do. I'm at the end of my rope."

Nehemiah was facing the impossible. No one in 120 years had even considered such a project as rebuilding the walls of Jerusalem. How could a bodyguard in a place 900 miles away—one who had no construction experience, little leadership experience on his résumé, and who was at the mercy of a pagan king—even consider such a foolhardy move?

Who could do that? A humble, committed, God-fearing person, that's who!

Nearly every person who experiences a miracle starts out thinking, *This is impossible. It can't be done. Why am I putting myself in this situation in the first place? What if I fail? I'll look like a fool.*

When Nehemiah received the disturbing news about his beloved home city, he was left wondering, *God, why haven't you done something about this situation? What can I do?* After a few hours of prayer, God came knocking on his door and handed him a commission to rebuild the walls surrounding Jerusalem. He then had to make a choice. Would he take a chance or not? The bodyguard answered the call, which opened the gates of Heaven's power to wash over the situation. God had a plan. Nehemiah said, "Yes," and the miracles started pouring out like a spring shower.

A few years ago, author John Ortberg wrote a book with one of my favorite titles, *If You Want to Walk on Water, You've Got to Get Out of the Boat*. This sentence resonates with every leader, who knows there are no sure things. Therefore, leaders must depend on the Almighty for empowerment, knowing an infusion of the Divine changes everything.

Our church leadership team tried to faithfully follow the "get out of the boat" principle.

IF YOU WANT TO SEE MIRACLES, YOU'VE GOT TO GET OUT OF THE BOAT.

Though our church was growing and healthy, we were, nevertheless, taking on significant new debt and increasing our utilities and maintenance exponentially. We wanted to do things so big that if God was not in it, we would be doomed to failure. When it came to finding a new home for our congregation, we pulled out all the stops and got our feet wet. Nehemiah was confident in the God who called him to this formidable task. The rest is history.

Food for Thought

1. When was the last time you did something so big that God had to be in it, or it would surely fail?
2. Are you presently facing an impossible situation and waiting on God for answers?
3. What communication and subsequent actions by a leader help followers to walk into the unknown?
4. When was the last time you tried a God-sized project and failed? What did you learn from the experience?
5. Read Acts 4:1-31 and examine how and why the Apostles were willing to try the seemingly impossible task of spreading the Gospel against all odds.

Bodyguard Tactic Five

LEADERS TAKE THE HEAT

*"Leaders own not only their shortcomings
but those of their followers as well."*

God chose Saul to be the first king of Israel, but he ultimately failed in his role as leader because he did not take personal responsibility for his actions and that of his army.

The study of Saul, the first king of Israel, and David, the second king, is one of contrasts. I believe God specifically planned this as a lesson for them and future generations. Saul was well-known among his people, a tall, good-looking man whom people loved. David was an unknown shepherd boy from an entirely different tribe, and there is no record that he was unusually tall. Saul was a native of the tribe of Benjamin, the least of the Israeli peoples, while David was from Judah, which would become the greatest of all the tribes and the one from which most present-day Jews trace their ancestry.

Saul began as a humble person, but power and position quickly went to his head, and he became a foolish, unproductive leader. David went from being nobody to Israel's greatest king, and when he or his people sinned, he took responsibility, albeit through an agonizing process. Saul consistently blamed others for his mistakes, even the prophet who appointed him king. He was what I call a "blame-shifter."

On one occasion, the wayward king blatantly disobeyed God by refusing to destroy the Amalekite nation, archenemies of Israel. God commanded that they *all* be put to death, including their livestock, but Saul spared their king and the best of the sheep and cattle, claiming that he wanted to sacrifice them to God. This foolish choice incited God to reject Saul as king.

In another situation, Saul faced the Philistine army, and instead of trusting God for his fate he became afraid and once again disobeyed. He consulted a medium instead of seeking guidance from God—big mistake.

Saul was a blame-shifter. He even turned against his son Jonathan. Then the king became paranoid and tried to kill David on several occasions. But God had already chosen David to become the next king, something Saul could never stop.

DON'T BE A BLAME-SHIFTER.

Saul's failure to take responsibility for his and his people's actions ultimately led to his downfall as king and his rejection as a leader by God. The first king of Israel is a cautionary figure of how critical it is for leaders to take responsibility for their actions. They must also claim culpability for those they lead.

Leaders who do not take responsibility for the failure of themselves or their organization are often viewed as lacking integrity and accountability. There are times when the most effective leadership tactic can be summed up in three words, "I was wrong," or "We were wrong." Blame-shifting is irresponsible and creates an environment where employees and followers lose trust in their leaders and become disengaged.

Leaders who reject accountability for the failure of their organization also fail to learn from their mistakes. Without accepting responsibility for the problem, they cannot fully understand the root causes of the issues and implement meaningful changes to prevent them from happening again. This fallacy can lead to a cycle of repeated failures and a lack of progress within the organization.

Another issue with leaders who do not take responsibility for the failures of their organizations is that they create a culture of fear and mistrust. Employees or volunteers who see their leaders shirking responsibility and placing blame on others become hesitant to speak up or share their ideas, as they fear being made scapegoats. This phenomenon stifles creativity and innovation and can ultimately lead to the stagnation of the organization.

In contrast, leaders who take responsibility for the failures of their organization are viewed as trustworthy and accountable. They take ownership of the problem, work to understand the root causes, and take action to prevent it from happening again. This leader creates a culture of trust and openness where followers feel comfortable sharing their ideas and taking risks. A culture of confidence, in turn, leads to increased innovation and progress within the organization.

Ron Gibori, entrepreneur and creative director at Idea Booth, explains that great leaders have one thing in common. They are willing to take the blame when necessary while allowing credit to go to other team members. Many leadership experts advise that the first step in solving a problem is taking responsibility for it.

> ## THE FIRST STEP IN SOLVING A PROBLEM IS TAKING RESPONSIBILITY FOR IT.

We learn that Nehma possessed this critical leadership trait of taking responsibility early in chapter one of the book.

When I heard these things, I sat down and wept. For some days I mourned and fasted and prayed before the God of heaven. Then I said:

"Lord, the God of heaven, the great and awesome God, who keeps his covenant of love with those who love him and keep his commandments, let your ear be attentive and your eyes open to hear the prayer your servant is praying before you day and night for your servants, the people of Israel. I confess the sins we Israelites, including myself and my father's family, have committed against you. We have acted very wickedly toward you. We have not obeyed the commands, decrees and laws you gave your servant Moses.

"Remember the instruction you gave your servant Moses, saying, 'If you are unfaithful, I will scatter you among the nations, but if you return to me and obey my commands, then even if your exiled people are at the farthest horizon, I will gather them from there and bring them to the place I have chosen as a dwelling for my Name.'

"They are your servants and your people, whom you redeemed by your great strength and your mighty hand. Lord, let your ear be attentive to the prayer of this your servant and to the prayer of your servants who delight in revering your name. Give your servant success today by granting him favor in the presence of this man." (Neh. 1:4-11 NIV)

Nehemiah was likely born in Persia to Jewish parents, and some believe his parents were people of consequence in influential circles. This social stratum might have allowed the young man to be recognized by royalty and aid his progress through the ranks to the high position of cupbearer and bodyguard to King Artaxerxes.

We are not aware of how much Nehma knew about the Babylonian captivity of his people and the Persian history of conquering the Babylonians. Still, he was sure to know some of the past, as would every Jew living in Persia and Judah. It was likely that he had close connections with at least a few people living in Jerusalem, including his brother.

So why would the distressed Jewish leader be so upset about the destruction of Jerusalem, and why would he claim any personal responsibility for the sins of his forefathers? Like any high-quality leader, Nehemiah knew that he and his family lineage were *all* part of the problem, and he was humble and penitent enough to admit it. Not only did he claim responsibility for his sins, but he interceded for his entire nation.

This factor alone made the future wall-builder a proper candidate to be used by God and to become a highly competent leader.

Famous coach Lou Holtz puts it like this by expressing the opposite characteristic of taking responsibility: "The man who complains about the way the ball bounces is likely to be the one who dropped it."

Food for Thought

1. How can leaders demonstrate that they are taking responsibility for their actions and holding themselves accountable to their team and stakeholders?
2. How can leaders ensure that they take responsibility for their decisions' long-term consequences rather than just focusing on short-term gains?

3. How can leaders foster a culture of taking responsibility within their organization, and what role do they play in setting this example?

4. When a leader is not directly responsible for a problem or failure, how can they still take responsibility and lead the way to find solutions?

5. How would you rate yourself on the "taking responsibility" scale, and how can you improve? Think of a time when you fell short of this trait. What happened? Why was this the case?

Read 1 Samuel chapters 13 to 15 and contrast Saul's leadership with that of Nehemiah.

Bodyguard Tactic Six

Beware The Success Syndrome

*"It was not those who aspired to worthy causes
but those who enjoyed the fruit of success
and its excesses who tumbled down the mountain
of success into the valley of despair."*

I had served Vibrant for twenty-five years and was proud of it! Too proud. The worst memory of my forty-year ministry was the entitled attitude I possessed for about a year at the arrival of my first quarter-century milestone. I had restarted this church many years previously and watched it grow from forty to five hundred in attendance. It was a healthy congregation, and I accomplished numerous goals throughout my tenure.

I am not prone to pridefulness in my career, so the whole success syndrome came as a surprise and took a while for me to recognize. Self-flagellation and never being good enough often indicated my attitude about my role. Pridefulness about my accomplishments was usually not an issue. My sin often involved me never thinking I was enough of a leader, and I spent way too much time comparing myself to my friends who pastored larger churches and figured there must be something wrong with me as a leader. Yet, it happened. I became full of pride.

I learned the elders and my assistant were planning a twenty-fifth-anniversary celebration for me. I don't remember how I got the information, but their plans became known to me and were not what I wanted. Furthermore, the planners did not consult my close friends about the events and gifts I might enjoy, which angered me. As weeks progressed, my temper repeatedly flared at home and with my close friends. It was disgusting and now embarrassing for a successful leader in my shoes to have behaved in such a manner.

I did my best not to make my disdain public, but those close to me knew what was happening. I felt that the leadership team, and indeed my assistant, knew how much my wife and I loved to travel. To boot, I had a couple of friends experiencing milestones in ministry, and they were sent on big trips, which was what I wanted. Instead, I received an expensive wristwatch. I still have the timepiece, not as a symbol of success but rather as a reminder of when my pride got out of hand. It will always symbolize shame for me, and a valuable lesson learned. I was always privately ashamed of how I conducted myself throughout what should have been a purely celebratory season. Still, I will forever be grateful for those who put up with my bad attitude during that period. Pride is an ugly monster.

Fortunately, that disgusting syndrome never conquered me again, and I learned my lesson.

SUCCESS IS MORE DANGEROUS THAN FAILURE.

Success can be dangerous for leaders because when they achieve success, they become overconfident in their abilities and strategies, leading to poor decision-making and a lack of flexibility in the face of changing circumstances. It also results in a sense of entitlement, a nemesis for anyone. A subtle and not-so-subtle mantra becomes, "You owe me, and I made this happen for you." More accurately, those in leadership positions are where they are because people are willing to follow them. If anyone owes somebody in this situation, it is the leader who owes the followers.

Another danger of success for leaders is that it can lead to losing perspective. Leaders who have achieved success can become so focused on maintaining their success that they lose sight of the bigger picture and the future needs of their organizations or communities. This kind of blindness can lead to a lack of innovation and a failure to adapt to changing conditions. "This has worked for me, so why should we change it? I know more about this stuff than you folks."

Success is also dangerous for leaders because it can lead to a lack of accountability. When leaders are successful, they can become insulated from criticism and accountability, which leads to poor governance and a lack of transparency. When the person at the top no longer gets any pushback, the organization is headed for trouble.

After many years of service, my board and staff trusted me so much that I could present pretty much any reasonable idea to them and they would approve of the proposal. Fortunately, I deciphered this lesson long after the event mentioned above, and the phenomenon made me wary of myself and my power. This awareness was good, especially since I came up with some exquisitely dumb ideas. I was so respected and loved because I had served Vibrant for many years, I was aging, and all but two of its members came into the church under my leadership. I became like a father figure to many, an older brother to others, and a benevolent uncle to some. They trusted me, but I had learned not to leverage their trust for my personal agenda. This church was God's work, not mine, and I would be wise to remember that fact when my next brilliant idea erupted.

Another danger of success for leaders is that it can lead to a sense of entitlement. When leaders achieve success, they may start believing they are entitled to continued accolades and do not need to work as hard to maintain them. This bloated self-assessment can demotivate even the best of leaders and make them fail to labor hard for continued success. Success is *always* hard work. Be wary of any achievement that costs you nothing. As King David once said, "I would never offer God something that did not cost me anything." (my paraphrase).

Finally, success can be dangerous for leaders because it can lead to a lack of humility. When leaders achieve fame, they can start to believe that they are infallible and that their way is the best or the only way. Famous football coach Tom Landry once said, "You're never as good they say you are when you are winning, and you are never as bad as they report when you are losing."

An inflated ego incites a lack of openness to new ideas and perspectives, which inhibits the growth and development of whatever you are trying to do. Furthermore, it leads to a lack of empathy. Empathy allows one to get inside another person's head (as much as possible) and perceive a situation from their point of view. Make no mistake, leaders need empathy to govern well. When subordinates sense their leader has no genuine concern for their welfare, productivity will decrease, and the leader will likely not even know it. People *do not* give their best to a boss who cares nothing about their lives.

The "big head" erodes one's ability to see things from the point of view of the "end user." Every—I repeat, *every*—endeavor is dependent upon the end user.

King David was a successful military leader and a beloved king of Israel. He led the Israelites to many victories and expanded the kingdom to new heights. However, as his success grew, so did his pride. King David became increasingly confident in his abilities and forgot that God had granted him victory. He was also weary after years of struggles against numerous foes of Israel and judging governmental matters daily. Weariness combined with pride is a formula for disaster.

King David's pride led him to conflict with God. The king's story began when he ordered a census of his kingdom. According to the Bible, King David wanted to know how many fighting men he had at his disposal and how powerful his kingdom truly was. This haughty act was a direct challenge to God's sovereignty and was seen as a lack of trust in God's protection and provision. God enabled David's success, but the Shepherd King's inflated ego forgot it.

As a result of his foolishness, God was displeased with His vessel and punished him. The census led to a rebellion, and many of the king's innocent subjects died. King David was filled with remorse and recognized that his sin resulted from his pride and lack of faith in God.

This story serves as a warning to leaders: Unbridled pride in your success and abilities will lead you to make foolish decisions resulting in severe consequences. This leadership maxim reminds us that true success comes from humility and obedience to God, and leaders must always be mindful of their actions and motives.

King David's humility in acknowledging his sin and seeking forgiveness is also a testament to the power of repentance and the mercy of God. Through his experience, King David learned to rely on God and trust in His wisdom and guidance, ultimately leading to his continued success as a leader. If, like David or me, you fall into this trap, follow David's example. Get on your knees, admit your foolishness, ask forgiveness, and accept God's grace.

The history of leadership is littered with success stories that went bad. The temptations are the same, from despots to department managers to church pastors. One person may have guided the ship, but the crew got them to their destination. Most team members will serve in obscurity, yet their labor and ingenuity are the energy needed to obtain success. A quality leader knows this truth and reacts accordingly.

> **ONE PERSON MAY HAVE GUIDED THE SHIP, BUT THE CREW GOT THEM TO THEIR DESTINATION.**

Nehma had plenty of history to teach him that his success would depend upon the person living across from the useless gate to the city, who he could motivate to do something about it. Ultimately, success did not go to his head when the walls stood tall again.

Beware of the success trap.

Food for Thought

Assessing humility after obtaining great success can be challenging, as success can often lead to feelings of pride and inflated self-importance. However, there are steps that leaders can take to assess their humility and maintain a healthy perspective. Consider these steps in your own experience and see how well you have retained the right attitude:

1. Reflect on your success. To whom do you attribute your success? Do you give proper credit to those who got you where you are?
2. How are you handling criticism? Do you seek honest feedback from team members and superiors?
3. How is success affecting your behavior? Has your accomplishment opened doors for harmful conduct? (David should have been leading his army one spring but instead stayed home and got himself into big trouble.)
4. Is your attitude causing riffs with family members, friends, or coworkers?
5. What is your "give back" score? Are you using your advancement to help team members, supporters, and the community?
6. Do you give proper credit to God for your success.

Read 2 Corinthians 10-12:13 to examine how Paul assessed his success.

Bodyguard Tactic Seven

If It Were Easy, Everybody Would Do It

"God never said it would be easy, did he, Eli?"

Theodore Roosevelt was born into a wealthy family in New York. He would seemingly have had every opportunity to be ahead of the curve toward success. However, his journey to fame was long and arduous.

Roosevelt had debilitating asthma as a child and was often bedridden. "Teedie," as he was called, could not participate in many of the everyday activities of a growing boy. He also suffered from severe headaches, toothaches, and abdominal pain.

Little was known about treating asthma in those days, and the young man suffered through all kinds of treatments, such as smoking cigars, drinking coffee and whiskey, and taking trips to the coast. Of course, none of those treatments worked, but Roosevelt's father constantly cared for his son, and they became very close. Finally, Mr. Roosevelt decided that the best treatment for his ailing son was to get into good physical condition, so he built his son a workout gym in their home. The father, who held to high moral and physical standards, told Teedie that one's mind could never be at its best until the body was in equally good shape.

Teddy was a determined person, and he started vigorously training, which included weightlifting, horseback riding, boxing, swimming, hiking, wrestling, and learning judo. As his body became more robust, his illness slowly subsided, and he ended up at Harvard.

But Roosevelt's troubles did not end with youth. One of our most effective presidents later experienced a personal tragedy when his wife and mother both died on the same day, which happened to be Valentine's Day. Teddy was devastated and sought solace in the western frontier, where he developed a love for the outdoors and the wilderness.

When Roosevelt returned to the east, he entered politics and served in various positions, including the governor of New York and vice president of the United States. He became the twenty-sixth president of the United States in 1901 after the assassination of William McKinley.

As president, Roosevelt faced numerous challenges, including a failing economy, political corruption, and labor strikes, but he used his leadership skills and determination to tackle these challenges and implement reforms that helped the country and its citizens.

Despite these obstacles and difficulties, Roosevelt remained determined and continued to work toward his goals, becoming one of the most successful and popular presidents in American history.

Most biographers agree that Roosevelt's years of struggle as a youth and learning to overcome illness and tragedy formed him into a formidable force for good in our nation and the world.

As our twenty-sixth president once stated, "Nothing worth having comes easy."

"NOTHING WORTH HAVING COMES EASY." —TEDDY ROOSEVELT

Hard work is necessary because it takes time and effort to master a subject, develop a skill, or achieve a goal. To be successful, you must be willing to put in the time and effort required to reach your goal. This means making sacrifices, staying focused, and not giving up even when faced with obstacles or failures.

Take, for instance, arguably the most famous rock band in history, The Beatles. By the time this group invaded the American scene and became wildly successful, they had already paid their dues.

Before The Beatles became one of the world's most successful and influential bands, they spent years honing their craft and playing together for thousands of hours. The Beatles formed in Liverpool, England, in the late 1950s and played in various clubs and venues in the city and later played in Germany, where they worked just shy of three hundred nights, four to five hours per night.

The band's dedication to their craft was evident in the amount of time they spent playing together. It is estimated that they played for over 10,000 hours before they came to America. This extensive practice allowed them to refine their sound and develop a unique style that would eventually set them apart from other bands.

Their hard work and persistence paid off when they were signed to a record label and released their first album, *Please Please Me*, in 1963. The album was a commercial success and marked the beginning of their journey to stardom.

The Beatles went on to conquer the world, revolutionizing popular music and inspiring generations of musicians. Their success was due, in large part, to their years of hard work and dedication to their craft. Their story serves as a reminder that success takes time, effort, and persistence and that extraordinary accomplishments can be achieved through hard work and determination.

The idea of 10,000 hours of practice as a key to success was popularized in Malcolm Gladwell's book *Outliers*, which was published in 2008. In the book, Gladwell argues that it takes approximately 10,000 hours of deliberate practice to master a skill or achieve expertise in a particular field.

Another of our presidents, Barack Obama, also stated, "Nothing in life that's worth anything is easy."

By the time God called Nehemiah into service, the bodyguard had long since paid his dues. Leading the large team of people who likely worked under his leadership was not an easy task, and if one made a grave mistake, it could cost the life of the king and likely his bodyguard.

When Nehma accepted the call to rebuild the walls around Jerusalem, he was signing on for a monumental task fraught with danger, frustration, opposition from within and without his ranks, and plenty of sacrifice.

Leaders often spend more hours, work harder, and take more responsibility than their team members to serve as the point person. Before you step into the captain's seat, be sure to count the cost. Count it, then double your number! Most of the time it will require more than you expected.

Food for Thought

An excellent way to count the cost of an upcoming endeavor is to perform a cost-benefit analysis. Begin by evaluating the magnitude of the project or program and listing all known benefits of its success. Then list all the costs associated with the undertaking, such as time, resources, cost, skills required, and the number of team members needed for accomplishment. This helps a leader not enter an operation blindly.

Do a cost-benefit analysis of Nehemiah's project.

Read 1 Kings 5-6 covering Solomon's building of the temple. Do a cost-benefit analysis of the project.

Bodyguard Tactic Eight

HEARING THE HARD THING

"A leader needs friends who tell it like it is."

Beyond my family, my variety and number of good friends are my most valuable asset in life. And the fact that many of my family members are also close friends is a double blessing.

It is often said of a leader that it is lonely at the top, which can be true. However, it is only lonely if you allow it to be so. The leader who lacks solid friendships not only misses the blessing but the precious value of relationships that make you better. Sometimes, that means telling it like it is.

A year or so ago, I embarked upon one of the most difficult conversations of my life.

I am lucky that my nephew, who is close in age, is one of my closest friends. We've enjoyed camaraderie since our youth and relished dozens of memorable seasons. We walked the 500-mile Camino Way trek across Spain a few years ago, which took forty days. This hike was an experience neither of us will forget. Joe is the only person with whom I could spend forty intense days, and never have an argument which is fantastic. I still marvel at that experience.

I invited my friend to make this journey with me and loaned him some money to help cover the costs. I know it can be dangerous, but loaning money is part of my DNA and gives me great pleasure. Unfortunately, Joe was unable to pay me back for several years. Meanwhile, my wife, who loved Joe dearly, was upset by what she considered his negligence and taking advantage of me. Gail did not always share my sentiments and was more frugal than me. Over that period, she sometimes fueled unhealthy feelings in me toward my nephew.

About a year ago, Joe approached me about possibly loaning him startup funds for a new business venture. Though I was excited about his project, for some reason the prospect of lending him money refueled unkind feelings toward him based on our situation in years past. I agonized for a few weeks about the entire possibility. Finally, I decided I needed to have a hard talk with him, the thought of which nearly nauseated me.

I wanted to share funds with him, but I needed to clear the air between us, something I should have done years previously. We spent the better part of an evening on the phone discussing the matter, me dropping my baggage in his lap. I think he was taken aback at first but listened intently. After some tearful discussion, we made up and went on our ways. As a close friend, I should have discussed the matter with him long before. His new venture is shining brightly, as is our relationship.

Good friends can share the good *and* the bad news, and in the process they both become better people. Everyone needs friends like that. Oscar Wilde put it so well when he said, "True friends stab you in the front." Henry David Thoreau expressed this truth as well, "True friendship can afford true knowledge. It does not depend on darkness and ignorance." And finally Proverbs explains, "Wounds from a friend can be trusted, but an enemy multiplies kisses" (Proverbs 27:6 NIV).

I cannot imagine not sharing numerous deep friendships, but many people don't cultivate them and take advantage of this blessing. We were not meant to exist like lone wolves but were created by a highly relational Being who designed us in His image. In short, we need each other.

Close friendships bring immense value to our lives. They provide us with emotional support and a sense of belonging, making us feel accepted and understood. A good friend allows us to have fun, experience new things, and create memories that last a lifetime. Having someone to confide in and share our triumphs and struggles with can be a valuable source of comfort and help us better cope with life's challenges.

A confidant provides numerous benefits for our physical and mental health. Studies reveal that people with close friends have lower levels of stress, depression, and anxiety. They are also more likely to lead healthier lifestyles, as they often engage in physical activities and share healthy habits. Furthermore, close friendships can also improve self-esteem and boost confidence. A "bro," "best bud," or "girlfriend" makes us feel valued, accepted, and supported. Proverbs 27:9 states, "Perfume and incense bring joy to the heart, and the pleasantness of a friend springs from their heartfelt advice."

Leaders need close friends for many reasons. Close friends provide a source of emotional support and can offer a nonjudgmental sounding board for your thoughts and ideas. In leadership positions, pressure and stress can be immense, and having a trusted friend to confide in helps you cope with the demands of your role. Having a close ally provides a sense of perspective and supports leaders in maintaining a healthy work-life balance, which is essential for well-being and overall success. Everyone needs someone to jerk a knot in their tail occasionally!

Enjoying the companionship of a compadre also plays a crucial role in helping a leader grow and develop. A leader needs people to challenge their thinking and provide constructive feedback. Caring, objective eyes help one identify areas for improvement. A close friend can inspire and motivate leaders to stay focused on their goals. I've been reined in numerous times by a caring friend who stopped me short of making a fool of myself.

A cohort of friends pursuing similar career paths helps one gain new perspectives and insights into different ways of thinking and problem-solving. A few years ago, I joined a discipleship cohort sponsored by my friends at Stadia Church Planting. Eight men, all serving in some vocational ministry capacity and of various ages and experience levels, met twice a year at a destination city. We spent two days "sharpening our swords" through topical discussions, a featured guest speaker, and plenty of sharing time over cigars and cocktails. Meanwhile, a regular flow of text messages still provides valuable information sharing, prayer support, and plenty of laughter. This group started four years ago and is still going strong. I know that when a text with nine members appears on my phone it will be good!

If you want to grow personally and professionally, find yourself some comrades and take on life together.

IF YOU WANT TO GROW PERSONALLY AND PROFESSIONALLY, FIND YOURSELF SOME COMRADES AND TAKE ON LIFE TOGETHER.

You will find emotional support, a source of perspective and feedback, and help with the challenge of keeping life in balance. Leaders with close friends are better equipped to navigate the demands and challenges of their roles and make better decisions, ultimately leading to more fulfilling and successful leadership experiences. He or she who finds a friend has discovered a treasure.

Nehma had friends, including his brother. Our story begins with a gathering of friends who care enough to reveal the hard things. I am sure it must not have been easy for Hanani to deliver such terrible news about their hometown and people, but he did, and because of it the walls around the Holy City rose from the ashes.

By the way, my friend and nephew is partially responsible for the expertise, encouragement, and determination it took me to write this book. What goes around comes around. If you want to succeed in life, find yourself some good friends.

Food for Thought

Who are the "comrades" in your life? Evaluate the value each one brings to the table of your existence, especially your leadership chops. What do you bring to each of them? When was the last time you thanked them for their contributions to your life and leadership?

It is helpful to have friends with special interests in different categories of life. For instance, friends that enhance your marriage or ones along your career path. Others might help with your "dark side," coming alongside to keep you morally, mentally, and physically in shape. Are there areas of your life in which you could use a new friend? What will you do about it?

Read 1 Samuel 20 and assess the value of David's friendship with Jonathan.

Bodyguard Tactic Nine

THE PEOPLE WHO GOT YOU THERE

> *"Behind every great project and healthy leader are the people behind the person."*

I have been good friends with my business partner and aide for nearly forty years. Not long after I started a pastorate that lasted thirty-eight years, Lori visited our church with her father, who I'd met at a wedding. We quickly became friends as she attended church regularly. Lori was studying to become a teacher, and before long the newcomer volunteered with the teen ministry, followed by the children's ministry, where she labored for many years. She worked on my staff as our children's director and eventually community outreach director for nearly thirty years. Her competence in both of those areas of ministry was outstanding, to say the least.

However, Lori also played another significant role in our staff. She is a relentless encourager and levelheaded advisor under challenging situations. During our tenure, we engaged in thousands of conversations in which she advised and challenged me in a manner that often helped me pursue our goals, especially when times were tough.

Since she and her husband, Rick, were my and my wife's close friends, both were there for us when my wife became ill with pancreatic cancer. Lori spent untold hours caring for Gail and encouraging me to keep going. After Gail's death, both of my friends have lifted me many times. Now she is a behind-the-scenes business partner overseeing my social media, calendar, speaking engagements, and research.

Since I often struggled with mild depression and foolish comparisons to other ministries, the support of this person aided me and thus our church and my family. Both my wife and Lori, like Aaron and Hur for Moses, uplifted my arms so that my leadership continued fruitfully.

Every leader needs a "Lori," or more accurately, *several* people who serve that role.

Another interesting note about the account of Joshua and the Israeli army fighting the Amalekites was the role of Moses and God (Exodus 17:8-16). They too were in a support role rather than on the battlefield. The Amalekites came against the Jewish people, so Moses instructed Joshua to gather an army and head to the battlefield. Meanwhile, Moses, Aaron, and Hur proceeded to the top of a hill overlooking the battlefield, Moses carrying his staff, which had wielded so much power in the past. Moses held up the staff, and Joshua's men started winning, but Joshua lost when the staff went down because Moses's arms were too tired to hold it up. Moses's role was to support Joshua in his unique manner by exercising his might when infused with God's power. But even Moses needed support. That's where Aaron and Hur came into the picture, as they held up the tired leader's arms. And *behind* all that action, God supported them in a background role. (Imagine that—God is in a background role.) Eventually, the Israelites won the day, and Moses built a shrine to memorialize the victory.

No leader possesses all the resources needed to carry out their work. Like grips in a theater production who prepare the stage for the actors, or sound and lighting techs who make the show come to life are those who carry the behind-the-scenes burdens for the lead actors or singer.

My daughter works for an events agency in Nashville, where she orchestrates significant events for the entertainment industry and large corporations. She serves as director of program management and executive producer leading their events.

As such, she often produces shows for well-known artists. I am sometimes privileged to watch her work and observe the results through Zoom and photographs. She is acutely aware of one thing. No matter how good, famous, or skilled a performer is, if the tech team is not equally excellent, the production will fall flat. However, no one ever sees the production crew. Their job is to make someone else look good. Who clients employ to produce their shows is of critical importance.

Surrounding oneself with the right people exponentially increases one's chances of success.

Consider Nehma's circle of supporters. The bodyguard maintained supportive relationships with people above him, horizontal and below him in the authority chain. Three critical people backed the future wall-builder from above his rank: Queen Mother Esther, Queen Damaspia, and King Artaxerxes.

Without the approval and support of these influential people, Nehma's project would have fallen flat before it ever got off the ground. Nothing significant in the servant's life would have happened without his friend the king's approval. It is reasonable to assume that both Queen Mother Esther and Queen Damaspia buttressed his requests. Nehma was a humble person willing to pivot to a life of serving a pagan king faithfully while not losing his identity as a Jew. Were he not well liked by these people, God would have needed to look elsewhere for a wall-builder.

Secondly, Nehma's brother and their group of friends arrived from Jerusalem with disturbing news. This group felt responsible for enlightening the bodyguard concerning his people in Judah, and then they cast their support for Nehma and his mission. Assuming Hanani was his brother reveals a family dynamic that does not always exist among siblings. The brothers must have maintained a loving, supportive relationship even though Nehma clearly surpassed his brother in status. There is no indication of jealousy among them.

Finally, there are the many servants who worked for Nehma in various roles. Nehma must have fostered quality relationships with cooks, delivery people, guards, and servers. In all likelihood, the cupbearer was training a successor to confidently step into the position in Nehma's absence.

Nehemiah cultivated fruitful relationships on every side, which garnered support when an opportunity came knocking to do something significant.

Let's look at some ways to cultivate support and supporters:

Support someone else. The way leaders learn the value of embracing assistance is by cheerleading others. Support for the success road is a two-way street. A leader is never so high on the ladder that they cannot have someone else to uplift regularly. Perhaps it is another leader, a spouse, a child, or a friend. Moses learned the value of support from the source Himself, so he knew how to help his protégé, Joshua.

Show up! Aaron and Hur didn't wait for Moses to get into trouble when his arms couldn't hold the staff; they *accompanied* their leader up the hill. They observed when he needed assistance and found solutions. His supporters allowed Moses not to be distracted when the going got tough.

Nehma's brother and friends knew they had news his brother needed to hear, though it was not an encouraging report. Providing and garnering quality support means associates provide both uplifting and not-so-encouraging news as required. Many leaders falter because their relationships foster fear, which causes supporters to withhold valuable negative information.

Leaders must be able to make informed decisions, and much of their knowledge comes from their associates above, on the same plane, and below their authority level.

Put others' interests ahead of your own, even if you disagree with them. Nehma did not follow the same religious system as his boss or oppressors, yet he found it helpful and wise to serve well and befriend his boss as much as possible. He wanted his friend, the king, to be successful.

Regularly inventory your circle of support. Who are the members, and what does each person provide? Are you lacking a helper in a critical area (e.g., marriage, parenting, employment, spiritual matters, hobbies and interests, education, etc.)? What can you do to change that situation? Are there those who you allow to critique you without becoming defensive? In whose circle are you, and what do you provide that person(s)?

Overall, be deliberate. The cultivation of an ever growing and changing support circle requires your attention.

The ancient bodyguard teaches us that behind every great project and healthy leader are the people behind the person.

Food for Thought

Do a support circle assessment and determine an action plan.

Consider where your lack of support held you back from pursuing your goals.

Read and consider lessons from Exodus 17:8-16.

Bodyguard Tactic Ten

CELEBRATE EARLY AND OFTEN

"A big win early in a project is a good thing, so celebrate the victory publicly."

Leading an organization and associated projects is like hiking a long distance over hilly terrain. Several years ago, I walked the famed Camino Way pilgrimage across Spain to Santiago de Compostela Cathedral. The first day of the hike is one of the most difficult. Over the course of the 500-mile trek, one crosses three mountain ranges. "Peregrinos," as trekkers are called, pass out of France, across the Pyrenees Mountains into Spain. The first-day trail is fifteen miles. During the hike, the elevation gain is nearly 4,300 feet, which makes it a real challenge.

About two-thirds of the way up the mountain, there is a small restaurant nestled along the side of the road. Besides indoor seating, it has two beautiful outdoor seating areas overlooking the majestic Pyrenees. Every hiker stops for a bite to eat and a beer. The atmosphere is festive, with trekkers from all over the world chatting and toasting to their uphill progress thus far. What most of them do not realize is that the most challenging part of the trail lies ahead.

However, the celebration and camaraderie boosts everyone's morale and energizes them for the remainder of the challenging climb and descent. It would be a long day coming, but the early victory celebration convinced the pilgrims they would succeed.

A wise leader understands the value of small achievement celebrations along the path to completion. Nehma both started and completed this project with public celebrations. Gathering the workers together to dedicate the completion of the first of many gates to be restored showed even the apprehensive among them what could be accomplished with resources and teamwork. The priests would be proud to show off their work and ready to encourage everyone else to do the same.

When a new building project ensues, the first important event is usually the groundbreaking ceremony. The leader realizes this is an important step for two reasons. First, placing a shovel in the ground, which is often done by several leadership partners, means that years of envisioning, planning, obtaining permits, fundraising, and numerous other preparations have finally come to fruition. This is cause for celebration. Second, when participants and partners gather to observe their leaders performing the physical act of shoveling, it demonstrates that the project is really going to happen. Constituents have listened to dreams and pitches for months, and now there is concrete action. In the grand scheme of construction events, this one is only symbolic but important, nevertheless.

During the twenty months my wife battled cancer, we spent countless hours in the infusion lab at Hershey Medical Center. This area of the hospital is not fun! Dozens of patients receive chemotherapy treatments, and the treatment rooms have a distinct odor not easily forgotten. There were, however, bright moments when the stillness of the lab was broken by the ringing of a large bell mounted on the wall at the entrance to the clinic. Every patient knew this meant someone was celebrating the completion of treatments. This small act of celebration is a powerful motivator for the patient pulling the clapper but also for their family, friends, and others receiving treatments. The bright sound of the bell means, "You can make it. I did."

Researchers have found that the act of celebration releases a feel-good chemical in the brain, which encourages people to continue their course of action. When done as a group, celebrating small victories binds people together, creating a sense of community.

I recently assisted my nephew and his wife in building out a new indoor archery range and pro shop, something that was a dream for several years. Several friends and family members worked long hours preparing the shop, range, and adjacent observation and party area. Part of the preparation included a food and drink menu for future customers, which would complement the grand opening. Finally, the exciting day came, and locals began streaming into the new addition to their community. Many joined us in the party room for a snack, a drink, and good conversation. The excitement was palatable, and new relationships quickly blossomed, ones that would bear fruit for the new venture. This event commemorated the "end of the beginning," and the hope of a bright future.

Food for Thought

Taking the first step of any project is often complicated and easily overlooked. Thinking of tasks that you manage, are you cognizant of small wins, and do you celebrate them with those involved? How could you improve? Sometimes it is good to appoint a "celebration officer" to ensure these crucial steps are not overlooked.

Read Nehemiah 3:1-2 "Eliashib the high priest and his fellow priests went to work and rebuilt the Sheep Gate. They dedicated it and set its doors in place, building as far as the Tower of the Hundred, which they dedicated, and as far as the Tower of Hananel. [2] The men of Jericho built the adjoining section, and Zakkur son of Imri built next to them."

How would you have felt watching the priests dedicate the first milestone of an enormous building project? How would it motivate you to complete your own part of the project?

Bodyguard Tactic Eleven

A View For The Long Haul

"Celebrate early but have a long view in mind."

I seriously doubt that Eli or Nehma had any idea that the Jewish Messiah would one day pass through the very gate that the fifth-century B.C. high priest rebuilt. The true Lamb of God Himself would be one of the thousands of sheep that would walk through this gate to be sacrificed for the people's sins. One never knows the downline impact of a project, program, company, church, or nonprofit organization. I am confident that if Eli had in mind that his Messiah would one day pass through his gate, he and his fellow priests would have given it their best effort.

The Apostle Paul put it like this: "And whatever you do, whether in word or deed, do it all in the name of the Lord Jesus, giving thanks to God the Father through him" (Colossians 3:17 NIV).

A few years ago, our friend Barbara asked our church to pilot a new program for a local organization with whom we partnered. We met Barbara at a nonprofit leadership event several years previous and enjoyed working with her on many occasions. The group wanted to try out a new volunteer workday concept in which volunteers would visit their clients and perform tasks they could not do. We agreed and gave it our all. We planned, promoted, recruited, and trained about 200 volunteers who went to several dozen locations throughout the region. The program was a great success, and the organization's national leadership took notice. Because we were willing to take a chance and do our best, this local caregiving nonprofit received large grants for several years based on the project's success. Who would have guessed?

On another occasion, our church piloted a program called Night to Shine, sponsored by the Tim Tebow Foundation. Night to Shine is a formal prom for individuals with special needs. The soiree included a delicious sit-down meal, dancing, walking a red carpet, limousine rides, photo ops, and even a dinner for the guests' parents and guardians. We pulled out all the stops to make this a spectacular evening for our special guests. As a result, Night to Shine became not only a regular event on our yearly calendar, but the program has also served thousands and thousands of individuals worldwide.

When I was a boy, my family vacationed in northern Indiana at one of the large lakes of the region. I fondly remember spending time with my parents, fishing from a fourteen-foot aluminum boat powered by a small Evinrude engine. I can still smell the aroma of night crawlers wiggling in my little fingers and the oil/gasoline mixture of smoke bellowing out of the outboard engine.

One day, I was fishing from the end of the long pier next to the beach in the little cabin community where we stayed. Like many little boys, my lack of finesse caused me to work the fishing line into a tangled mess. I worked feverishly to straighten out the twisted jumble, to no avail. I was nearly in tears when a large man approached me on the pier. He noticed my pathetic situation as he greeted me. "Hello, there, young man," he said as he sat down beside me. Our legs dangled over the water as he quietly asked, "Would you like some help with that?" I nodded in defeat as I handed him the fishing pole and the mess. In a few short moments, the kind man untangled my line and gave me the rod. He smiled, then promptly rose and walked away.

I've never forgotten the kindness of that fine man, and many years later, his good deed came to mind. I was grateful for the lesson he taught me, but I realized there was more to the incident than face value. Little did I know that as a pastor, I would spend most of my life helping people get their lives untangled. I have passed along his kind deed many times.

I'VE PASSED ALONG HIS KIND DEED MANY TIMES.

The fact is that we are all influencing people around us in ways that we will never realize. We *all* lead people daily without knowing it, and this truth is especially applicable to those who officially lead.

WE ALL LEAD PEOPLE DAILY WITHOUT KNOWING IT.

Quality leaders have the long haul in mind, knowing their decisions today will influence future generations.

Nehma and his people experienced vivid examples of leaders making foolish decisions, resulting in dire consequences for poor souls way down the line. He and his nation suffered deportation and humiliation for generations because their leaders rejected wisdom and integrity. The bodyguard was determined to break that chain and start new patterns of thinking and behavior that would enhance their society for generations to come.

Food for Thought

Can you think of a time when something you did or said had much more significant consequences than expected? If it was good, what made it so?

Consider how you are the product of those who came before you and had the long view in mind. How will those down the line from you benefit from your story?

Consider from Genesis to Revelation how God's long view of humanity has affected your life.

Search the internet to read the story of the events that led to Billy Graham's conversion. It is a classic example of this leadership principle and a great story.

Bodyguard Tactic Twelve

Communicate Thoroughly and Often

Perhaps Nehma's most valuable leadership asset was his ability to communicate effectively. The old axiom is true; it is nearly impossible to over-communicate. He painted a compelling picture of his vision and combined it with a strategy to solve the problem from start to finish.

His humble but captivating approach to the king won him full support. Nehma pulled on the king's and his wife's heartstrings. One can almost hear her saying, "Come on, Art, you've got to help this man. He has been a faithful and trustworthy servant for so long." Stating that the "city where my ancestors are buried lies in ruins" is a powerful picture for anyone concerned about ancestral heritage. Certainly, uber-powerful kings and queens understand the significance of one's ancestry. His official name, Artaxerxes, was the fifth in the "King of Kings" line and he was probably born during the reign of his grandfather, Darius I. His father, Xerxes, was murdered by members of his ruling council, and Artaxerxes avenged his death by having everyone involved put to death. This Achaemenid dynasty was the most prominent sovereignty in Persian history. The rulers were buried in the famous "Tombs of the Kings," cut into a mountainside and ornately decorated. Nehma's friend and boss understood his servant's dismay about his hometown's situation.

Nehma's presentation was a simple yet calculated explanation of his predicament. The bodyguard's communication skills became vital when he reached Jerusalem where he gave moving speeches, detailed instructions, powerful rebuttals, and rebukes. He provided a constant flow of information to keep the people motivated and the project moving forward despite much opposition.

Many organizational, marital, and friendship failures relate to lack of communication or miscommunication. A good rule for keeping an organization or family healthy and growing is for the leader to say it, repeat it, rephrase it, and say it again, then repeat.

SAY IT, REPEAT IT, REPHRASE IT, AND SAY IT AGAIN, THEN REPEAT.

Leaders also tend toward a "style" or approach to leading. Good leaders know their default leadership tendencies but can adjust to different styles as the situation commands. There are four generally recognized leadership styles. **Autocratic** – The person at the top makes all critical decisions and then instructs followers on what they want them to do. **Democratic** – Most high-level choices are discussed with the team, and decisions are based upon input from team members. **Laissez-faire** – This leader finds competent followers and then empowers and trains them to make decisions apart from their direct involvement. **Transformational** – This leader defines and inspires followers toward a grand vision to be realized through teamwork and collaboration.

Around 2008, during the recession in the U.S., our church had recently completed a capital fundraising campaign. The church was receiving committed funds for some time to do a building addition and renovations on our church. Unfortunately, the recession caused our general fund donations to decrease significantly. This lack meant it was necessary to redirect campaign funds to support the general budget. Designated funds should never be repurposed unless open, abundant communication is made to donors, with the opportunity for them to deny the change in appropriation or ask for a refund. When donors give to a specific project in good faith, they expect their money to be used for the intended purpose. If it is not, the breach of trust will damage future donations from supporters.

I prepared and distributed communication pieces to the congregation but did not do enough. Although original campaign pieces also had the caveat of this possibility, it was not highlighted enough, nor did we contact people personally about their donations. Though most people were untroubled about the situation and understood, a few were irate. We handled complaints as wisely as we knew how, and the problem seemed to subside.

All was well until it came time for the next campaign. As soon as the effort was announced, a handful of people remembered the previous campaign and did not trust another ask. We produced additional informational materials and handled questions both individually and in group settings. The campaign was successful but not without unnecessary travail on my part. We could have saved ourselves a lot of hassle had we communicated more thoroughly and often the first time around.

Here are some thoughts on effective conveyance in any situation.

* **Does my communication appeal to the head or the heart?** Sometimes people need facts. Sometimes they need feelings. The head usually follows the heart, but both kinds of information must be provided. It is helpful to assess both the situation and the person(s) receiving information. Detail-oriented people like accountants, lawyers, and engineers often respond well to abundant facts more so than the average person.

* **Is my communication clear?** Clarity results from editing by several readers. The communicator must be humble enough to accept helpful advice. What seems perfectly clear to you may be cloudy to someone else. It is also beneficial to finish a communique, put it down for a day, then return to edit the work. The short time away gives the creator fresh eyes on their work.

* **Is my communication appropriate for the audience?** Different people receive communication differently. A common mistake is to produce informational materials that are precisely the same for everyone in an organization. It is wise to identify your audience(s) and group them according to how they receive news and how the information being transmitted affects them. A good communicator contours the message to fit the audience.

* **Is my communication consistent?** 2020 and 2021 delivered massive changes and trauma to humanity through the COVID-19 pandemic. The already enormous problem was exacerbated by inconsistent information from the political and medical communities. Various leaders produced con-

flicting decisions that were then thrust upon large population segments. Develop a quality, detailed information piece and be sure all the key players know and understand the message. Messages handed down through the leadership should be consistent and accurate.

* **Are all the key communicators relaying the same message?** It is helpful to get the leading players together, decide on the story to be told, and ensure everyone is telling the same narrative.

* **Am I adequately updating people through the process?** Effective communication is an ongoing, never-ending process. Leaders often deliver information well at the start of a project but fail to provide adequate progress reporting.

Communication is the grease that keeps the engine running. Too little and too sparse an information flow will make the engine eventually lock up. Nehma was a transformational leader who could achieve maximum results in minimal time through quality communication skills.

Food for Thought

As you read through Nehemiah's story, identify the different people and groups to whom he had to communicate. How did the bodyguard relate to each differently?

Evaluate the different audiences to whom you usually communicate. How do you convey information to each group or individual? Do you understand in what manners these groupings receive communication differently? Are you relating to each appropriately?

Bodyguard Tactic Thirteen

Don't Forget To Honor Your Team

As a leader, I was known as an inspirational visionary. I nearly always had a picture of a preferred future in my mind and challenged followers to pursue the goal with me. Visionary people are usually one or two steps in front of the crowd, making these gifted individuals necessary for any growing organization. However, there is often a downside to this kind of personality.

As my organization pursued a substantial project, people got excited and made rapid progress. But as I realized we would accomplish the goal, my focus sometimes morphed into a new project. I occasionally lost interest and mentally moved on to the next big thing. My followers became frustrated because I did not take adequate time and planning to celebrate our victories. I failed to "stop and smell the roses." One of the essential measures of an organization is the frequency and quality with which they celebrate wins. Without celebration, there is no recognition of work performed and goals reached. It's all about the next hill to take. This kind of leadership is demoralizing. People need to celebrate.

Nehma understood this axiom. From the very beginning of their massive undertaking, he was already planning the party at the end and other smaller celebrations along the way. A good celebration says "thank you" to those who contributed to the project. People feel appreciated and will more likely want to follow the leader in new endeavors. When the leader neglects to recognize accomplishments, followers can feel used. "I'm just a stepping stone on someone else's road to glory."

There are usually a few people in any organization who know how to throw a good party. Put them to work. Nearly every program or project contains predictable milestones. Recognize and celebrate milestones along the way, and when the goal is reached, salute and honor the workers who made it happen.

SALUTE AND HONOR THE WORKERS WHO MADE IT HAPPEN.

In a seminal article, Karl E. Weick of Cornell University proposed that "small wins" are integral to solving enormous problems or tasks. The average person can be challenged to achieve a big goal while at the same time be demoralized by its mammoth nature. Rebuilding the walls around Jerusalem was a gigantic undertaking beyond the scope of its citizens' imaginations to solve, as evidenced by the fact that the fortress had been in its present state for about 120 years. The people were paralyzed until a leader could identify small steps leading to more significant wins and, ultimately, a restored wall. It was critical to recognize those baby steps to maintain high morale.

Studies reveal that recognizing wins releases dopamine, a feel-good chemical, in the brain. This chemical is connected to motivation and is needed to spur people forward.

It is important to note that God is a being who enjoys celebration. When the Father first delivered directives to His newly called-out nation, the laws required several celebratory occasions each year. Some observances lasted a day while others a week or more, and every fiftieth year was set aside as a "Jubilee" when the entire society reset. Nearly every major biblical Israeli victory or accomplishment was accompanied by a celebration, and at the culmination of all things, God has already planned a titanic celebration and banquet. Our God likes to party, and we should too.

Celebration reinforces the sense of community, so vital to the health of an organization. It reminds people that "we did this, *and* we did it together." At the same time, the ritual of celebration buttresses the worth of each individual by reminding them that at whatever their level in the organization, their personal contribution counts and is recognized.

Eli and his fellow priests completed the first significant goal of the wall restoration project: the Sheep Gate. Two factors in this accomplishment were worth celebrating. First, the rebuilding was done by the leading priests in the community. Their involvement meant that the principal community leaders were on board with the effort and willing to put their hands to work along with everyone else. They were leading by example, which is a powerful and effective motivator. Secondly, the Sheep Gate was important to the citizens of Jerusalem. This famous gateway into the city meant that sacrificial animals were entering and offered on their behalf. The Sheep Gate not only represented the restoration of a wall but the reformation of their relationship with God. That is worth celebrating, which is what Nehma planned and executed. The party was a confidence builder for everyone.

Food for Thought

* Are you a "celebrating" visionary? Would the people you manage agree?
* Do you usually plan celebration events into strategic plans?
* Who is in charge of celebration events in your family or organization?
* How do you mark special days and accomplishments in your family?
* If you are a church leader, what is significant enough to warrant a celebration in your congregation?
* How do you celebrate employees and volunteers?

Read Nehemiah 3:1-2, which describes the recognition of rebuilt gates. This was a significant milestone in this project. If you are in the midst of, or planning, a new or updated program or project, what are the mile-markers along the way that should be celebrated? Who will be the focus of that recognition?

Bodyguard Tactic Fourteen

Tell Me
The Story

*"People need success stories to tell around
the dinner table. The rebuilding of the walls
has inspired people for generations."*

When someone says "poster child," what comes to mind?

Most of us know of a famous young character named Tiny Tim, the fictional disabled boy who was the motivating force behind Ebenezer Scrooge's transformation from "Bah! Humbug!" to "A merry Christmas, Bob!" The imagery of the disabled kid on crutches quickly became a staple in American culture, featured in dozens of films. From 1901 to 2009, *A Christmas Carol* was portrayed fifty-six times in movies and animated feature films. The story was told on thousands of stages and sold millions of books. But that was not the totality of Tim's influence. The little fellow also inspired a concept with which we are all familiar.

The term "poster child" has been used since 1737 when William Hogarth painted a picture of a child on a hospital coat of arms and asked people to donate to the hospital. Hospitals have used poster children to raise money ever since. The first use of a "real" child took place in 1947. A six-year-old boy named Eugene Anderson appeared in fundraising marketing for March of Dimes. Anderson had been a patient in a Shriners Hospital, whose members recommended the young polio survivor for the role. The photos showed little Eugene leaning on a hospital bed and another of him proudly walking like a child with no disabilities. "Poster people" have been a significant part of financial appeals for decades.

Why is that? What makes the image of a child or a person suffering from starvation so powerful?

The old saying "a picture is worth a thousand words" is true, but if you add enlightening facts to explain the photo, the message becomes even more motivating. Add to these factors the ability to support the cause with ease and haste, and a fundraiser achieves maximum probability of success.

More importantly, a poster person helps both marketer and marketed stay on point. "We are not doing this campaign for self-aggrandizement, big numbers, or glowing reports; we are doing it for this person." A poster person or people helps keep everyone focused on the endgame, which is vital since contributors like to be recognized, and executives like to report "big" results to their constituents and boards. Amid trying to be successful, we sometimes lose sight of why we were doing this in the first place.

Stories are powerful motivators. A picture tells a story, whether it is written, spoken, photographic, or an artistic depiction, narratives provide context for passing along information. A wise leader understands and practices the art of storytelling.

STORIES ARE POWERFUL MOTIVATORS.

It's time to take the leap!

My wife and I enjoyed snow-skiing, and one year we took the opportunity to visit Whistler/Blackcomb ski area in British Columbia with our family. Whistler has the highest vertical ski slopes in North America and can be very challenging. It is also an exquisite journey to drive, with magnificent scenery the entire ascent. We were anticipating a fantastic few days in the snow with our children.

Gail was a better skier than I and could descend a slope looking like grace in motion. On the other hand, I resembled a drunken bear lumbering down a ridge. One morning we decided to ski Blackcomb Glacier. We started our trek up the mountain by riding four lifts and then hiking several hundred yards before we reached the summit. But it was worth the hassle.

We rounded a slight rise in terrain when the magnificent mountains were before our eyes, with glistening snow and a sky as blue as Caribbean water. Gail went ahead a bit and edged toward the precipice of the glacier. I could tell by the look on her face she was astounded. I slowly approached the rim but had to push gently over the edge of a giant bowl, Blackcomb Glacier. People at the bottom looked like ants, and I was quickly petrified. *What the in the world have I done?!* But there was only one way down, and I would have to take a chance sooner or later.

Gail shoved off first, and I watched her as she beautifully traversed the white wonderland. I knew I had to go next, so I ever so slowly pushed my ski tips over the edge. They were jutting into the air before I could even see my destination. Would I go or just keep standing there, becoming more afraid as each minute passed?

Hamilton, you know you'll love this experience, so get on with it. Like jumping off a cliff, I took off, gathering speed quickly enough to become out of control. However, I caught myself and started weaving down the mountain. Slowly and not so surely, I made it to the bottom of the vast run, where I met Gail. She was chuckling with glee as she watched me blunder down the slope.

But I made it without falling and continued down the four-mile run without incident.

I have pondered this experience many times, and we shared the story dozens of times through the years. Every time I read the account of Jesus calling Peter out of the boat and onto the water, I think of Blackcomb Glacier and think, *If you want to walk on water, you've got to get out of the boat.* These two far-flung events remind me of this profound truth, and I think I have a taste of how Pete felt when he dangled his toes into the sea.

Stories serve as a means of transmitting cultural values, beliefs, and traditions from one generation to the next. Stories have the power to engage, entertain, and educate, making them an essential part of our social and cultural heritage.

TELL ME A STORY AND I WILL REMEMBER IT.

Stories evoke strong emotions and inspire bold action. They can evoke feelings of fear, sadness, joy, and excitement, and can catalyze change. They can challenge our beliefs and values and help us to see the world from a different perspective. Whether they are told orally, written down, or acted out on stage, stories have the power to inspire and motivate people to act, making them an essential tool for social and political change.

The power of stories can be seen in how they shape our beliefs and attitudes. They can help us understand our place in the world and our relationships with others, and they can give us a sense of identity by giving us a shared history and culture.

The story of Nehemiah and his bold undertaking teaches many lessons in a manner that no other method can do as well. Wise leaders continually develop a scrapbook of stories that can be pulled out and told at the right moment. Indeed, a picture is worth a thousand words.

Food for Thought

Are you a good story keeper? Are you a proficient storyteller? What could you do to improve?

If you are presently amid or contemplating a large project or program, is there a story or two you can use to help people see your vision and discover the motivation to act?

Read Matthew 13 and ponder Jesus's effective use of stories to explain profound spiritual truths.

Bodyguard Tactic Fifteen

SERVANT LEADERSHIP

*"A humble leader is a beloved leader
who many will follow."*

Pride is the original sin. A haughty spirit caused Lucifer to challenge God and attempt a Kingdom coup along with a hoard of soon-to-be demons. Spurred on by the fallen angel, pride incited humans to challenge the Almighty, resulting in all of us getting kicked out of the Garden.

Every person must deal with the pride monster on some level. Even the humblest sometimes shake their fist at their Maker and proclaim, "You're not the boss of me!" Arrogance combined with leadership has a trickle-down effect on followers. This defect is often reflected in group dynamics, whether in a small group or a large organization. Some people cower under the hubris of a boss, while others rebel, often passive-aggressively. And finally, some groups choose to make pride the corporate culture.

In his famous 1970 essay, Robert K. Greenleaf coined the phrase "servant leadership," though I would contend that Jesus beat him to the principle.

Our friend Nehma was a well-educated person with powerful connections in the government. He dined on choice meals and lived in luxurious surroundings. The bodyguard to the king had many reasons to be full of pride, yet pridefulness was not a characteristic of this servant leader.

"I confess the sins we Israelites, including myself and my father's family, have committed against you. We have acted very wickedly toward you. We have not obeyed the commands, decrees, and laws you gave your servant Moses" (Nehemiah 1:6b-7 NIV).

Nehma's knee-jerk reaction to the disturbing news about his hometown was to fall on his knees and pray. His invocation reveals much about his character. After recognizing the supremacy of God and His loving nature, he launched into a series of confessions concerning the disobedience of his people. The acknowledgment includes the sins of both himself and his family.

There is no particular reason why Nehma would have had any part in the disobedience that caused the downfall of his nation. However, his character demanded he accept a level of personal responsibility for the condition of Israel. Humbling himself before God and claiming his share of the guilt reveals his self-effacing nature.

Jesus, the most extraordinary leader of all, had much to say about leaders having a servant mindset.

There is a humorous episode where two of Jesus's followers, James and John, dubbed "the sons of thunder," approached the

Teacher with a request. They brazenly asked that they might be exalted to sit on His right and left side in Heaven. Their request indeed took chutzpah, but as always Jesus firmly but gracefully put them back in their places. Nicely, the Servant Leader declared, "Absolutely not," and then He explained that the decision was not His to make.

The actions of the two brothers made the rest of the disciples indignant, and they were ready to chew them out when Jesus sat them all down for one of His typical experiential lessons.

"Jesus called them together and said, 'You know that those who are regarded as rulers of the Gentiles lord it over them, and their high officials exercise authority over them. Not so with you. Instead, whoever wants to become great among you must be your servant, and whoever wants to be first must be slave of all. For even the Son of Man did not come to be served, but to serve, and to give his life as a ransom for many'" (Mark 10:42-45 NIV).

We can only imagine James's and John's reactions, but it is reasonable to picture the two proud brothers lowering their heads, wishing they could crawl under the nearest rock.

The Apostle Paul writes in the letter to the church at Philippi that humility made the Savior forfeit the glories of Heaven for flesh and blood, ending in miserable death.

Nehma proved himself a truly great leader. He followed words penned by the famous devotional writer Andrew Murray: "Pride must die in you, or nothing of heaven can live in you."

"PRIDE MUST DIE IN YOU, OR NOTHING OF HEAVEN CAN LIVE IN YOU." — ANDREW MURRAY

Food for Thought

Thoughtfully read the following five pitfalls of pride and discern their truth and how it could apply to your situation.

Pride creates a false sense of security.

Pride blinds the bearer from reality.

Pride diverts responsibility from the bearer.

Pride depends too heavily upon positional rather than relational leadership.

Pride impedes your ability to learn.

Read Philippians 2:1-11, which defines the basis of servant leadership as exemplified by Jesus.

Bodyguard Tactic Sixteen

THE FEAR FACTOR

"Leading this undertaking was the scariest thing I've ever tried, but anytime someone steps to the front of the crowd, they will experience the fear factor."

Leadership is scary, but it's part of the job. If you step up to lead most anything, one normal emotion is fear. How you manage it makes the difference between success and failure.

Arash Javanbakht and Linda Saab, assistant professors of psychiatry at Wayne State University, explain that fear is a powerful motivator and a source of empowerment that can be harnessed to propel one forward.

Steve Farber describes pivotal times in leadership he calls "Oh S**t! Moments" or (OS!M). OS!Ms are life-altering junctures when a leader finds themselves face to face with a significant decision that might propel them forward, but the outcome is not fully known. They can choose to face their fears and take a leap or retreat. He explains that you know you are a leader when OS!Ms cross your path.

If you've led much of anything, you have experienced OS!M situations firsthand. There are numerous possible outcomes, both productive and counterproductive, from the fear experience. Here are a few.

Fear is a natural and universal human emotion, and it can have both positive and negative effects on leadership. On the one hand, fear can motivate leaders to work harder and strive for excellence. On the other hand, fear can also cause leaders to become overly cautious, indecisive, and paralyzed in the face of challenges.

One of the most common fears that leaders face is the fear of failure. Unmitigated fear of failure can cause leaders to avoid taking risks and limit their ability to innovate and succeed. Fear of failure can also lead to a lack of delegation and a desire to control every aspect of a project, which can negatively impact the leader-follower relationship and result in burnout.

Another fear that leaders may face is the fear of rejection or criticism. This condition can cause leaders to avoid confrontation and difficult conversations, leading to missed opportunities and ineffective decision-making. Fear of rejection or criticism can also cause leaders to become overly defensive, leading to a lack of trust and collaboration among team members.

Fear can also impact a leader's ability to inspire and motivate followers. Fear-driven leaders may become overly controlling, micromanaging their followers, and failing to trust them. Loss of trust will lead to a toxic work environment and a demotivated workforce.

In 1932 Franklin D. Roosevelt was inaugurated thirty-second president of the United States. His inaugural address, which lasted only twenty minutes, became one of American history's most powerful and mountain-moving orations.

America was in the throes of the Great Depression, with unemployment reaching over 25 percent. Farmers were losing their land, banks closed their doors, and twelve million people were out of work. The country was in dire circumstances, and fear was rampant. In the speech, Roosevelt identified fear as the enemy and described it like this:

So, first of all, let me assert my firm belief that the only thing we have to fear is fear itself—nameless, unreasoning, unjustified terror which paralyzes needed efforts to convert retreat into advance. In every dark hour of our national life, a leadership of frankness and of vigor has met with that understanding and support of the people themselves which is essential to victory. And I am convinced that you will again give that support to leadership in these critical days.

Roosevelt, who suffered from polio, overcame his fears to help American citizens do the same. He took decisive, well-planned action and dramatically expanded the executive branch's power, as would be done in wartime. The convincing argument emphasized the country's condition of being at war, therefore requiring strong leadership authority that could take swift action. He became one of America's most effective presidents, navigating World War II and leading America to emerge as the wealthiest and most powerful nation on earth.

All this is because our thirty-second president conquered fear and used it as its own worst enemy. Fear can be debilitating for a leader, or it can be harnessed for decisive, effective action.

Nehemiah took the same route as our president. He was placed in a fearful but influential position, which made him God's choice for the restoration of Jerusalem's defenses and the integrity of his people.

In the month of Nisan in the twentieth year of King Artaxerxes, when wine was brought for him, I took the wine and gave it to the king. I had not been sad in his presence before, so the king asked me, "Why does your face look so sad when you are not ill? This can be nothing but sadness of heart."

I was very much afraid, but I said to the king, "May the king live forever! Why should my face not look sad when the city where my ancestors are buried lies in ruins, and its gates have been destroyed by fire?"

The king said to me, "What is it you want?"

Then I prayed to the God of heaven, and I answered the king, "If it pleases the king and if your servant has found favor in his sight, let him send me to the city in Judah where my ancestors are buried so that I can rebuild it." (Nehemiah 2:1-5 NIV)

"I was very much afraid . . ." These are the words of an honest, forthright person, a sign of strength in leadership.

One can imagine what might have gone through the bodyguard's mind. *Oh, geez! It's time to step up to the plate, old boy. God, I hope you are paying attention because I am a dead man without you.* He was having an OS!M!

But this was only the first of one fearful time after another when he embarked on his journey. He would need to fearlessly face down strong political and social opposition and hostility from Jewish leaders and convince the masses to join his effort.

Fear can be harnessed toward resolute determination. The following are a few suggestions for taking fear by the horns.

* Know what scares you and reason through the issues by comparing the probable results of inaction against the possibilities of follow-through.

* Don't sabotage yourself by thinking you are an imposter. It does not matter if others under your mantle are smarter or more skilled. Do what you do best and invite the rest to help you.
* Be open and honest. You don't know everything and cannot do everything—that is called being human. Don't try to hide your insecurity in any unsure situation.
* It is said, "Courage is fear that has said its prayers." Nehemiah was praying *through* his fear.
* Stop the fear of failure. If you are not failing, you are likely not doing much. The only people you won't find failing are in your local cemetery.

Every leader often faces the fear factor, but it need not stop you.

Food for Thought

When you are facing a fearful situation, ask yourself these questions.

1. What is the source of my fear, and how can I address it realistically?
2. What is the worst-case scenario, and how likely is it to occur?
3. What resources and support systems do I have in place to overcome this fear?
4. How can I reframe this situation in a positive light?
5. Have I faced similar fears in the past, and what did I learn from those experiences?
6. What are the potential benefits and opportunities in this situation?
7. How can I use this fear to motivate me toward growth and progress?

8. Who can I turn to for guidance and support in overcoming this fear?

Read Joshua 1. God repeatedly told Joshua to be strong and courageous. Why is this injunction used so often for the new leader of the Jewish people?

Bodyguard Tactic Seventeen

CREATE YOUR TEAM

"Leadership success is dependent upon those whom one gathers around them."

There is no such thing as a self-made man or woman. We are inextricably interlocked with other humans in more ways than can be defined or recognized. One generation stands upon the accomplishments of those who have gone before. Our family and community structures shape us, and we move forward or backward, yoked with fellow travelers on similar paths. Whom we gather around us will define how far we will go.

I recently watched an exciting college basketball game. Both teams were of high caliber, and the score seesawed back and forth the entire game. Though I was unfamiliar with players on either team, one guard began to distinguish himself. He was an outstanding player and could dribble and move the ball well. However, it was evident that he had an inflated view of his value to the team. Commentators agreed that he dribbled way too much and took impulsive shots.

The clock wound down, and the other team was up by one point. The noted player and his team had one last chance to win. Make note that I said, "and his team." Somehow, he didn't get the memo and tried to win the game independently. The opposing team had also noted what the commentators reported, so they double-teamed him on the last play. He lost the ball, and the opponents ran the court and the clock to win the game.

Interestingly, they were the underdogs. Basketball is a team sport, and so is life. As the John Maxwell proclaims, "Teamwork makes the dream work."

Leading a good team is like conducting an orchestra. Outstanding conductors gather the best musicians they can find, unite them around a stated purpose, and then artfully draw the best out of each instrumentalist at just the right place and time. Without the conductor, an orchestra is a jumbled mess of dissonant notes.

Culture creates superstars. Coaches create teams. Nehma's roster started with King Artaxerxes and ended up including the entire community of Jerusalem.

CULTURE CREATES SUPERSTARS. COACHES CREATE TEAMS.

The bodyguard, for whom we have no previous leadership record, knew that this project was well beyond his scope of ability or resources. So Nehma turned a ragtag group of downtrodden citizens into a building and fighting force. As author Jim Collins wrote in the classic leadership book *Good to Great*, leadership involves getting the right people on the bus in the right seats.

Leaders foretell their story by those they gather around them. You will become whom you make your partners, and the same group can predict your success.

LEADERS FORETELL THEIR STORY BY THOSE THEY GATHER AROUND THEM.

Gather a diverse group depending upon the need. Do not choose only people like yourself to join your team. One of the most effective presidents in history was Abraham Lincoln. The outstanding book *Team of Rivals* explains how Lincoln was savvy to gather a group of cabinet members, nearly all of whom were political and philosophical rivals—some even his own political enemies. This group of men brought many ideas and methods to the table and Lincoln had the ability and authority to focus them on their mission—to save the Union. Their diversity was the genius of their team. Which leads to another team builder value.

Listen to your team members. We choose team members because each one brings something unique and valuable to the table. But if one chooses not to listen because of an inflated ego or insecurity, the team and subsequent mission loses.

I just finished reading the compelling book *Sea Stories* by Admiral William H. McRaven, which chronicles the exemplary life of this Navy SEAL from his days struggling to become a SEAL, all the way to being the commander of all U.S. Special Operations forces. The work is a handbook on team building at every level of operations and so exciting as to make it a true page-turner.

The last chapter of the book explains the story of the removal of Osama Bin Laden. The number and diversity of military representatives, political figures (all the way to the president of the

United States), and agencies involved was astounding. Numerous possible methods of conducting the raid were presented from various sources. The strike took months of preparation, culminating with actual rehearsals of the operation until they were honed to perfection.

Admiral McRaven was leading the operation and if you read the account, this consummate leader reveals a critical leadership lesson. Listen. Ask questions and listen. Listen with complete focus. Invite all the appropriate team members to the table and solicit their input.

Read, study, and listen to podcasts presenting stories and methods of great coaches, military leaders, presidents, CEOs, and successful pastors. One can learn from anyone who has built good teams. It is helpful to study team leaders from diverse kinds of organizations. For instance, the systems of military leaders differ from those of most sports coaches, and CEOs often work only with high-capacity individuals who are already proven, while nonprofit leaders often work with volunteers. There is much to learn from a variety of styles and systems. A church leader who only learns from other church leaders will develop a myopic view of team building.

Get on a team of which you are not the leader. This often involves participating in an organization outside your normal job. If you enjoy sports, find a team to join, or if you like to volunteer, find an organization that does work about which you are passionate, and get on one of their teams.

Working with a team that is outside our norm allows us to see teamwork and its leadership from a different perspective. One can learn much from the successes and failures of other team leaders.

Find a quality leader to be your boss. Success is not only about those on a horizontal plane of colleagues, but vertical as well. One of the most effective ways to learn leadership is to work for a competent boss. Mike Krzyzewski is the winningest NCAA Division I basketball coach of all time. Coach K coached forty-seven seasons and 1,202 games while winning five national championships.

The G.O.A.T. of college basketball got his start playing for legendary coach Bobby Knight at Army, where he went on eventually to become the head coach, being recommended by Knight. Coach K later served as Bobby's assistant at Indiana, who also recommended him to coach at Duke University. Knight made popular the motion offense in college basketball, which Coach K used his entire career. Though their coaching styles were radically different, and their relationship eventually deteriorated, Duke's legendary figure learned much about leadership from "The General,. as Knight was deemed.

Most great leaders have worked for great leaders who not only mentored and coached them, but also promoted them along their road to success. Nehma's leadership acumen was gained in part by observing the most powerful leader in the world as his employee. If you want to learn leadership, go to work for a great leader.

Food for Thought

When Jesus started a movement, He deliberately chose twelve key players to "be with Him," along with a handful of others. Why did this master leader pick these people?

Character, chemistry, and competence are the three stool legs of a quality team member. What do you believe is the order of importance of these traits and why?

Most leaders would agree that character is requirement one. Without it, everything eventually falls apart. I believe chemistry is number two. Jesus picked leaders with whom He could work well and bought into His dream. One can have impressive competence but still not fit the team. One must choose the level of competence *required* for the job, knowing that other competencies can and should be learned.

Take note: All leaders eventually choose someone who does not work out for the team. Don't be discouraged. Even Jesus picked Judas.

The most significant impediment to team development is an insecure leader. Insecure leaders draw people they can control and who generally have lower competencies. The insecure leader wants to be the "smartest" and most powerful person in the room. Most leaders possess one to three core competencies, so they develop a team of people who are more proficient in other areas of expertise and allow them to run with the ball. Insecure leaders drive off the best players.

Read Mark 3:13-19 to observe Jesus's team-building methods.

Bodyguard Tactic Eighteen

BE A GOOD FOLLOWER

"Genuine deference fosters loyalty from those who can help a leader's cause."

A strong leader is also a good follower. Eleven of twelve Apostles became outstanding leaders who initiated a movement that is still going strong 2,000 years later. None of these men were formidable leaders until they followed the master leader for three years. When they called out people to become dedicated followers of Jesus, they knew the role firsthand since they too were followers.

A STRONG LEADER IS ALSO A GOOD FOLLOWER.

Given this truth, quality followership garners little attention. There is no end to books, classes, articles, speeches, and leadership talks. Schools that offer MBA degrees tout their leadership development programs since not many students are looking for advanced degrees in following, yet to become an outstanding leader they must gain followers. Leadership requires learning followership, and leading unwilling, untrained, and under-sourced supporters is difficult at best.

Since everyone experiences both sides of the leadership-followership coin, it is essential to understand what makes a good follower. Practicing appropriate deference is the starting point. Deference means that one practices humble submission and respect to someone—in this case, a leader. This trait often defines the gap between failure and success.

Nehma's first act of deference was with God. Nehemiah 1:4-7 demonstrates his approach to those in more powerful positions.

When I heard these things, I sat down and wept. For some days, I mourned and fasted and prayed before the God of heaven. Then I said:

"Lord, the God of heaven, the great and awesome God, who keeps his covenant of love with those who love him and keep his commandments, let your ear be attentive and your eyes open to hear the prayer your servant is praying before you day and night for your servants, the people of Israel."

As Leonard Ravenhill said, "The person who kneels before God can stand before anyone." Nehma understood that without God's blessing, his endeavor would fall flat before it even started. His simple request was that the Almighty grant him favor with the king. Jesus's brother wrote that God gives grace to the humble but opposes the proud.

Nehma will now go before the king and ask for help, and he explains about himself, "I was very much afraid." These are not the words of a person who has determined that he had no concerns since God was on his side. Nehma's words reveal a deep understanding of authority and a willingness to follow well. As a result, Artaxerxes bestowed his blessing upon his faithful servant and thus began the restoration project. Effective followership now placed Nehma in a position of leadership. Both God and the king blessed the upcoming endeavor and the person who would lead it.

Nehma positioned himself with his boss, the king, in a manner that garnered support. He served many years as a humble servant to the ruler, who repaid him with respect and empathy. Deference does not pay off with some leaders, but most appreciate and are loyal to those who approach their guidance with proper regard.

Jesus was the most influential leader in history, and He started a movement over 2,000 years ago that is still healthy and growing throughout the world. As a follower of Jesus, I would contend there is a divine element to the success of the church, but even considered from a purely human perspective, this man has accrued more dedicated and competent followers than anyone. So what is His secret?

Jesus looked for people willing to commit, not just to Him but to His cause. The road of followership would be fraught with many temptations to turn back. Only fully devoted disciples would finish the course.

Jesus looked for people willing to sacrifice. When He called the twelve Apostles, they left everything to follow Him. He told His acolytes they would sometimes be required to give up their family, friends, wealth, position, and even themselves.

Jesus looked for teachable people. Teachable people know that they don't know and are willing to learn. A lifelong study of any leader is the art of recognizing the myriad of information and wisdom they do not know and allowing what they *hought* they knew to morph.

Jesus looked for open, honest people. The disciples were brutally honest and transparent about their questions and shortcomings. The follower who maintained the most secrets turned out to be the traitor who betrayed the Master—Judas.

Jesus looked for courageous people. Effective followers must be willing to encounter new and sometimes fearful situations with their leader. The Teacher's devotees would be persecuted and even die for their beliefs.

Jesus looked for people of action because he needed doers, not just talkers. Considering both teams, ninety-two players and thirty coaches are suited up for NFL games. Those statistics place 122 participants in the average game. The average seating capacity of an NFL stadium is 64,444, and 64,000 to 122 is the comparison between people playing the game and those simply watching. Jesus enlisted players, not gazers.

Jesus looked for people who would persevere. Every organization, from families to giant corporations, experiences tough times. Jesus told his followers that they would share many troubles in life and the crown goes to the disciples who kept the faith.

People who follow Jesus's leadership model exhibit these qualities in abundance, and they are all rooted in their deference to his leadership.

Food for Thought

What words describe you best as a follower?

When have you decided to stop following someone and why? Was your decision wise, or would you have changed your action?

How would your family, friends, and associates rate you as a follower? Why? It might be helpful to ask those close to you what they think of you as a follower.

Read the following scriptures to be reminded of the cost of following Jesus: Luke 9:57-62, Mark 8:34-38, and Matthew 10:5-42.

Bodyguard Tactic Nineteen

Leadership Teachers Are Everywhere

"God uses who He wishes to mentor our development, and the teachers sometimes come from unexpected places, so a wise leader remains open-minded and learns."

Much of my early leadership development was derived from Boy Scouting. Scouting started me on the leadership journey and is where my leadership chops sprouted. A quality scout troop requires a strong leader, and I was lucky to have a scoutmaster named

OK Friend. Yes, that was indeed his name. I rose quickly through the scouting ranks until I reached the honor of Eagle Scout and then Order of the Arrow. Few Boy Scouts reach this milestone, but I loved everything about the club, whose members dressed in army green and held high moral and ethical standards.

My scoutmaster saw potential in me that I did not discern, placing me in leadership positions for special events, camping trips, scout camps, and, most importantly, patrol leader and senior troop leader. I learned many leadership maxims that served me well throughout my life from a man named OK Friend.

I worked in a warehouse in my late teens and drove a delivery truck for a frozen-food distributor. It only took me about three years to deduce that working at twenty-two below zero was not going to be my vocation! During those years, the warehouse manager to whom I reported taught me much about leading as well. The difference between him and my Boy Scout leader was that he was an incompetent manager; I learned how *not* to guide people.

His directions were often delivered at one hundred decibels with a scowl on his face and filth erupting from his mouth. He was intent on making employees miserable eight to ten hours a day.

During this period of employment, I experienced a religious revival. I became a Christian at age twelve but spent many years on a prodigal journey before becoming a dedicated follower of Jesus. When my boss learned of my transformation, he spent much energy testing me with unreasonable demands and demeaning conversations. Most days, his first words to me were, "F-you, Hamilton." I also quit smoking cigarettes during that period, which irritated him as a fellow smoker. He regularly blew smoke in my face, trying to get a rise out of me. Generally speaking, he tried to make my life hell. This man was an unlikely source of leadership development but taught me much despite himself.

We tend to hold predetermined views of the mentors and partners God might use to move us forward. For instance, we might think the person must be a dedicated Christ follower, spiritually mature, and possessing time-tested leadership experience. We could assume the person must be of the same sex and more aged. However, our determination of whom God would use to move us forward versus the Almighty's view can be very different.

When Solomon became king of Israel, he aspired to construct the temple his father, David, had envisioned but was not allowed to build. The project would require large quantities of lumber and skilled labor. He wrote to King Hiram, a Phoenician, requesting him to partner with him in this endeavor. David had cultivated a good relationship with this monarch, and Hiram was favorably disposed toward David's son. He agreed to sell Solomon the lumber in exchange for wheat and other supplies, and the Phoenician king assisted young Solomon through the entire project. One would not expect a pagan king to mentor a Jewish leader through partnering to build a temple for their God. As a result, the two leaders' partnership resulted in the magnificent structure known as Solomon's Temple.

God used the Persian kings Cyrus and Darius to allow Jewish captives to return to Judah and rebuild the temple destroyed by Nebuchadnezzar. They also provided resources and guidance for the effort.

Nehma was a Jewish person of great integrity and latent leadership skills. He must have spent many hours observing the king's leadership style and likely managed numerous cupbearers and butlers in the monarch's court. The position was prestigious and well paid. Where did he get his leadership chops?

One would not assume to learn these skills from a person holding you as a forced servant, deported from your homeland. Nevertheless, Artaxerxes was the monarch of over half the world's population, covering twenty-two million square miles. He oversaw numerous colossal building projects and led thousands of troops.

God used this unlikely king to mentor Nehma's leadership development.

We sometimes limit the possibilities of those who can help us in our journey because of our predetermined picture of who those people will be, including their characteristics. For instance, it is easy to reject a coach or mentor because they have different opinions and views. Being narrow-minded can cause us to refuse assistance from someone supportive but not like us.

I wonder if Timothy, the Apostle Paul's protégé, would have envisioned the hardheaded, outspoken, determined Apostle to the Gentiles as his mentor and coach. In Paul's writings, the former Christian hater describes his young follower as soft-spoken, timid, and fearful. One would think Timothy would have desired a mentor whose personality was more like his own, but the opposite proved true. Timothy was self-aware, making him willing to learn from a more decisive, demanding leader than himself. How much less of a leader would the young man have been if not challenged and prodded by a strong character like Paul?

Though we can and should choose mentors who we think will help us grow, we must also be aware that good leaders learn from many sources, some of which we do not expect.

Food for Thought

Consider the various sources of leadership development in your life. Do you reject possible resources because someone holds differing values, political views, ethnicities, prestige, gender, or religious beliefs?

Read Nehemiah 2:1-9. What leadership cues are revealed in the conversation between Nehma and Artaxerxes?

Bodyguard Tactic Twenty

RESOURCE YOUR TEAM

"Those whom God calls, God equips."

Life is an internship.

Both my youngest and oldest birth daughters married men who had three children from previous marriages, and neither of the girls had children before that. Both families also have a child with disabilities. Andrea and Kristin were thrown into the water to sink or swim and, to my delight, are swimming well.

I believe God called my children to this opportunity knowing they have the parenting chops to provide their children with a quality upbringing. Fortunately, ours was a healthy family, which allowed my four daughters to learn parenting skills in an uplifting environment. Growing up, they learned more about parenting than they realized until they found themselves in their new families. God had been preparing them their entire lives for this vocation, and I frequently listened to their recollections of how their mother handled different situations.

Kristin relates her story:

My Bible verse for becoming a mom on my journey has been from the story of Esther. Like some of the other biblical examples you mentioned, I think Esther is another amazing example of a leader who felt inadequate but placed her ALL in God and trusted Him as He called her to something risky and great at just the right time, preparing her long before she ever knew what her journey would be.

"Who knows if perhaps you were made queen for such a time as this?" (Esther 4:14b NLT)

When I read this verse, I often hear God speaking it to me this way:

"Who knows if perhaps you were made their mom for such a time as this?"

Many times, circumstances in life place us in situations where we feel incompetent. The Bible is replete with examples of men and women fearing failure because they did not feel qualified for specific tasks. Moses argued with God about his lack of speaking and leadership abilities, yet he saved an entire nation and led two million Israelites for the last half of his life. Joshua was intimidated when the younger leader was required to step into Moses's shoes and lead the new nation into the Promised Land. God repeatedly instructed him to be "strong and courageous" and that He would never leave his side. David seemed to be the least qualified of his brothers to become a king, but he became the preeminent monarch in the nation's history. Peter felt that his denial of friendship with Jesus disqualified him for future leadership in the new kingdom, but Jesus had other plans. One would be hard-pressed to find twelve people less likely to start and lead a worldwide movement, but Jesus called the twelve Apostles and spent three years equipping them to do just that.

Apprenticeship is an excellent equipping method, and God places people in our lives to show us how to become proficient in whatever He assigns us. Apprenticeship does not have to be "official" to be valuable, so it is wise to surround oneself with people a few steps ahead of us and pay close attention to their lives. It is unwise and unnecessary to go it alone.

SURROUND YOURSELF WITH PEOPLE WHO ARE A FEW STEPS AHEAD OF YOU AND PAY CLOSE ATTENTION TO THEIR LIVES.

Their names are "Jim and Jim." The two Jims were instrumental in my initial discipleship development and subsequent leadership and ministry growth.

I became a dedicated Christ follower at age twelve when I accepted an Easter sermon invitation to put my trust in God and get baptized. I walked from the back row of the large church (my typical seat) and told Pastor Kineman what I wanted to do. He smiled and asked me to repeat my confession of faith in Jesus which I proudly verbalized. Within a few minutes, I was entering the baptismal waters, and to the amazement of my parents and other relatives, little Donnie had given his life to Jesus. Fast-forward a few years.

As I mentioned in the last chapter, most of my Junior and high school careers were spent on a prodigal journey that went from bad to worse. When I read about the younger brother in Jesus's famous story, I get it. Likely, many of you reading this get it as well.

It's a long story, but in my late teens, I was married and still partying. My cousin and great friend kept inviting me to attend the new church started by the one where I grew up. They talked about how I would like the pastor and the exciting atmosphere. It took a long time and some serious prompting from the Holy Spirit before I decided to give it a try. I was blown away. The atmosphere was electric, and these folks seemed excited about church and it was like they possessed a sense of purpose that eluded me. Cousin Eddie was right. I was sold.

At Southern Heights, I became friends with the youth pastor and his wife, Jim and Vicki Harless. Jim was a fellow hunter/fisherman and a good friend of my cousin. They invited me to hunt with them, which was a blast! *You really could have fun without drugs and booze*, I thought, even though alcohol still had some hold on me. Jim saw something in me I did not see in myself. I could communicate and lead reasonably well. I had potential. It must have been a taste of what Jesus saw in a few fishermen.

JIM SAW SOMETHING IN ME THAT I DID NOT SEE IN MYSELF.

Jim and I started meeting regularly. I worked nights, so I frequently met him with a box of doughnuts and coffee early in the morning at his office after my shift. The youth pastor had become my mentor. Jim challenged and taught me in many ways, and before long, I was a youth group coach and Sunday school teacher. Through our doughnut meetings, Jim taught me what it meant to follow Jesus while he and his wife *showed* me the same. **Teach, show, apply**—that is called apprenticeship, and it works. Within a few years, under his guidance, I decided to enter ministry. I ended up there for over forty years and am still going strong. By the way, I highly recommend coffee and doughnuts for discipleship training.

I've always liked big cities, and during my sophomore year at Johnson Bible College (now Johnson University), I was given the opportunity to serve a church on Long Island, about an hour from Manhattan. Jim Hamer was the pastor of this healthy church, and he was passionate about ministry in New York and the Northeast, one of the least churched regions of the United States. He and his wife, Bonnie, would later become my in-laws since I married her sister. Jim and I hit it off quickly. We were both vocal and opinionated, loved to laugh, and shared nontraditional views of the way churches should operate. Jim's words and actions ignited in me a holy challenge, vision, and proper outlet for my somewhat rebellious spirit. "You should come to the Northeast and plant a church after college," he said. Though our original plans for my work with him on Long Island did not work out, I came to a region that desperately needed healthy, soul-reaching churches and served there for thirty-eight years. During that time, I've watched this dedicated man's determined spirit never waver, and it made me want to do the same.

These men not only challenged me but equipped me to step up to the challenge. When God calls someone, He provides the necessary tools to meet the challenge. Those tools usually arrive at your doorstep through people He brings into your life, people the Teacher knows will help you take your next steps.

Dave Ferguson, Patrick O'Connell, and Warren Bird explain how this process works in their book *Hero Maker*. *Hero Maker* reminds us that Jesus's method was simple. Pick a few dedicated people and spend enough time with them so that they "rub off" on you. That is the story of the Apostles, who changed the world. Leadership is not so much taught as it is caught.

Nehma was likely equipped by his predecessors in the cup-bearing and bodyguard business and learned leadership qualities from the king. Since the monarch was famous for building projects, Nehma would have enjoyed ample time to learn the art and science of construction projects. He also had a wealth of biblical information at his disposal—stories of men and women who led God's people throughout the ages.

God does not call people to a job without equipping them with the time and resources to accomplish it. Our leadership paths often come from unlikely sources and from those we have yet to meet. Wise leaders learn how to work in partnership with God's plans.

Food for Thought

Consider your proficiencies. Who are God's people in your life to coach and mentor you? Are you maximizing growth opportunities in your network?

It is a maxim of professional sports and executive leadership that the further one goes and wants to grow, the more coaching one needs.

Check out Mark 3:13-19, Luke 9:1-6, and Luke 10:1-12 to observe Jesus's methods.

Bodyguard Tactic Twenty-One

FIND A NEED AND FILL IT

"Leaders see needs others disregard or overlook and want to act."

A couple of years ago, I became a board member of a new organization called Unchained, which is a coalition purposed to fight human trafficking, especially of children. Most of the organization's work is in two South American countries. Human trafficking is a tragedy of enormous proportions, and I was honored to be part of this effort to fight it.

A friend started this effort after witnessing firsthand the trafficking business while serving abroad in the military. Scott saw young women being exploited by ruthless people who made huge profits from buying and selling innocent victims, most often for sex. Globally, slavery is a $150 billion a year industry.

Interestingly, many soldiers also witnessed this activity during their tour of duty, but one person chose to do something about it—my friend Scott. There are two differences between leaders and the general population. First, torchbearers often see problems that others overlook or turn their heads and walk away from. Second, a catalyst considers a dilemma and wants to act on it.

A few years ago, I became aware of a sad problem in our community. Our church owned a fifty-three-acre campus that we developed into a community park over many years. At one point, our next project was to construct a small playground. As we considered what kind of playground to build, our community outreach director received a call from a church member. This person became aware of a playground accessible to children with disabilities. Our director visited the playground, which community volunteers built, and immediately called me. She explained that once I had seen this playground, I would want to create something similar, so I should visit.

I drove into the township park and pulled up to the playground, which was very large. As I walked up to the fenced-in recreation area, I noticed a child in a wheelchair rolling around the playground and enjoying the amenities designed for those with special needs. I was astounded! It dawned on me that children in wheelchairs or with physical disabilities could not play on average playgrounds because the surface was not navigable for them. Honestly, it was embarrassing. Tears came to my eyes as I watched this young person playing and smiling. Our outreach director was right; I immediately decided this was the kind of structure we would build.

Over the next two years, we raised over half a million dollars, involved 1,400 volunteers, and built a two-acre playground complex that was fully accessible to all children. We also built public restrooms and a large pavilion for family picnics and entertainment. Since that time, thousands of community members have enjoyed Adventure Zone Playground.

Leaders see needs and act to meet them. They raise public consciousness, develop a plan, recruit team members, raise funds, and do whatever is necessary to accomplish the goal.

LEADERS SEE NEEDS AND ACT TO MEET THEM.

Candy Lightner is one such person. In 1980, Candy's daughter, thirteen-year-old Cari, was walking along a quiet road headed to a church carnival. She was struck by a drunken driver who had been arrested on several drunk driving charges and had hit another person just the week before striking Cari. Cari was killed in the incident.

Candy was inspired to research laws and attitudes concerning drunk driving and discovered that most offenders are released with minimal penalties while thousands of people died yearly due to intoxicated drivers. She found that her daughter's killer would likely receive little punishment since drunken driving was not considered a serious offense at the time.

As a result, Cari's mother started an organization called MADD, or Mothers Against Drunk Driving. She believed drunken drivers killing people was "the only socially acceptable form of homicide." The year Cari died, 27,000 people died from alcohol-related accidents. She lobbied California's political figures, including the governor, who enacted legislation for more severe penalties for this crime. Repeat offenders could now go to jail for up to four years.

By 1985, MADD had over 600,000 members and influenced laws across the country, making driving while intoxicated a severe crime. The minimum drinking age was raised to twenty-one, as states that did not implement these laws were barred from receiving federal funding for highways. The national legal blood alcohol content was also lowered and tied to federal funding. By the twentieth anniversary of MADD's inception, alcohol-related fatalities had decreased by 40 percent.

In 1970, a woman living near Niagara Falls had two children who contracted rare illnesses. She soon learned that nearly every neighbor in the Love Canal neighborhood suffered from strange diseases. She began researching the problem and discovered they lived next to a waste site where 20,000 tons of toxic chemicals were dumped. The concerned mother and leader started a protest movement, and 800 neighbors were relocated. Ultimately, Lois Gibbs was the catalyst for the U.S. Environmental Agency to create the Superfund to clean up toxic waste sites across the country.

I have a friend named Jossy Chacko, who is the president of an international organization that aims to transform villages and communities by training and mobilizing men and women to share the Gospel and provide vocational education. His story is a fine example of how leaders are different from the masses.

Jossy Chacko was a successful Asian Indian businessman when he experienced a life-altering encounter in his personal life while traveling to visit the Taj Mahal with his newly wedded wife. A little boy named Raju, holding a broom in his hands, approached the newlyweds on the train they were riding and asked permission from Jossy to clean his cubicle on the train.

This chance meeting for Chacko and his wife, and the domino effect of this rendezvous would have profound implications. They asked Raju a string of questions and learned that this illiterate orphaned boy had endured much suffering and had no prospects of anything better.

This street urchin's misery forced Chacko to take a serious look at the trajectory of his current path. He began asking himself questions like, "What is my life's purpose? Why am I here, and what does God expect of me? Am I to be a successful businessman who makes copious amounts of cash, live on a ranch, and savor my success, or is there something else, something previously hidden from my sight?"

Jossy's heart was pierced, and this savvy businessman would embark on a new journey that continues to change thousands of lives.

Chacko began to think beyond his comfort zone and his life's definition of success; he began to think about the millions of under-resourced people living in physical and spiritual darkness and determined that he should do something about it.

At last, he made a decision that changed his destiny and that of many others. He forsook his desire of enjoying a posh retirement. Instead, he set out with his leadership and entrepreneurial skills, along with the wealth he had accumulated, to start an organization that would champion the cause of the lost and suffering people of southern Asia, one of the poorest places on earth where millions of people have never even heard the name Jesus.

His life was transformed, and the journey of transforming people and communities began. The one-person mission has now become an international army with many staff members and 2,500 social workers fulfilling the vision of transforming poor communities by providing vocational training and spiritual truth. His project would also feed thousands, care for the homeless and orphans, and train Indigenous leaders to carry out the mission.

Josey set a goal of starting 100,000 Indigenous churches by 2030, and his dynamic organization is on track to exceed that goal. Hundreds of leaders have been trained and deployed, and a movement has ensued. The man whose life was changed by a chance encounter has become a model leader. What was the celebration of a new marriage turned into an international movement. Mr. Chacko has the long view in mind.

Leaders see problems others overlook or ignore, and they go into action. Jossy Chacko is one such person, and thousands of lives have been transformed because of his actions.

Occasionally, someone would approach me with a statement like, "Pastor Don, I've noticed such and such is not happening, and it really should happen," expecting me to agree and then do something about it. I then did something they did not expect. I laid the idea back into *their* lap. "You know, I think you might be right. What are you going to do about it? You should do something about that. How can I help you take charge and make it happen?" I've witnessed many countenances change when the ball is returned to their court. Within a short while, I would learn if this person was a leader, a potential leader, or simply someone with a complaint.

Nehma was one such leader. Jerusalem was laid to waste for over one hundred years, yet no one, not even the ones who lived there, tried to do anything about the plight. No one except Nehma. Fast-forward 2,500 years later and one can still view the remains of the wall built through the efforts of this mover and shaker.

Food for Thought

There is a vast chasm between seeing something that needs attention and responding to it. Can you think of times when you or others have exhibited this leadership principle? Can you think of instances where people simply passed by an opportunity to make a difference? Are there people in your organization who identify needs and want to do something about it? How do you facilitate these individual's actions.

Find a Need and Fill It

Read Luke 10:25-37. The story of the Good Samaritan is an excellent example of this chapter's leadership point. Would you consider this man a leader? Perhaps not in the traditional sense, yet we still follow his standard 2,000 years after the tale was told.

Bodyguard Tactic Twenty-Two

Nothing Is Ever Easy

Solutions to big problems usually take more time and effort than planned.

I have always led people and projects adhering to this maxim. Significant accomplishments take more time than you expected, cost more than you thought they would cost, and involve more work than you anticipated.

I started writing a book in August 2020. It was my first stab at creating an entire book, but I was excited to become an author. I considered the subject of a book for many months, and then after a period of adjustment after retiring from being a full-time pastor I was ready to begin. I figured it would take a year at most.

Along the way, a local publisher asked me to write another small leadership book. So I began writing that one as well. That "small" book expanded into a much larger project resulting in the material you are presently reading. I started this one in October of 2021, thinking I would finish in 2022, but now 2022 has passed, and I'm still writing. My other book is half completed and waiting for me to circle back to it. I will be pleased if I get one book published in 2023, but I hope to finish two. Writing is hard, slow, and sometimes agonizing labor.

If my axiom is accurate, and I think it is, what is needed to finish what we start? Three characteristics are required: vision, determination, and encouragement.

Vision is a mental picture of a preferred future. Famous author and speaker Napoleon Hill wrote, "Whatever your mind can conceive and believe, you can achieve." I can "see" myself holding a hardcover book in my hands authored by Don Mark Hamilton. I envision a leader sitting alone reading this book and gleaning helpful insights garnered from years of training and experience. That is the vision. Vision can be organizational, family-oriented, or personal, but a painting of the finished work must be in your mind.

The other side of the coin is that as you pursue a vision, it morphs and fully develops over time. Changing your mind as you navigate the path toward fulfillment is okay. It is also true that sometimes we pursue a dream and along the way the vision is no longer something we desire or is helpful for the organization. Wise people know when to let go and don't consider it a failure. What we learn in pursuing a dream is often more important than accomplishing the objective itself.

People succeed not because of immense talent but because they outlast and work harder than everyone else. One of the keys to my success in life was a recognition that I am often not the most brilliant or talented person in the room, but I will outlast everyone and keep learning along the way. Dogged determination is key to success. You will lose many battles, but perseverance drives you to get up, evaluate your mistakes, and learn from them. Then you must get back in the race, and you will be a better runner than you were in your last effort.

JUST GO ON ANYWAY!

Moving forward in life requires courage. It takes courage to sign up for college while you are working full-time. If you want to learn a new language, you will need the courage to take a chance and try to speak your new tongue with someone who has used that language their entire life. It takes courage to apply for a job and bravery to take the leap and get married. Audacity is required to start a new project or do something differently than it's always been done. Only the daring rise early every day and face the challenges of a life that seems to be falling apart. Gallantry defines the person who walks into the chemotherapy lab for treatments that will nauseate them and make their hair fall out, but they do it anyway.

I love the word "encourage" because it literally means "to fill with courage." Every human being, especially those who step up to lead, needs copious amounts of this success driver. Between the excitement of a new endeavor and the thrill of crossing the finish line, many moments will need a secret ingredient. That recipe requires external motivation from encouragement sources: cheerleaders, experts, prayer warriors, and motivators. Behind every successful leader, you'll find encouragers. A wise leader identifies those critical people and gathers them around for support. Leaders fall, get tired and frustrated, and want to give up. Sometimes they need a good word from their team, and other times they need a kick in the pants. That is the job of your "E" team.

EVERYONE NEEDS AN "E" TEAM.

Nehma experienced frustrations accompanied by significant achievement. It was at least four months of waiting before he could begin to pursue his desire to rebuild the walls and restore dignity to his people. Beyond that, we do not know precisely how long he waited until all the preparations were made for the trip. It was November or December when he received the disturbing news about his homeland, and March or April before he could do anything more than pray and plan. But after the slow buildup, it took the Israelites only fifty-two days to complete the project.

Along the journey to success, he met with frustrations and setbacks, but likely, his brother and friends pulled him back up and sent him moving forward again. Not to mention he knew that he had the might of his friend the Persian king backing him.

Food for Thought

What part of accomplishment do you find most challenging—vision, perseverance, or encouragement?

Do you remember a time when you did not finish a project? What was the cause? Was it a case of no longer desiring that dream, loss of vision, lack of persistence, or need for encouragement? What did you learn from this experience?

If you were Nehma, would the wall have been rebuilt?

Read John 1:15-23. Peter possessed a vision of himself as the most stalwart follower of Jesus, more faithful than any other. He was vocal about his convictions and guaranteed Jesus that he would never forsake him, even unto death. But within a few hours the man whose name means "Rock" denied knowledge of Jesus, and he turned out to be much more like sand than rock.

Bodyguard Tactic Twenty-Three

TIMING IS EVERYTHING

"Timing is crucial and takes patience to perceive."

Sometimes we find ourselves in the wrong place at the wrong time. Sometimes we are in the right place but at the wrong time. And there are situations where it is the right time, but we're in the wrong place! King Solomon stated that timing is everything.

For everything, there is a season, a time for every activity under heaven. A time to be born and a time to die. A time to plant and a time to harvest. A time to kill and a time to heal. A time to tear down and a time to build up. A time to cry and a time to laugh. A time to grieve and a time to dance. A time to scatter stones and a time to gather stones. A time to embrace and a time to turn away. A time to search and a time to cease searching. A time to keep and a time to throw away. A time to tear and a time to mend. A time to be quiet and a time to speak. A time to love and a time to hate. A time for war and a time for peace. What do people really get for all their hard work? I have seen the burden God has placed on us all. Yet God has made everything beautiful for its own time. (Ecclesiastes 3:1-10 NLT)

The most encouraging words in this paragraph are the last: "Yet God has made *everything* beautiful for its own time."

The situation for the Jewish people was dire. Haman, a racist, high-ranking, power-hungry political leader in Xerxes's government, plotted to annihilate the Jews by royal decree. The dastardly figure convinced the king that it was in his best interest to encourage all his subjects to kill all Jews and plunder all their wealth. Though the general populace was bewildered by the decree, it was now law.

Meanwhile, Esther, a Jew, had been elevated to the position of the queen as Xerxes's wife, which infuriated Haman. Esther had an uncle, Mordecai, who adopted her when her parents died, and he served as a constant advisor. He learned of the evil plot and implored Esther to talk to the king about rescinding the order. Esther was sorely afraid, but her uncle was convincing and ultimately made a famous proclamation to the queen: "For if you remain silent at this time, relief and deliverance for the Jews will arise from another place, but you and your father's family will perish. And who knows but that you have come to your royal position for such a time as this?" (Esther 4:14 NIV).

Esther was in the right place at the right time to save her people. The Jewish queen developed a plan to catch Haman in his intrigue and convince the king to spare her people. And in a turn of irony, Haman was caught and impaled on the same pole he set up to kill Mordecai.

Meanwhile, Esther admonished the king to save the Jewish nation. Though his former mandate could not be altered, he created another edict allowing the Jewish people throughout the kingdom to defend themselves, kill anyone who attacked them, and plunder their estates. Someone who discerned proper timing saved the Israelite nation.

This story, as well as that of Nehma, reminds us of several factors about timing.

Proper timing is learned through experience. Inexperienced leaders sometimes make rash decisions that end up hurting rather than helping their cause.

Proper timing is discerned through forbearance. Too much too fast reveals a lack of patience and maturity. Too little too late shows a lack of courage.

Proper timing must be approached with boldness. Sometimes the right time is scary and intimidating, but, like Esther, one knows the time is right. It is time to act.

Proper timing is intuition based upon facts that point to certain conclusions, resulting in action. Since no one can foretell the future, instinct-based decisions are a step of faith. One cannot see into the next hour, but experience and evidence guide leaders to take steps of faith intelligently.

The proper time is sometimes missed but be patient—what goes around comes around. There is always a second chance though it may be a while before it emerges. The Apostle Peter is the king of second chances.

The constant pursuit of wisdom, discernment, and knowledge enlightens one to position themselves in the right place at the right time.

Nehma waited patiently on the Lord's timing before he approached the king. He steadied his emotions and thought through his timing and approach. During the waiting period, he also developed plans to show the king he was prepared for such an undertaking.

Food for Thought

When was a time you acted rashly to your chagrin? Think through the process and discover why and how your decision was made. How could you have performed more effectively?

Review the five factors of proper timing. Which ones tend to be your strengths and your weaknesses? How can you improve? If you are amid a significant decision, filter it through the five factors.

Read 1 Samuel 13:1-14. What precipitated Samuel's exclamation to Saul, "You have done a foolish thing!"?

Bodyguard Tactic Twenty-Four

TAKE A CHANCE

*"Leaders must take calculated risks
and step forward in faith."*

There is a reason why Abraham is called "the father of faith." I re-read his story recently, and every time I think, *I cannot believe this guy thought he heard God speak to him, told him to leave his happy home with his entire family in tow, and travel who knows where.* But that is precisely what he did—all because he believed in God.

This man's life leaves me with more questions than answers, but isn't that what faith is all about? The Hebrew writer explains that faith is *feeling* confident of what we hope will happen and using our hope as evidence for things we cannot see. Nearly every aspect of Abe's story displays the Hebrew writer's definition. Consider a few questions about this gutsy old fellow.

* How did he know God was talking to him? It could have been a lousy mutton steak the night before or a little too much wine after dinner. What made him so confident?

* What did God look and sound like to him that made him sure this voice was God?

* How did he convince his wife he had chatted with the Almighty? Did Sarah think he was nuts? And what about his dad? What would he think? He would have needed to explain, "Hey, Dad, I know this sounds crazy, but I spoke with God last night." His father might have thought, *I always thought there was something strange about this kid.* Abe would continue, "He told me to load up the wife, kids, relatives, servants, and everything I own and head south." "Where are you going?" "Uh, I don't know exactly." Terah: "So you are packing up my daughter, grandkids, and the rest of my relatives and going *somewhere*?" "Yep, God said I've gotta go."

* What did everyone else in the family and household think about this decision? "Oh sure, whatever Abe says is fine with me."

* And what about this circumcision thing? I'm not thinking that was fun. Couldn't we have just had a secret handshake or something?

* "What is that you said? We're going to have children?" "I've got to cut back on the wine. It's making me delirious."

On and on the story goes, leaving us with one question after another. And yet, something is inspiring about this man's life. I want to be like Abraham. I want to lead like Abraham. To do so, it's obvious that faith is the secret ingredient. But faith makes me uncomfortable, especially when I'm leading something. I'd rather *know*. I want a sure thing. I'll try to cover all my bases of certainty before I jump in. What about you?

But here is the quandary. Promising opportunities accompany significant risks, but these risks also afford the chance for severe failure. Unpredictability is always the conundrum of forward-thinking leadership. However, if you are not failing, you are likely not moving forward, and the results of inaction are a far greater risk than taking a chance and doing something.

When evaluating risk, consider these factors:

* **What is the present atmosphere with my team or organization? Where are we on the bell curve of organizational life?** Rapidly moving up, plateaued, or nearly so, just crossing over the top and slightly downward, or a downward slide? Attitudes on the left side of the curve are usually positive and can do. At the top, they are, "We made it. Let's take a break and enjoy success." On the downside of the curve, leaders will hear comments like, "We've tried that, and it didn't work. We are not going there again." Or, "We could lose everything. Is it worth the chance?" Wise risk managers consider these factors, which require different styles and methods of communication. Nehma arrived in Jerusalem when his people were near the bottom right of the curve, which made progress a formidable task.

* **What are the ratios between challenges and opportunities, success, and failure?** How are we going to mitigate the challenges and seize the opportunities?

* **Who and how will we need to address each group if we take this risk?** Nehma knew he must address community leaders first, including priests and officials, and decided to

appeal to their sense of cultural pride and heritage while making his plea personal by involving their families and children in the request. The wall-builder knew his audience and addressed them accordingly. He also determined who needed private conversations to be convinced. There is always a hierarchy in the communication chain, and each level must be approached appropriately.

* **What is the worst and best that could happen? Is it worth the cost?** If the worst happens, what will we do? If the best happens, what will we do with success? Success is often more dangerous than failure.

* **How is my ego involved?** Coach K, perhaps the greatest NCAA Division I basketball coach in history, retired recently. In his MasterClass on leadership, the famous leader humbly reveals a personal issue from his last home game.

The Duke Blue Devils lost their final home game to their cross-state rival, North Carolina. For the occasion, the hall was packed with well-wishing fans, including a hundred or so former players, to honor him. He was applauded for such an outstanding career. At that moment, he explains how he allowed his ego to get in the way of the team. The game became more about him than his team. He initially blamed his players for the loss until a day or so later when he realized and admitted that *he* lost the contest, not his players. Even a person as wise and seasoned as this uber-successful coach allowed his ego to get in the way of his organization, causing him to make bad decisions. What distinguishes Coach K from many is his self-awareness, honest personal evaluation, and humility to admit it to himself and his players. That is what great leaders do! No one is exempt from allowing pride and self-service to get in the way. When assessing risk, check your ego at the door.

WHEN ASSESSING RISK, CHECK YOUR EGO AT THE DOOR.

In ancient times, monarchs maintained strict policies about who, when, and how anyone, including the queen, could approach them. Someone who breached a policy could be put to death. Many early rulers considered themselves gods or divinely appointed agents for the gods, and one does not approach a god without serious consideration.

Nehma knew he was taking a considerable risk if he approached Artaxerxes in a manner unpleasing. Still, the leader was so determined to help his people that he was willing to imperil his life. The king trusted Nehma, and God went before the bodyguard to prepare his boss's heart to be receptive to the servant's request. But the choice to take a chance was Nehma's alone. He made the gamble, and the walls went up.

Food for Thought

How much of a risk-taker are you on a scale of one to ten?

Are there instances where you feel you should have taken more extraordinary steps of faith than you did? If so, what held you back?

If you were in Nehma's shoes, would you have made your request to the king?

One way to intelligently approach risk is to conduct a risk assessment. List the possible benefits of the decision and potential threats. Does the payoff justify the gamble? How can the possible adverse effects be managed if they happen?

Read Esther chapters 4, 5, & 8 to study another considerable risk taken by an unexpected leader.

Bodyguard Tactic Twenty-Five

DEEP ROOTS

*"Wise leaders expectantly pray, fast, meditate,
and wait for God to show up."*

Shepherd trees grow in the Kalahari Desert, and by chance, drillers of groundwater wells learned that they develop the deepest roots of any tree. In search of water, their roots grow to a depth of 230 feet, three-quarters the length of a football field.

Wise leaders are like shepherd trees; there is much more beneath the surface than seen above ground because they constantly search for spiritual nourishment.

In the middle and late '90s, I found myself near burnout. I had four daughters, a brother-in-law, and my sister-in-law's family all living in my home. I was also completing my doctoral studies, conducting a capital fundraising campaign for our church, and pastoring a growing, healthy congregation. My mother was diagnosed with ovarian cancer and died seven months later during the same period. I was exhausted!

Fortunately, a close friend urged me to increase my quiet time with God, journal, and take regular days off. Later, other friends flew my wife and me to Colorado and set us up in a mountain condo for a week of rest and relaxation. These factors refreshed my spirit and mental attitude, and I returned ready to go back to work.

When I returned, I forced myself into a rhythm of daily quiet time and regular days off. These "behind-the-scenes" exercises kept me in ministry, improved my marriage and fathering skills, and kept me sane. I weathered the storms and came out of the other side deeper and wiser.

Leaders are judged by what they accomplish "on the outside." However, an essential part of their success is found on the "inside." Like the roots of plants, leaders need to constantly search for water and nutrients in publicly unseen places, especially when they are in a season of high demand. Like shepherd trees in the Kalahari Desert, the drier the conditions, the more they need deep roots.

Without warning, Nehma faced a dire situation that rocked him to the core. He was living in luxury while his compatriots were suffering. He could not erase his love for Israel and the Holy City from his mind, and now he was confronted with the stark reality of their plight.

The terrible news devastated the exiled man. You can tell a lot about a person by what brings them to tears, and Nehma's flowed freely upon hearing this message.

> **YOU CAN TELL A LOT ABOUT A PERSON BY WHAT BRINGS THEM TO TEARS.**

The bodyguard's knee-jerk reaction *literally* brought him to his knees: "When I heard these things, I sat down and wept. For some days I mourned and fasted and prayed before the God of heaven" (Nehemiah 1:4 NIV).

Nehma *mourned, fasted, and prayed*. He was upset about the condition of his homeland and more importantly why his people were in this position. His final prayer contained a confession of the sinful state of his nation, including himself. He knew his people had brought this tragedy upon themselves. God exacted punishment upon them, and the Almighty was the only one who could remedy their sad situation. For Nehma, fasting was both an act of repentance and a show of dedication and desire.

Sometimes, prayer is almost an afterthought. We do our best to solve a problem, and if our savvy doesn't seem to work, we turn to God. Nehma's reaction was the opposite because he talked with God often and instinctively knew that the solution to this problem was in God's hands, so the Lord was the first place he went.

Many leaders suffer from a malady author Charles Swindoll calls "promotion erosion," a downward character slide caused by success and promotion. As I've stated elsewhere in this book, success is often more dangerous than failure. The natural human reaction to achievement is pride. Pride wants to replace God's part in our accomplishments with *our* part, causing lesser dependence on the Almighty and problem-solving independent of God's blessing.

Successful leaders are people of action, but prayer does not feel like action. Martin Luther is credited with the statements, "If I fail to spend two hours in prayer each morning, the devil gets the victory through the day," and, "I have so much to do that I shall spend the first three hours in prayer." We're not sure if the great reformer said these words, but we do know he was a person of prayer, and the results of his prayer habits speak for themselves.

The temptation to abandon prayer and fasting increases the higher one climbs up the ladder. As one commentator stated, high status means more work and stress, which tends to erode the unseen world of the leader. Luther's logic is upended and more accurately stated as, "I have so much to do today that I can only spend three minutes in prayer."

Nehma knew better. His high governmental position drove him to greater dependence on God. When tragedy struck, his knee-jerk reaction was to fall on his knees, not run to a solution without consulting his heavenly Father. His prayer and patience with God resulted in the blessing and partnership of his boss, Artaxerxes.

Food for Thought

There is nothing like a crisis to reveal the depth of our spiritual roots. How would you rate your spiritual practices, such as Bible reading, meditation, prayer, generosity, service, journaling, Sabbath practice, etc.? If you are not a person of faith, how are you developing deep roots?

Have you ever faced a crisis that revealed your lack of depth? How did you react? What have you done to enhance your development as a leader and as a follower of Christ?

Read Esther 4. Evaluate the reactions of Mordecai and Queen Esther upon hearing the king's devastating edict.

Bodyguard Tactic Twenty-Six

MAKE INFORMED DECISIONS

*"Action without knowledge is re-action
and causes more problems than it solves."*

General Colin Powell was one of the exceptional leaders of the last generation. Powell served as a diplomat and politician and was the first African American secretary of state. Famous writer and speaker Oren Harari wrote two books on the renowned military leader and statesman who, as chairman of the Joint Chiefs of Staff, handled twenty-eight crises, including Operation Desert Storm. In an article on GovLeaders.org, Harari quotes Powell on the wise use of information in decision-making.

General Powell recommended using the 40/70 rule. He taught that when you need to make a tough decision, you should gather at least 40 percent of the information concerning the problem up to a maximum of 70 percent. No less than forty and no more than seventy. In that range he said, "to go with your gut." He explains that if you wait until you gather more than 70 percent, the opportunity has likely passed.

A common mistake for novice leaders is acting impetuously without adequate knowledge of the issue. Often these decisions are driven by emotion. However, seasoned leaders also make this mistake. It is helpful to do your homework before you make a significant decision, but if you wait until you have 100 percent assurance, you will miss opportunities.

Here's a checklist for your decision-making homework.

* **Learn what you don't know.** It is easy to make assumptions about matters beyond our expertise. Therefore, it behooves a decision-maker to recognize the limits of their knowledge and seek assistance from an "expert" to get their take on the issue.

* **Weed out information that doesn't genuinely relate to the decision.** When studying an issue, it is easy to go down rabbit trails that do not concretely relate to the problem. This wastes time and energy. If the leader does not exercise this discipline, they will end up with information overload and become paralyzed. Also, gathering information often causes team members to come up with related ideas, which may be good ones, but are not appropriate to address at that time. Make a list of opportunities to study another time.

* **Learn what you can know from people who know more about the situation than you.** We cannot see the future or mitigate every possible scenario resulting from our deci-

sions, but we can gather enough accurate intelligence to make an informed choice. Your knowledge and expertise is limited so be humble enough to solicit help.

* **Assess the risk factor with the information you have gathered.** What is the worst and best that could happen from this course of action? What will we do if the worst or best happens?

* **Marry information with timing.** One can obtain adequate research pointing to forward movement, but is it the proper time to act? One might get themselves on the right dock only to find the ship has already sailed or it will not dock until tomorrow.

* **Evaluate your emotional involvement.** Too much emotion, and logic goes out the window, and too little emotion, people get unnecessarily hurt. Some very good decisions get made that seemed illogical at first. Other choices are made because the leader has too much emotional attachment to the issue or wants to save face.

* **Prepare to pivot.** Circumstances change daily, and what worked yesterday may not go so well today. Don't allow yourself to be so rigid that you refuse to adjust to changing circumstances. Most large projects morph and grow or diminish, given unforeseen circumstances. One often encounters changing conditions that require strategy adjustments. Like a championship football or basketball team, during halftime, the game plan adjusts to the challenges presented by the opposing team.

As I write this chapter, a young NFL player lies in critical condition in a hospital. In the middle of a game, Damar Hamlin of the Buffalo Bills collapsed on the field from cardiac arrest. Tens of thousands of hours of planning and practice could not have prevented this tragic situation. Though it could hardly be considered a loss by either team, everything about the game changed in an instant. Coaches, managers, trainers, officials, and players had to immediately pivot their concerns and focus.

* **As much as possible, prepare for failure.** No matter how much evidence you've gathered, nothing is guaranteed, and "stuff happens." Thomas Edison once said, "I have not failed ten thousand times—I've successfully found ten thousand ways that will not work." The law of averages tells us that the person willing to try ten thousand different ideas will finally come up with one that works. When "this" method doesn't work, just go on anyway with something else that might.

Taking a crisis to some people is like pouring gasoline on a fire. Instead of looking for solutions, this person reacts emotionally and makes the situation worse. Others who are wiser handle "fires" by pouring on water. Which kind of a leader are you?

Nehma was confronted with a crisis that rocked him, but he waited several months before acting. During that time, he could consider options and formulate plans for solving the "wall" problem in Jerusalem. Had he quickly run to the king upon hearing the bad news, he would have been unprepared to field questions from his boss and show the king he had a workable plan. He would still have been overly emotional and risked looking foolish before the king.

When Nehma arrived in the Holy City, he remained quiet about his intentions. This subtle approach allowed the builder to assess the situation closely and develop a plan that included not only the construction itself but, more importantly, the process of enlisting residents to get on board with the project. One can sense that Nehma's night ride around the city brought clarity and helpful ideas that culminated in a strategy that would work. The wall-builder's night-riding team contributed valuable insights as well.

Food for Thought

Information is a double-edged sword. On one side, there is the need for adequate decision-making data, while the other edge is trying to collect enough intelligence to guarantee success. Most leaders tend toward one side or the other until they are seasoned enough to maintain balance. On a scale of one to ten, one being impulsive responses and ten being reluctance to decide, where do you fall?

What kinds of situations cause you to lean one way or the other? What are your thoughts about Colin Powell's 40-70 percent probability of success in decision-making process? How do you presently make important decisions?

Read the following scriptures that demonstrate rash decision-making by the Apostle Peter: Matthew 16:21-28, Matthew 26:31-35, and John 18:10-11. Peter was known for making rash statements, not knowing the implications of his thoughts.

Bodyguard Tactic Twenty-Seven

ASSEMBLY REQUIRED

"Vision is born of need and cultivated by carefully examining and evaluating the circumstances surrounding it."

Tim Tebow is an outstanding individual. Among his numerous benevolent and life-changing programs, a new one emerged in 2014: "Night to Shine." This is a special prom event held for people with special needs who are rarely, if ever, celebrated. By 2020, Night to Shine proms were held in 721 churches in all fifty states and thirty-four countries. Two hundred fifteen thousand volunteers hosted

110,000 guests with disabilities, which grows yearly, even during a worldwide pandemic. But how did all this come about?

At fifteen, Tim traveled to the Philippines on a mission service trip. While on this journey, Tebow met a boy named Sherwin whose legs were turned backward, and he could not walk. Villagers believed he was cursed, so they ostracized the young man. Sherwin had two young friends who took responsibility for his care since no one else would associate with him.

Sherwin stole Tim's heart and changed his life forever. To the chagrin of many villagers, the future Heisman Trophy winner carried Sherwin throughout the village to teach the community that God created Sherwin and that He loved him, and so should they. Tim's encounter with this young Filipino boy created in him a vision to give his life to help those who cannot help themselves. The Tim Tebow Foundation has come alongside countless people worldwide and garnered the support of churches, corporations, wealthy individuals, and celebrities.

Nehma and Tim Tebow share similarities. They were both confronted by injustice, a dire need of their fellow man, and that revelation rocked their world. The news created a vision, a picture of a preferred future, that consumed them and invigorated them to action.

The seed of vision is created when a person observes a need, is moved by the plight, and is motivated to improve the situation. Ideas come in all shapes and sizes, but it has these familiar ingredients. From that spark, a leader begins to examine and evaluate the trouble to make the solution more apparent, and a plan is born to solve the problem.

As the father of four daughters, I spent numerous Christmases assembling everything from dollhouses to Easy-Bake Ovens. I don't like to read directions. After all, I possess a doctorate and have done many projects throughout my life. Why should I need guidance to build a child's toy? On numerous occasions, I opened the box, took out parts, and jumped into putting things together—without the benefit of directions.

READ THE DIRECTIONS!

Directions to just about any "assembly required" project start by instructing one to lay out all the parts and match them to the assembly list provided by the manufacturer to determine if they are all there. My assumption? "Of course they are all there. Why would a toy manufacturer ship toys with missing parts?" Mistake! I can't tell you how many times I got well into an assembly project only to determine that it was missing parts. Meanwhile, I wasted two hours getting to that point.

I've purchased numerous items from the IKEA chain of stores. The Swedish behemoth produces hip, affordable furniture. But there's one catch. The new owner must assemble the product. When you look at the finished product in the showroom, you think, *Wow, I like that, and it looks easy to put together. I can do that.* You take the new bed home and spend the next four frustrating, sometimes maddening hours turning a hundred parts into a piece of furniture. Some projects appear simple until one tries them. Then simplicity turns into a complicated monster. A good leader does their homework *before* assembly. As I stated previously, it will take longer than you expected, cost more than you thought, and be much more labor than you imagined.

During Nehma's time of mourning, prayer, and fasting, a game plan developed that first involved the king's support and, ultimately, the citizens of Jerusalem. When Nehma arrived in Jerusalem, he did not jump into action. He quietly assessed the situation, asking, "What are the people like? How do they feel? How responsive might they be to rebuilding the walls? Who will oppose us, and how will we overcome them? What resources will it take to rebuild this wall?" Nehma rode around the city late at night and evaluated each gate, home, and section of the decimated defense system. Out of close examination and evaluation arose a vision and strategy. Now he was ready to take the next steps by getting people on board with his plans.

Food for Thought

What is the difference between a vision and a dream, a visionary and a dreamer? Which one gets things done and why? Can a dream become a vision? Consider Dr. Martin Luther King Jr.'s famous "I Have a Dream" speech.

Some leaders try to bypass the tedious examination and evaluation process only to discover that their original vision is not feasible or preferred. On a light note, men are often accused of refusing to read directions only to find well into the construction that they have missed several vital steps in the process. They are also accused of refusing to ask for travel directions and end up lost. What kind of leader are you?

Read Luke 14:25-34. What did Jesus say about a person with a dream but who is not willing to examine and evaluate the cost? Have you ever done this?

It is common for a visionary to overestimate the scope of a vision and underestimate its cost. How do examination and evaluation aid the process of honing a vision?

Bodyguard Tactic Twenty-Eight

HOMEWORK REQUIRED

"A vision without a plan is nothing more than a pipe dream."

In the eighteenth and nineteenth centuries, opium was widely used by English writers and was smoked through a long pipe. In 1895, the *Fort Wayne Weekly Gazette* made the first reference to dreams incited using the opium pipe, called "pipe dreams." Many people have visions of grandeur but do not make the effort necessary to turn the dream into a reality. They have pipe dreams.

Visions are easy; plans take work, lots of it. My wife worked as a nurse practitioner for several years at a drug rehabilitation facility for teenage boys. Most of these young men were getting their final chance to stay out of jail since they had committed numerous crimes in their quests for drugs. Many of her patients were from the inner city of Philadelphia and had less-than-ideal family histories.

VISIONS ARE EASY; PLANS TAKE WORK, LOTS OF IT.

A large percentage of these young drug users dreamed of playing professional basketball since this sport is popular on inner-city courts. They spoke seriously about their desire but could not realize how important it is to curb their drug habits and do the hard work needed to become proficient at basketball. My frustrated wife often came home saying, "These boys say they want greatness, but their ideas are just pipe dreams." Unfortunately, their dreams never turned into workable plans to accomplish their goals.

Once Nehma had a vision of rebuilding the wall around Jerusalem, he formed concrete plans to see his dream become a reality. During the four-month interim, he likely had further conversations with his brother and friends to obtain information on what it would take to complete the project. He also needed a plan to approach the king for permission and assistance. Once the king gave him the go-ahead, Nehma prepared and traveled to Jerusalem.

Interestingly, Nehma kept his plans on the down-low when he arrived and did nothing for three days. He was a stranger to the community's citizens, who had long since acquiesced to their plight, and they would need some assurance of his integrity and ability. To approach the citizenry with nothing more than a dream, he would be shut down before he even started. The wall-builder set out on horseback late one night to survey the decimated walls. He took a team with him, and they spent most of the night studying the situation. By the time he returned, his strategy had materialized, and he now had enough information for him and his partners to develop a workable plan to get the job done. The design had enough details to convince some of the most jaded residents and leaders. He also knew that he already possessed the resources, both financial and otherwise, to reassure the project could be supported.

As a visionary leading a healthy, growing church, I often had big ideas about the next steps for our church. I worked with a board of elders and always wanted their support with a significant initiative. I knew each man on our board very well, and they each approached big decisions differently. These leaders were men of great faith and wanted our church to advance with Kingdom victories. A common saying among them was, "We want to do things so big that if God is not in it, it's doomed to failure." However, their positive attitudes and confidence in me did not mean they gave me carte blanche approval for everything I presented. Accountability was good because my ideas were not always the best, and sometimes needed numerous modifications.

One necessary ingredient to a successful presentation answered the question, "Did you do your homework?" Lawyers, CEOs, CFOs, PhDs, and just regular guys comprised our board through the years. Accountants, lawyers, and engineers live in a world of details. I was generally a strategic but not detail-oriented leader. However, I learned that to convince some of these solid leaders, I would need to do the research and make it part of my presentation. There was always a healthy skepticism in the room, which made me and the team more effective.

One of our elders was a friend and mentor who retired from the Navy and worked as chief financial officer at a large local non-profit organization. Tom was a wise person of great integrity and did not take significant decisions lightly. As the "financial guy" on the board, he always had three questions: "How much is this going to cost? How will we pay for it? Is this God's plan or yours, Don?" Wowzer! I quickly learned that it would be unwise to make a presentation for a new idea without addressing those questions. Tom has since passed but left an indelible mark on my life and leadership acumen. Do your homework! Tom was a person of considerable faith and willing to take *calculated* risks. He taught me a lot about pursuing new endeavors wisely.

Each congregation has various personalities, passions, education levels, and career paths. An influential captain presents communications appealing to a broad spectrum of constituents, and Nehma did just that and convinced the crowd to follow him.

Food for Thought

Do you know your personality type (e.g., Enneagram, DiSC profile, Myers-Briggs, StrengthsFinder, etcetera)? If not, it would be worth learning, and I recommend one take at least two tests. If so, how do you relate to the point of this devotion? How would you have approached Nehemiah's project?

Read Matthew 5, 6, & 7. At the end of the Sermon on the Mount, Matthew states that people were amazed at His teaching, for He spoke as one with authority compared to their religious leaders. How and why could people discern between the Pharisees's and Sadducees's preaching and Jesus's instruction? How do present-day leaders gain followers in the same manner?

Bodyguard Tactic Twenty-Nine

CONCENTRIC CIRCLES

*"Influencers must be enlisted and excited
for a great endeavor to succeed."*

In every group of people, there are concentric circles of influence. If you identify the key players and win them over, they will carry the message to their networks, which in turn will take the communication to a broader and wider audience. Jesus spent most of his time influencing a handful of future leaders, knowing that the success of his movement rested upon their shoulders, and the plan worked brilliantly.

In my church experience, circles of influence started with the key staff members, then elders, followed by ministry team leaders, and a handful of prominent members. Often, influential people in a group do not hold a position, but many people look to them for guidance. They will not nod to a significant endeavor until they see this predominant person do the same. Some influencers even shrug off attention and office, but their position beyond the church walls, life experience, and generosity make them thought-shapers. Inexperienced leaders sometimes wrongfully assume that only those in "official" positions wield power. Real power doesn't need a title.

REAL POWER DOES NOT NEED A TITLE.

In my church, a good friend owned a successful business, and he was well-known in the community for his generosity and support of enhancement projects. Charlie (not his real name) did not hold any formal church office and disdained the idea. He did not like to be "upfront" in any manner and had no desire for attention. Most of his volunteering occurred behind the scenes doing jobs that few people knew he performed. However, Charlie influenced the entire church family. He was generous with his significant wealth and quietly helped numerous needy people within and outside the congregation. The dedicated Christian and prosperous businessman was indeed a key leader in our church.

As such, I often met Charlie for lunch, and when I considered a new idea or endeavor, I bounced it off him for his opinion and clarification of my aims. He had no problem asking me the tough questions and challenging my thoughts, and I always came away from our encounters the better for it. I could often tell by the look on his face if my idea was less than desirable.

On one occasion, I felt like our church was becoming stagnant. Financial times were tough, and we seemed to use the lack of funds as a weapon to shoot down any new initiatives. "We don't have the money right now. These are hard times, and we cannot take that chance." I was finally tired of our excuses and decided it was time to get on with it. The result was Project 21, an amalgamation of programs and tasks that covered a wide gamut. I sat down with Charlie for his thoughts. I explained that numerous people would think taking on this many tasks was too aggressive. I knew there would be pushback as there is with any significant progress. After a short discussion, he stated, "Don, say you only finish twelve or fifteen or seventeen of these goals? In the end, you will be far ahead of where you are now." After the elder team approved, the aggressive plan went into action. Within around two years, the church had accomplished twenty of twenty-one tasks, and we celebrated each accomplishment publicly along the way. The more checkmarks on the Project 21 poster in the lobby, the more people got on board. Charlie and the elders were unabashedly and vocally behind it; the rest followed.

Once the elders, staff, and key influencers were on board, we took the plan to the next wider circle. We gathered the ministry team leaders and small group leaders, with the elders and influential people present, and presented the idea. Those leaders then impacted hundreds of our church family through their networks, so there were enough members to get the ball rolling.

This method is sometimes slower than we prefer but will yield far better results than simply trying to railroad or subversively pursue a corporate goal.

Nehma started to sell his idea by gathering the priests and community leaders. He made his case and presented a concrete, doable plan. His speech raised the collective conscience to a problem they were ignoring every day, and it stung. Once he rested his case, they agreed and got to it.

Food for Thought

Who are the key leaders in and outside official positions in your organization? Do you devote time and energy to developing friendships with these influencers? Can you identify a program or project where you failed to follow the concentric circle principle to your peril? Is there some goal you hope to accomplish presently, and are you using Nehma's approach to get there?

For Jesus, his concentric circles looked like this:

* The Inner Circle: Peter, James, and John
* The Twelve Apostles and a small band of close followers
* The 70 or 72 Jesus sent out to preach
* 120 in the upper room after Jesus's ascension
* 500 believers to whom Jesus revealed himself risen from the dead
* The crowds who followed

Paul also describes the concept in 2 Timothy 2:2, where he talks of four generations of disciples. We see him use this principle in all of his church-planting travels.

Bodyguard Tactic Thirty

GO FOR THE HEART

"People follow a story. Ventures of consequence must be initiated through people's hearts before their minds are convinced to join the effort. Get the heart on board, and the head will follow."

The fortieth president of the United States was dubbed "The Great Communicator." Ronald Reagan will forever be known for his powerful, convincing rhetoric. Reagan attributed his ability to communicate effectively to two factors: being honest and truthful, and being in touch with your audience.

Much of the great speech-giver's genius was his ability to bring the belief in lofty ideals to the level of the person on the street. In 2010, it was discovered that the great orator collected a large file of

4x6 note cards placed in keeping in a shoebox. The speech cards were a collection of quotes, poems, and stories from various sources collected over many years. Reagan said that a great speech must address significant matters and then bring those matters to meet the ordinary person where they are. Many of his compelling orations spun stories of real-life people who put flesh and blood into noble ideas and causes.

Jesus loved to tell stories that left the listeners with a question about their moral. Perhaps this one is the most famous. Many people who have never darkened the doors of a church or cracked a Bible know this one well.

But he wanted to justify himself, so he asked Jesus, "And who is my neighbor?"

In reply, Jesus said: "A man was going down from Jerusalem to Jericho, when he was attacked by robbers. They stripped him of his clothes, beat him and went away, leaving him half dead. A priest happened to be going down the same road, and when he saw the man, he passed by on the other side. So too, a Levite, when he came to the place and saw him, passed by on the other side. But a Samaritan, as he traveled, came where the man was; and when he saw him, he took pity on him. He went to him and bandaged his wounds, pouring on oil and wine. Then he put the man on his own donkey, brought him to an inn and took care of him. The next day he took out two denarii and gave them to the innkeeper. 'Look after him,' he said, 'and when I return, I will reimburse you for any extra expense you may have.'

"Which of these three do you think was a neighbor to the man who fell into the hands of robbers?"

The expert in the law replied, "The one who had mercy on him."

Jesus told him, "Go and do likewise." (Luke 10:29-37 NIV)

The story carries the ideal, applies it to everyday life, and leaves the hearer to decide how to use its meaning in their own life.

Nehma understood the wisdom of stories to inform and invigorate people toward an extraordinary cause: "Then I said to them, 'You see the trouble we are in: Jerusalem lies in ruins, and its gates have been burned with fire. Come, let us rebuild the wall of Jerusalem, and we will no longer be in disgrace.' I also told them about the gracious hand of my God on me and what the king had said to me. They replied, 'Let us start rebuilding.' So they began this good work" (Nehemiah 2:17-18 NIV).

Verse 17 identifies a problem that everyone knew existed, but no one cared to address it up to this point. The predicament seemed beyond their grasp, so the entire community simply swept it under the rug and went on with life—yet the embarrassing issue lay dormant in the hearts of the residents of what they considered their Holy City. They were waiting for someone to address the problem and didn't even know it. Nehma called it a "disgrace" and a situation that should be remedied.

TOUCH THE HEART AND THE HEAD WILL FOLLOW.

Once Nehma touched their heartstrings, he turned to the story of God's hand upon him in the presence of the king who controlled their destiny. He brought both human and divine authority into the situation and revealed that their God was already at work. They had but to get on board with what the Almighty was already doing. Now the decision was theirs. "So they began this good work," explains their response.

Once their hearts were moved, their heads would begin to develop solutions that ultimately put them all to work on this noble project. To move people forward, one must move the heart, and the head will follow. A formula for quality communication looks like this: **Story + Decision + Application = Commitment + Strategy + Labor = Finished Product.**

Story: Any human endeavor starts when someone identifies a problem. The problem always ends with an adverse effect on real people. Much problem-solving is not a matter of something new that should take place but learning how to do something better that is already taking place. Human beings are always the end game of a problem, which a leader turns into a possibility and convinces others to get on the solution bus. Since people are the bearers of such problems and opportunities, human stories resonate in a manner that sheer facts and figures cannot. To start a movement, find a story and tell it well.

Decision: The story leaves the listener asking, "So what? How should I be involved?" The leader defines the "what" by implying that the hearer can and should do something to help alleviate the issue. The best presentations give the receiver a clear option to act or pass by without caring. Essentially, he or she is saying, "Now it is decision time."

Application: A presenter accompanies the problem/solution quandary with possible strategies and resources, or at least seeds of these critical components. "Here is one way we can do something about it. Perhaps you will think of others." The communication circle is not complete until some kind of application happens.

The results look like this:

Commitment: "What level of engagement are you willing to make?" Many strategies involve several levels of allegiance, and a wise leader makes these degrees clear. If the proposition is all-or-nothing, valuable contributors will be run off before the project begins.

Strategy: A movement leader might initially present possible strategies, enough to start the thought process of team members, but leave the ultimate plan up to them while the leader provides guidance and resources.

Labor: Multi-talented actress, writer, singer, and activist German Kent once accurately stated, "There is no shortcut for hard work that leads to effectiveness. You must stay disciplined because most of the work is behind the scenes." If anything is to be done, everything ultimately amounts to hard work and focus. One can strategize until the cows come home, but if a project is to be completed, somebody's got to get to work!

For many months, Nehma labored intensely toward one goal and only one goal. Many leaders are ineffective or do not reach their potential, not because they do not work hard but because they work on too many things. In turn, they often make their followers do the same. Great leaders are not jacks of all trades.

Food for Thought

Do you agree that storytelling is a crucial motivational force? Are you proficient at telling stories? Storytelling is an art that can be developed by anyone who understands its significance in the human spirit. What are some of Jesus's other stories that moved people to action?

Read 2 Samuel 12:1-25. Note how a story changed the course of history.

Bodyguard Tactic Thirty-One

BE A CATALYST

"The visionary raises consciousness of a forgotten or unseen problem that the community can solve with their involvement. Leaders are catalysts of movements."

In 1852, public opinion of slavery in the northern states and much of the world changed abruptly with the publication of Harriett Beecher Stowe's book *Uncle Tom's Cabin*. Stowe, the daughter of a minister and an ardent abolitionist, wrote the book to describe the plight of those held in southern slavery. The famous book sold 300,000 copies in its first year of publication, and by 1857 the number hit 2,000,000 worldwide. It was so popular that a legend developed concerning Stowe's first meeting with President Lincoln.

Lincoln is said to have gazed upon Harriett and proclaimed, "So this is the little lady who started this big war."

The abolitionist movement, though relatively small in numbers, became a powerful anti-slavery force in the northern states. The vivid descriptions of the everyday lives of enslaved people taken from interviews and writings of formerly enslaved people tore into the souls of sympathetic readers. Stowe wrote the book in protest of the Fugitive Slave Act of 1850, which required escaped enslaved people to be returned to their owners. Regardless of their views on human enslavement, northern citizens were expected to aid law enforcement in acquiring and capturing runaway slaves. Local officials were paid for each slave they apprehended and returned.

During this period, many northerners were slaveholders but did not favor expanding slavery into newly acquired territories. Many northerners simply turned the other way and paid little attention to the issue. *Uncle Tom's Cabin* changed the collective conscience by vividly revealing the brutality of this mostly southern institution. *Uncle Tom's Cabin* played a role in the American Civil War by making people aware of the horrors of enslavement.

Leaders raise awareness of a formerly ignored or unseen injustice, causing a placid population to face the issue and act for or against it.

After Nehma examined the condition of the city walls and devised a workable plan to address the problem, his next step was to awaken citizens to the disaster their eyes had long since refused to acknowledge.

In all our lives, situations need our attention, yet we often put them off, sometimes even to the point we forget the problem persists. For several years, the Hamilton household experienced what we fondly call "trash wars." Our kitchen trash can sat against the wall opposite the sink and stove. Like any kitchen trash can, it could, at any given time, contain days-old food, junk mail, used paper towels, and various other articles of refuse. As the receptacle slowly filled, each family member kept stuffing more trash into the can until it was a solid block of smelly garbage. Nobody wanted to take out the trash. This negligence began a war of attrition as to which person would be the final poor soul required to empty the can and replace it with a new bag. During this stand-off, each of us did our best to look the other way every time we were near the refuse container. The battle was real!

Every day, residents of Jerusalem walked out their front door to see the remains of a glorious wall that existed to protect the community. Stones and bricks lay in heaps, gathering trash, while the smell of burnt wood filled their nostrils each time they passed one of the many dilapidated gates built to enter the city.

To a visitor, the site was disgusting, but not to the people of the city. They had looked upon this mess for so long that they didn't even see it for what it was. The condition was now part of their unconsciousness, and no one had a mind to do anything about it—that is, until the bodyguard shook them all up!

Nehma roused community leaders and residents and painted a vivid picture of their embarrassing condition. As their eyes were opened, he also presented a solution and a plan. Then he gave a call to action and showed them how and where to sign up. The people were moved, the work began, and in a few months they threw a party to celebrate a new chapter in their city's history.

Food for Thought

Can you think of a situation in your church or community in which the process of raising congregational or organizational awareness to a problem was unveiled? Were you a part of the process? Analyze the unfolding and completion of this accomplishment.

Nehma's effectiveness was based upon a three-pronged approach:

1. Tell a powerful story. Nehma explained why and how he got to Jerusalem by the mighty hand of God, something to which they could all relate. The story appealed to their higher sense of purpose.
2. Make them aware, or remind them vividly, of the problem using their own personal experiences. His plea forced them to consider their families and how the situation affected their loved ones.
3. Present a workable plan that would instill confidence in his ability to solve the problem. The project might morph, or a new plan could even emerge, but they needed to know Nehma had the chops to make it all happen.

Food for Thought

Are you presently aware of a problem in your family, friendships, church, community, or even your nation where a champion like Nehma is needed? Are you being called to become the catalyst for a movement?

Google Harriett Beecher Stowe and read the history of a world-changer.

Bodyguard Tactic Thirty-Two

WASHINGTON'S SECRET

"Humility is the lynchpin of outstanding leadership."

By the end of the American Revolutionary War, George Washington was nearly worshipped by his troops and the colonial people in general. The general and his army had defeated the most well-trained and equipped military force on earth—the British. Washington stood nearly a head taller than most of his contemporaries and adhered to a strict set of Rules of Civility, which he developed at age fourteen. The commander was an excellent horseman and often led his troops riding his favorite horse, Nelson, alongside them rather than from behind. The general also possessed the ability to withstand the most severe conditions, making him a formidable foe.

During his youth, Washington was not an exceptionally humble person. The young Virginian recognized that he was handsome and could attract women easily. He was an adept social climber and possessed a volatile temper. As a soldier, the wealthy farmer looked stunning in a military uniform. However, through the years, he learned to eschew his base desires and act with deference and respect, which are the traits that eventually marked his personality.

When the British were defeated at the peak of Washington's power, the victorious general refused to claim a dictatorial regime common among military leaders of the ages. He soon retired to Mt. Vernon, just south of Washington D.C., on the Potomac River. A few years later, he was pressed into service as the first president of the United States, considering the role a citizen's responsibility. Though Adams, Hamilton, and others wanted his title to be "His Excellency," the first commander in chief refused. He also refused to wear his military uniform but chose civilian clothing, representing his ideal of the president as a people's servant. Nearing the end of his second term, the aging head of state made it clear that there needed to be a new president and refused to accept the office again. He was also suffering the numerous ill effects of aging by this time.

George Washington was indeed humble. However, it is essential to note that humility often requires bold, courageous, and decisive leadership. One must take charge and chart the course to serve and lead others well.

Jesus Christ was the most outstanding example of servant leadership to walk the earth. The most famous account of the Master's humility is found in Paul's letter to the Philippian church. He starts what will be an explanation of the following charge to his readers and then explains in detail what the Apostle means.

Do nothing out of selfish ambition or vain conceit. Rather, in humility value others above yourselves, not looking to your own interests but each of you to the interests of the others.

In your relationships with one another, have the same mindset as Christ Jesus:

Who, being in very nature God, did not consider equality with God something to be used to his own advantage; rather, he made himself nothing by taking the very nature of a servant, being made in human likeness. And being found in appearance as a man, he humbled himself by becoming obedient to death—even death on a cross!

Therefore God exalted him to the highest place and gave him the name that is above every name, that at the name of Jesus every knee should bow, in heaven and on earth and under the earth, and every tongue acknowledge that Jesus Christ is Lord, to the glory of God the Father. (Philippians 2:3-11 NIV)

This is called the "kenosis" passage based on the word translated to mean "emptied," and it describes how Jesus willingly emptied Himself of His heavenly glory to take on human flesh and blood. It is unfathomable for mere humans to capture the profound magnitude that the Creator of the Universe—by whom, through whom, and for whom all things exist—was willing to cast off all this glory, power, and majesty to take on human form and ultimately die a miserable death for ungrateful humanity. Yet the deeper one understands its grandeur, the more like the King we can become.

A LEADER'S PRIME DUTY IS TO SERVE THEIR FOLLOWERS.

Perhaps the critical principle for a leader to consider is that Jesus did not view his divine power as something to be utilized and exploited for leadership purposes. He defined his foundational leadership principle as being a servant. This guidance translates into us, as human leaders, regularly quizzing ourselves concerning our motives. *Why* we do what we do is as important, if not more so, than *what* we do. The temptation to use our influence, acumen, and achievements for our own glory can be overpowering. It is far too easy to credit accomplishments to ourselves instead of Jesus's work through us and the labor of our followers.

It is wise to gather around you people who will take you down a notch when your pride swells because of position or accomplishment. I've heard numerous movie stars and politicians explain that they may climb on their high horses, but when they walk through the doors of their homes, either their wives, husbands, or children promptly knock them off, which is a good thing.

I recently watched an interview with the famous Beatle, Ringo Starr. When asked about the dynamics within the band during the height of their fame and fortune, the drummer said, "When one of us got the big head, we had our mates to set us straight. Pity the famous person who has no one to ground them" (my paraphrase).

Nehma arrived in Jerusalem with an entourage of officials and soldiers that must have been impressive. Though he did not reveal his intended purpose immediately, there must have been a buzz through the community. "Why would the king send this kind of group to our city? Have we done something wrong? Are they here in peace or to harm us? Will they take more of us into exile to become servants of the Persians?"

Many citizens of Jerusalem would not have known Nehma, but he was clearly a person of great importance. Yet the king's bodyguard did not depend upon position or power to recruit the residents and their leaders to take on this project. He approached them as God's servant and appealed to their sense of community and heritage. Nehma knew that if anything good was happening on his mission, it was because God was in the driver's seat. He had no grandiose visions of power-grabbing when the project was completed. However, like George Washington and many other accomplished administrators, Nehma was willing to step up and take responsibility for a task no one had yet completed.

Food for Thought

Leadership expert John Maxwell explains that "positional leadership" is the lowest form. The person who depends heavily upon their title to get things done usually does so out of the extremes of pride or insecurity. Neither are solid foundations needed to move people into action, especially long-term. Sooner or later, positional power implodes because the same people who allow one to lead can also take them out.

On the other hand, the "relational leader" guides others through the development of mutual connections and respect. This person influences others to follow through a collective sense that each person brings value to the table and is essential to the team.

Which direction do you lean—position or relationship? Why?

What answer would those under your leadership give to this question?

Have you ever worked under one who leans heavily upon their position to get things done? How does that feel? Is it motivational?

Perform a leadership critique concerning how well you are emptying yourself of personal glory to serve your team. Does anything need to change?

Read Matthew 20:20-28. Compare the disciples' views of authority to that of Jesus.

Bodyguard Tactic Thirty-Three

START A MOVEMENT

"Leaders turn their cause into the people's cause."

"If you think you are leading but no one is following, you're only taking a walk." —John Maxwell

A leader must acutely understand that movement is dependent upon followers. Someone can own a great cause but fail to employ the skills needed to produce followers, which leads to frustration for everyone.

A fascinating account in the New Testament book of Acts enlightens this point.

When they heard this, they were furious and wanted to put them to death. But a Pharisee named Gamaliel, a teacher of the law, who was honored by all the people, stood up in the Sanhedrin and ordered that the men be put outside for a little while. Then he addressed the Sanhedrin: "Men of Israel, consider carefully what you intend to do to these men. Some time ago Theudas appeared, claiming to be somebody, and about four hundred men rallied to him. He was killed, all his followers were dispersed, and it all came to nothing. After him, Judas the Galilean appeared in the days of the census and led a band of people in revolt. He too was killed, and all his followers were scattered. Therefore, in the present case I advise you: Leave these men alone! Let them go! For if their purpose or activity is of human origin, it will fail. But if it is from God, you will not be able to stop these men; you will only find yourselves fighting against God." (Acts 5:33-39 NIV)

In an attempt to provide the Sanhedrin with some rational thinking, respected teacher Gamaliel presented a history lesson about leadership. He reminded the council of two "would-be" great leaders, one named Theudas and another dubbed Judas the Galilean. Each of these men started religious movements that ended with no lasting accomplishments. Gamaliel points out that the movement died after the revolutionary catalyst was removed. These people were following a person rather than an ideal. When the person died, the crusade vanished with it.

Not so with Jesus. The Master Teacher drew followers, but not just to Himself, though that would have been a worthy goal in itself. Jesus instead appealed to an even deeper vacuum in the human soul: "How can a flawed human have a personal relationship with God?" And secondly, "How can I make a difference in the world? How can I leave my mark?" In both the pagan and Judean religions, one could never be good enough to obtain secure favor with "the gods" or God. That is why gods are gods, and they/He is "other" even in Jewish theology. One must attempt to adhere perfectly to a set of laws and offer sacrifices to atone for their shortcomings. This approach to God is the foundation of nearly every religion. The wonder of Jesus as a leader is his ability to effectively answer all of those questions and provide a path for their realization.

Wise leaders help followers embrace "the main thing," and they keep the main thing the main thing.

Jesus expressed succinctly "the main things," which are to love God and love others as you love yourself. Every noble attribute and action can find its roots in these two ideals. Many Christian organizations stray from the main Christ-honoring thing. Why? Because they do not keep asking "why" questions. God is more interested in *why* we do good deeds than the *what* and *how* of the matter.

LEADERS MUST KEEP ASKING "WHY?"

When Jesus returned to Heaven, he left behind a group of people sold out to the truth that anyone could obtain good standing with God through His Son. This was indeed "good news" and the Teacher had trained them so well that what was His cause was now their cause.

I remember standing before a large chamber of commerce gathering with my community relations director. We were invited to share and solicit assistance for a large community project our church was developing. The room was filled with influential and affluent businesspeople, none of whom knew us, and many were not Christians. We were both nervous to say the least. How could a couple of pastors convince successful men and women to help us in twelve minutes? However, a few were aware of our church's ministry because of our focus on community involvement.

In the short twelve minutes we had to present our case, we each told the true and compelling stories of specific children with disabilities who could never roll onto a playground and play with the other children. Most playgrounds are not accessible to children with physical disabilities. We could sense the emotion building in the room. We then presented a plan, including a brochure, explaining our solution to the problem: to build a fully accessible community playground with community funds and physical assistance. Finally, we made the ask and sat down. The room erupted in applause, and both the organization and specific individuals got on board. We left that meeting praising God, who would use us for such a good work. *Our* cause became *their* cause in short order.

Nehma was passionate about his purpose but could never accomplish his calling alone, even with all his power and resources. He needed to enlist followers that could gain the same devotion to his cause. The bodyguard did this by coming prepared with resources to provide hope and prove his dedication. He recruited vital influencers by sharing his "God story" about the king and appealing to their personal pride and responsibility. Ultimately, he was also willing to pick up a hammer and get to work, which was his request to everyone. Before long, Nehma was a leader with committed followers.

Food for Thought

How does one know if they genuinely have followers? Followership must be put to the test by expecting action from those doing the following. Do you have disciples? How do you know?

Do people follow you because they must do so based on your position or because you endear them to your leadership and cause?

A ruler can rule and still not lead. A leader can lead and not be a ruler.

Read Acts 2. Analyze Peter's sermon and determine how the Apostle's speech enlisted followers who would join his cause.

Bodyguard Tactic Thirty-Four

GIVE THEM TOOLS

*"Leaders must equip the team.
Proper equipping is where many leaders stumble."*

One of the highest organizational costs is under-developed and under-utilized employees or volunteers. Many for-profit and non-profit organizations fail to provide ongoing employee and volunteer development, which ultimately hurts the operation. Equipping those serving to pursue corporate goals is time and money well spent.

For many years, our church had no "newcomers" class or event. This sometimes resulted in people becoming members of the church but having little idea of our theological position on matters that were important to us. Our church placed high value on the ordinance of water baptism by immersion. In fact, to become an official member, one had to have been baptized in this manner at some point in their life. A few times in the early years, a person joined the church only to discover eight months later our view on baptism was a perspective they did not hold. Some very difficult discussions could have been avoided if we had done a better job of equipping prospective members.

We also developed a specific mission, vision, and set of core values, which included church attendance, generosity, structure, and participation in ministry. Since many people became part of our church who had migrated from other congregations, they had no way of knowing any of these matters, and of course those new to the faith had no idea either. I guess we assumed they would gain this knowledge through osmosis. Finally, we came up with the bright idea of a newcomer seminar where I spent several hours explaining all these issues and more. This one piece of equipping began to change the level of commitment to the church's identity, beliefs, and future goals It is not good to ask people to become part of something without providing the knowledge, tools, and training to make them successful.

I was recently invited to function on the board of directors of a large nonprofit providing services the disability community in our region. UCP of Central Pennsylvania employs many people with varying levels of responsibility. I have been friends with three presidents of this organization, and I highly respect them. However, I hold the current president in the highest esteem. She has worked her way up the ladder in this organization, holding several positions and obtaining a master's degree in the field. Janeen knows the value of quality training and education to maintain high standards of service to the community.

Before I was inducted, one of my first jobs was to introduce myself to a packet of information about UCP. This document explained several essential aspects of the nonprofit of which I was unaware. I was then asked to attend the annual meeting where employee awards were bestowed, a year-end report was presented, and the primary responsibilities of board members were shared. The program then turned to new member induction, which included me. I have since received an in-depth job description, including how each support team fits into the organization's mission. Afterward, I met meet with Janeen personally for a complete orientation concerning my position.

From the beginning of my relationship with UCP, I have been impressed by the level of equipping the company provides to employees and volunteers. This training makes me excited and hopeful about my role in our mission. Janeen and leaders before her have understood that turning someone loose on a job without adequately equipping them is a recipe for disillusionment and low-quality work.

TURNING SOMEONE LOSE ON A PROJECT WITHOUT TRAINING AND RESOURCES IS A RECIPE FOR DISILLUSIONMENT.

Before Nehma even left Persia, he recognized the future need for numerous resources, including official passage documents, lumber and other building supplies, and money. These items became part of his request to King Artaxerxes. When we arrive at the third chapter of the biblical account, the wall is being rebuilt in an orderly manner as laid out by Nehemiah and his team. Various groupings of Jerusalemites performed work on selected sections of the wall. A short statement in the third chapter reveals that Nehma had adequately resourced these work teams: "The next section was repaired by the men of Tekoa, but their nobles would not put their shoulders to the work under their supervisors" (Nehemiah 3:5 NIV).

Some slugs refused to get on board, as could happen in any project or organization. In this case, the "nobles" of Tekoa likely felt they were too good for physical labor. A key indicator of quality equipping is shown when the account records that they would not work under their "supervisors." Nehma knew he could not personally manage this large project alone, so he recruited supervisors who could serve as guides and expertise providers who could also report back to Nehma and his team. These leaders freed Nehma to move about the entire project site to evaluate and encourage the builders. He provided a sound leadership structure in which resources could be delivered quickly and without hassle.

Later in the story, we note that Nehma gathered the people and had the Law read in their presence. The commands and historical examples would remind them of why they did the work and how they could maintain a society that would facilitate this debacle not happening again.

Food for Thought

If you lead a team or an entire organization, what are your systems and channels for equipping employees or volunteers? Do you know if it is working?

How much time do you spend on "people development" each week? Are you strategic and purposeful about this endeavor?

Can you identify an experience when a person or organization did not give adequate attention to this matter? What were the clues that exposed the problem? How could they have been avoided?

Read Exodus 18 concerning Moses's father-in-law's wise advice about equipping the entire nation.

Bodyguard Tactic Thirty-Five

Always A Foe

"No significant project was ever completed without facing opposition."

"Don't go to church!" The statement appeared on several prominent billboards in our area one year. The signs were bright orange with prominent white lettering, and they were an invitation to join our church in serving the community on a particular Sunday morning. We also mailed 30,000 postcards to our community with the same message. Near the bottom of each advertisement was a website address where one could sign up to serve and the church's phone number to call for more information.

Oh, did we get calls! There were irate Christian community members who reached out over phone lines to express their disdain with such an idea as not holding worship services and instead going into our community to meet needs. Rarely a day passed that I did not need to console one of our office assistants after being chastised by an angry Christ follower. Our Faith in Action program was not popular with many.

But there was also opposition to the idea within our church family. Some of them had the same disdain for this idea. "How dare we close worship services!" I preached a series of messages leading up to the big day of serving, and after catching a lot of flak, Faith in Action happened. We met at the church building, prayed, and took communion, then dispersed into our entire area doing everything from cleaning gutters to washing floors and painting rooms. A handful of old-time members left the church.

Of course, my smart-aleck self was saying, "Yes, how dare we actually do what we talk about every week!"

Others were afraid we would forfeit offerings because there was no offering time in service (this was way before online giving). So, we placed buckets at the doors where members could put their offerings as they left the church building.

Faith in Action was an astounding success, but it came with a price. The following year, we did it again and prepared 100,000 meals for hungry people in our region and Haiti. This activity sparked unprecedented growth in our understanding and application of community involvement, which became the hallmark of our congregation.

If it's worth doing, expect to be opposed in one way or another. A proverb states, "What doesn't kill you will make you stronger." Perhaps this is not always true, but it is often spot-on. Opposition to new ideas, improvements, and changes is part and parcel of forward movement. There is another saying for those leading such initiatives: "If you can't stand the heat, stay out of the kitchen!"

My friend, Tim Harlow, leads a very large church in suburban Chicago. As church leaders with similar stories of changing traditional churches into forward-thinking, relevant ministries, I highly respect him. Tim has served this congregation for many years, and today it would appear as a successful juggernaut. Though the church has experienced God's power and fruitfulness through Tim's tenure, it was not always this way.

When Tim began ministry with this church, it was a small, traditional, locked-in group that was not reaching their community or their potential. This young pastor had no intention of his congregation remaining tepid and out of touch, so he started changing a few things, then a few more, and so on. Now the church baptizes hundreds of Christ followers every year on multiple campuses. Tim describes the process of improvement and the opposition he received in this manner.

Nehemiah completed the wall in fifty-two days. I knew that we couldn't push that hard. It took well more than fifty-two months! And yet, even in the slow roll, we kept the principle of one hand on the sword and one hand on the trowel. I believe that means we can't get so distracted by the opposition that we forget what we're building. Perhaps the sword analogy seems too harsh, but I believe it's not that far off. We have to fight to stay on mission.

It becomes even more difficult when the opposition is from our own team. Someone once told me that turning a church around is really the process of killing one church and starting another. Unfortunately, there is some truth in that. Not everyone—well, sometimes not anyone—is really all that interested in change, no matter what they say.

And it didn't take long for those people who were eager to hire a twenty-eight-year-old guy with very little experience to realize that my lack of experience was not going to keep me from doing what God called me to do. What God called all of us to do, actually—reach those who are lost.

We reached the point where we had to decide when to appease the already found, and when to ignore them and go searching for the lost. That's the crux of Jesus's parable in Luke 15. It's interesting to me that the Shepherd who had a large flock (one hundred) was so concerned about the one lost sheep that he left the other ninety-nine in the "open field" (Luke 15:4).

Do you think the ninety-nine were happy about that? They were vulnerable in the field. They didn't have the care of the Shepherd. And what if he got lost or hurt and couldn't make it back? Was it really worth it for that one stupid sheep that shouldn't have wandered off?

When you study this Nehemiah story, it's hard to determine what the enemies were really worried about. But at some point, they were threatened by what Nehemiah was doing. It was obviously going to affect them somehow.

So, for thirty-three years, I've been leading our people to become comfortable with being uncomfortable. And if they can't take it, they leave. Which is honestly really hard. It's hard to pour your life into sheep for years and then have them decide they want to go to another flock. But that's the only way we've been able to stay focused on the ones who are lost. I haven't had to use the sword on anyone, yet, but the enemies always know I have one.

Leaders must expect and prepare for resistance, which arrives both internally and externally in an organization trying innovation. Nehma knew these principles well, and when the opposition came he was ready with a prayer and a plan.

NEHMA FACED OPPOSITION WITH A PRAYER AND A PLAN.

Leaders of several area tribes were accustomed to harassing the citizens of Jerusalem, and the arrival of a new governor from the king did not sit well. To them, it would be a cold day in hell when the walls of Jerusalem would be rebuilt, so they began their dastardly work. They banded together and devised plans to discourage the workers and instill fear in their leaders.

The historical description of the subsequent events is choice: "Hear us, our God, for we are despised. Turn their insults back on their own heads. Give them over as plunder in a land of captivity. Do not cover up their guilt or blot out their sins from your sight, for they have thrown insults in the face of the builders. So we rebuilt the wall till all of it reached half its height, for the people worked with all their heart" (Nehemiah 4:4-6 NIV).

Nehma's knee-jerk reaction was, once again, prayer. He dropped to his knees and invoked God's favor, appealing to the Father's sense of pride in his children. "Lord, you see what is happening, and if you want this wall rebuilt, you will have to take care of business."

Then the record casually states that the work continued until the wall reached the halfway point. The footnote is that it went up because the people bought into the project with all their heart and soul.

Opposition was far from over, but Nehma prayed and responded with a plan with each wave. Perhaps the worst opposition was yet to come, and it was not from outside sources but inside his own ranks. There would be a mutiny of sorts.

Food for Thought

What is your knee-jerk reaction to opposition? Does it usually help or hurt your cause? Some people handle wildfires by throwing gasoline on them, while others think, develop a strategy, and extinguish the problem.

How would you have handled Nehma's problem?

Read Nehemiah 5:1-13. Note how the bodyguard handled internal issues.

Bodyguard Tactic Thirty-Six

Don't Lose Your Cool

*"A leader must learn to manage anger
and frustration well during an initiative.
If they do not, the person at the top may be the
person who derails everything."*

In his autobiography, Martin Luther King Jr. discusses how he learned to manage anger. During his early days as a reformer, he was often met with fierce opposition. King regularly lost his temper, spoke rashly, and was indignant. One day he returned home from a meeting and a wave of guilt swept across him. In a meeting, the civil rights leader had returned unbridled anger with the same.

That day he finally realized that if he allowed his temper to get out of hand, he would have a more difficult time solving problems with opponents and colleagues alike. He would also become bitter, which would not help his cause. From that time forward, he was determined to remain calm in every situation and turn his anger into constructive action.

A leader's anger can be harnessed for tremendous good or become a force toward their demise. King experienced more than enough injustice and suffering, including his home being firebombed with him and his family inside, yet the great civil rights leader did not allow frustration to master him.

Leaders are often under pressure to make crucial decisions, meet deadlines, and lead their teams effectively. These expectations can lead to frustration and anger, which have negative consequences if not managed well.

When a leader displays anger in the workplace, it can create a toxic environment for employees and damage morale. Employees are likely to feel intimidated, stressed, and demotivated, leading to decreased productivity and high turnover. An uncontrolled temper can cause a leader to make impulsive decisions that they may later regret. This can harm the reputation of the leader and the organization, and potentially damage relationships with stakeholders.

Moreover, leaders who struggle to manage their anger will find it harder to communicate effectively. Anger can cause leaders to be confrontational and difficult to approach, which hinders collaboration and cooperation with colleagues, partners, customers, or volunteers. Angry outbursts can negatively impact the success of projects and initiatives, as well as the overall success of the organization.

A leader must learn how to manage their anger effectively. This discipline requires developing self-awareness, using stress-management techniques, and seeking support when needed. When leaders can control their emotions, they create a positive work environment, make better decisions, and communicate effectively with others, ultimately leading to their success as leaders and the success of their organizations.

CHECK YOUR UNMANAGED ANGER AT THE DOOR.

It was my second mission trip to Bangkok, Thailand, leading a small group of church members who were new to mission travel. We arrived at our first stop, the Detroit airport, where we would disembark and wait for our flight to Tokyo to depart.

I had gate checked my small suitcase and was waiting for its arrival up the lift at the end of the jetway along with several other passengers. One by one, each traveler picked up their luggage until only two of us were left. The man next to me was waiting on his small briefcase containing his computer. The lift started its way up once more, and his briefcase was only half on the platform. As it rose toward us, we both noticed that the case would not get through the tight area. But the lift kept ascending. We watched for the next few moments as his case and computer were crushed between the lift and its frame. As you can imagine, he was not a happy camper.

He finally left while I still waited for my baggage, and I waited and waited. Finally, I walked to the gate check area and explained my situation to the attendant. She was obviously not sympathetic but proceeded to call the luggage handlers. They told her a bag was left, but it had no gate-check tag, and they were not allowed to send it up. I would have to get it in Tokyo. I showed the attendant my tag and identification and insisted they send me my bag. Not happening.

As we discussed the fate of my luggage, I explained that it contained my computer, medicine, reading materials, and personal items, all of which I would want on the upcoming twelve-hour flight. I was met with a stern frown and repeatedly told I would not get my luggage until we arrived in Tokyo. I was getting angrier by the second, raising my voice to a level that could be heard several feet away. We argued for several minutes until I finally conceded.

Meanwhile, my little cadre of missionaries were watching their pastor lose his ever-loving mind. None of them had ever seen me lose my temper, and they were astounded. It suddenly dawned on me that I had made a fool of myself and simultaneously disappointed my team. We left the area and gathered elsewhere, where I repeatedly apologized. What a fantastic start on a mission for God! I have never again lost my cool in such a manner at an airport.

Anyone who chooses to lead must learn to manage their anger and keep their cool.

Nehemiah was no stranger to leadership anger.

Moreover, in those days, I saw men of Judah who had married women from Ashdod, Ammon, and Moab. Half of their children spoke the language of Ashdod or the language of one of the other peoples, and did not know how to speak the language of Judah. I rebuked them and called curses down on them. I beat some of the men and pulled out their hair. I made them take an oath in God's name and said: "You are not to give your daughters in marriage to their sons, nor are you to take their daughters in marriage for your sons or for yourselves. Was it not because of marriages like these that Solomon king of Israel sinned? Among the many nations there was no king like him. He was loved by his God, and God made him king over all Israel, but even he was led into sin by foreign women. Must we hear now that you too are doing all this terrible wickedness and are being unfaithful to our God by marrying foreign women?"

One of the sons of Joiada son of Eliashib the high priest was son-in-law to Sanballat the Horonite. And I drove him away from me. (Nehemiah 13:23-28 NIV)

When the bodyguard returned to Jerusalem and became aware of the numerous ways his people had backslidden, he went off like a rocket. Nehma had every right to become incensed, and in this unusual situation he needed to take drastic measures, which he did. It would be rare for a leader today to experience anything like Nehemiah's discovery, and his angry actions were justified. However, it should be rare for a quality leader to lose it on his followers.

Here are some steps that a leader can take to manage their emotions effectively:

1. **Practice mindfulness:** Take breaks throughout the day to clear the mind and refocus. If something is happening that is igniting what will become unmitigated anger, a leader should walk away for a few minutes and gather their emotions. This helps to reduce stress and prevent anger from escalating.

2. **Identify triggers**: Leaders should understand what causes them to become angry or frustrated so they can anticipate and avoid these situations if possible. If a leader knows they will be in an unavoidable anger-triggering situation, they can prepare ahead of time how they will keep their cool.

3. **Use relaxation techniques:** Take a walk, do breathing exercises, and/or chat with someone who is calming.

4. **Remove yourself from the situation:** Staying near the problem that is enraging you is unwise. Step back and return later when you've regained your composure.

5. **Communicate effectively:** Actively listen and try to see things from other people's perspectives. Communicate clearly and calmly, even in challenging situations.

6. **Seek support**: Seek support from a trusted colleague or a coach, and don't be afraid to ask for help when you feel overwhelmed.

7. **Give yourself grace**: Leaders should treat themselves with kindness and understanding, and acknowledge their emotions without judgment. Everyone eventually loses their cool.

8. **Apologize and ask forgiveness if appropriate**: A leader who is willing to admit their mistakes and take appropriate action to rectify a relationship is wise. People respect leaders like this.

Food for Thought

When was the last time you lost your cool? What triggered your anger, and how did you handle or mishandle the situation? Do you implement the steps presented above? Are there ways you can improve?

We can learn a lot about ourselves and others by *what* makes us angry. It is healthy to study what made Jesus mad. How do events that made the Master angry compare to what makes you lose it?

Read Mark 3:1-5 and Matthew 21:12-17.

Bodyguard Tactic Thirty-Seven

DECISIVE ACTION

"When the tipping point that might lead to failure rears its head, the leader must act."

It is called the "Miracle on the Hudson." On January 15, 2009 an Airbus A320 left La Guardia airport in New York headed for Charlotte then on to Seattle. Shortly after take-off, the plane was intercepted by a large flock of birds that destroyed all engine power. Chesley (Sully) Sullenberger was piloting the plane, and given their low altitude and proximity to an airport, he and his co-pilot decided to ditch the plane in the Hudson River just off Midtown Manhattan. Sully had been a fighter pilot, and at fifty-seven he had logged over 19,000 hours in the air. He quickly realized the plane would not make it back to La Guardia or another airport in New

Jersey, so he decided to down the plane in the Hudson. The plane hit the water at about 140 miles per hour, bounced once, and then glided slowly to a stop. He immediately instructed evacuation of the aircraft, and many of the passengers stood on the wings of the plane while others swam to safety. There were 155 people, and everyone on the plane survived as Sully reentered the plane twice to be certain every person was evacuated.

"When the tipping point that might lead to failure rears its head, the leader must act."

Sully was presented several awards, and a movie starring Tom Hanks told his story. On that day the decisive action of a leader saved many lives.

In March 2020, the COVID-19 pandemic struck our country. In the course of a week or two, everything changed, especially for churches. As pandemic news crowded the airwaves—opening the door for large-scale panic—political, corporate, small business, nonprofit, and church leaders were treading new territory, ground that could rock their organizations' stability or even existence. Public gatherings were banned, hospitals shut their doors to visitors and were overwhelmed with patients. Cell phones, computers, and flatscreens suddenly and without warning grew in importance tenfold. These were dire, strangling times for the entire planet. What would everyone do?

Answer: They turned to their leaders for answers and assistance.

With the onset of this tragedy, churches could no longer hold live services, which meant they needed to broadcast online. Many churches were not previously using the online medium to transmit worship services, meetings, and study groups. Other churches were way behind in their ability to facilitate online donations. If church leaders did not act quickly and decisively, the threat of their church going out of existence was real. Along with many small businesses and nonprofits, many *did* close their doors forever.

In our case, we were in the middle of a senior leadership transition since I was to retire in a few months. My successor started working with Vibrant in January with plans to take the helm in June. However, Drew had much more experience with live media transmission than I. Along with several other media-savvy staff members and volunteers, our church was able to pivot quickly and effectively. I was convinced that, for all practical purposes, I needed to hand over the reins then and there. My new leader and I discussed the matter within a few days and came to the same conclusion. I would continue to serve as the head of the congregation, but he would bring us up to speed in the online world. This would give him the ability to quickly gain respect among the people he would soon be leading solely while not needing to take full responsibility for decisions during the next few months. The transition was made quietly with critical members aware, and he went to work. The church pivoted rapidly and maintained healthy (as possible) communication with our members and supporters. The pivot plan worked, and the church stayed healthy. Drew did an admirable job in this new role.

When the tipping point that might lead to failure rears its ugly head, good leaders act decisively.

Nehemiah 4:9 is reminiscent of a famous statement made by President Ronald Reagan near the end of the Cold War. Negotiations were taking place concerning restricting nuclear warheads between Russia and the U.S. An American scholar who met with Reagan frequently, Suzanne Massie, taught the president a Russian proverb, "Trust but verify," which the leader used at nearly every meeting with the Russians. Trust but verify!

Nehma stated his response upon learning of enemy plots, "But we prayed to our God and posted a guard both day and night to meet this threat" (Nehemiah 4:9 NIV). The wise leader realized that prayer should be the first reaction but not *the only* response. God often uses us to fulfill our own prayers, so He expects us to turn to Him and trust Him, but we will also act. Nehma was unwilling to stay on his knees and wait for God to work a miracle when he knew there were effective strategies he could implement. This pattern continued in response to every challenge Nehma and his people encountered—and it worked!

Food for Thought

In response to a challenge, are you characterized as a "thinker" or a "doer"? Nehma was both. His willingness to first consider matters in the presence of God shows that he contemplated solutions. But then his penchant for action was put into gear.

It is said that it is better to act and make a mistake or not be entirely correct than to do nothing. Inaction is itself an action.

Can you imagine situations where you "thought" too long and lost an opportunity? Or the opposite, acted too quickly and caused yourself more problems?

Can you think of examples you have witnessed of others making these errors? What other solutions could they have used?

In Acts 10, both Peter and Cornelius were decisive leaders. Note how they reacted when they perceived the Lord presented a challenge. Why would going to Cornelius be a difficult decision for Peter? Why would sending for a Jewish teacher and leader be a problem for Cornelius?

Bodyguard Tactic Thirty-Eight

DEFINE YOUR ENEMY

"Recognition of a common enemy and a solid plan to defeat them is a powerful motivator."

Sometimes the enemy can be standing right in front of us, but we do not recognize them. Such was the case with Judas, who betrayed Jesus and his friends. The disciple-turned-traitor of the Teacher lived, ate, slept, observed, and listened among them for many months, yet only Jesus recognized his presence.

I am reading my friend Albert Tate's new book, *How We Love Matters: A Call to Relentless Racial Reconciliation*. Several years ago, I enjoyed the opportunity to visit Israel for two weeks with Albert and several other pastors and Christian leaders. Most evenings, Albert and our friends gathered for a delightful ritual of enjoying a good glass of wine and a fine cigar. Through hours of discussion, I came to respect this fine pastor's sincerity, wisdom, and talent.

How We Love Matters was born in Albert's mind as the result of our country's racial divisions in the past few years, especially during the COVID-19 pandemic. The precipitating act was the murder of a black man, George Floyd, by a white police officer. The officer, Derek Chauvin, was later convicted of murder, and it became known that the killing was racially motivated. Albert calls to account numerous other murders and hideous acts perpetrated by racist White Americans against Black Americans. Tate explains how he concluded that he could no longer remain silent on such a tragic and pervasive injustice that has its earliest roots in American history.

Masterfully and lovingly, Tate calls upon both the White and Black communities to come to grips with the unfortunate and undeniable truth that American history up to the present has created an often unseen enemy that wreaks havoc on both White and Black Americans and clandestinely divides the races. The author contends that "whiteness" is the ultimate standard by which much of our culture judges and provides the opportunity for advancement. In a grace-filled and genuine manner, Albert identifies our hidden enemy and how it manifests itself in our daily lives. He also provides evidence that the same standard prevails in the Christian church. What we fail to see is hurting us all.

WHAT WE FAIL TO RECOGNIZE IS HURTING US ALL.

The book is a rallying cry, especially for the Christian community, to identify and combat this evil persistently and aggressively. In a real sense, Tate is tasked with just the opposite of our friend Nehma. Instead of rebuilding or bolstering walls of separation between factions in this nation, we must tear down those walls that divide us to our peril. The author does not simply leave us with a clear picture of the present evil; like Nehma, he provides a plan to get the job done. The enemy has been revealed, and Albert calls his readers to act.

A few years ago, my wife was standing in front of the mirror in our primary bathroom, noticing that she was losing weight at an alarming rate. She was already thin and fit, so it was not difficult to identify this phenomenon. But why? Why was she shedding unnecessary pounds? It was time for action, so she arranged a meeting with her doctor, who immediately ordered rounds of testing. Within a couple of weeks, the verdict arrived. Gail had the dreaded pancreatic cancer, which is a near-certain death sentence. Twenty-two months later, my wife passed.

Throughout the entire battle, we often wondered how long this hideous disease had been attacking her body with no outward manifestations. Gail was a nurse practitioner and understood that this form of cancer often goes unnoticed until it is too late, making it deadly.

However, once the culprit was identified, a small army of family, friends, doctors, nurses, and administrators was mustered and deployed. The war was on, and we did not plan to lose. Gail was blessed that she suffered minimal pain until the last few months of her life. Meanwhile, her care on every front was miraculous and inspiring. During her illness, she started a new ministry and raised over a half-million dollars to support under-resourced women in southern Asia to receive vocational, health, and biblical training. Gail may not have won the battle, but she won the war. She now sits in the presence of God, fully healed.

A leader's job is to identify threats, raise awareness, and present a call to action. When a common enemy is identified, people rally, and resources come to bear.

When the bodyguard received news of the enemy's attack on his beloved home, he called people to join a movement that would remedy a hundred-year-old blight on their lives. This insidious enemy existed among them for many years, yet the citizens refused to acknowledge and face their problems. Once a new leader stood among them, calling them to recognize and address the problem, it was soon solved.

As I write, Russia continues to attack Ukraine. What was expected to be a short war and subsequent takeover of Russia's neighboring country has turned into a war of attrition. Neither side plans to give even an inch, and Putin, the leader of Russia, has been unpleasantly surprised at the determination of the Ukrainian people.

Ukraine's leader is a former actor and comedian, Volodymyr Oleksandrovych Zelenskyy. This Jewish leader was an unlikely choice for president but has done a masterful job of uniting Ukrainians and much of the world from whom he garners support against a far superior force. To date, Russia has yet to overthrow Zelenskyy and his people.

A wise leader knows that identifying and describing a threat or an issue can rally people into a formidable force. Every church has a common enemy, Satan, who should be regularly called out as such. Unfortunately, many allow other so-called threats to shroud the real foe and draw attention and resources from the church's mission.

Food for Thought

In what ways have you been either a leader or follower and witnessed a story like Nehma's? Can you identify the steps that were part of the process? How did the leader(s) get people to recognize an issue and address it with action?

If you lead a team, family, or organization, who or what is your enemy, and how can you exploit your adversary to unify your group?

Read Nehemiah 2:17-20. Who would the citizens of Jerusalem normally have thought of as their enemies? How did Nehma redirect their thinking so they could identify their "real" enemy and show them how to defeat this foe?

Bodyguard Tactic Thirty-Nine

THEY WANT TO KNOW WHY

"The why is more potent than the what."

God cares about the "why" questions.

After God rejected Cain's offering, the farmer became angry. Then God spoke to the disgruntled man and inquired, "Why are you angry, Cain? Why is your face so downcast?" (Genesis 4:6 NIV). God wanted Cain to examine his dispostion so that he would not end up doing something foolish.

When the angels visited Abraham and Sarah in their old age and told them that Sarah would have a newborn son within a year, Sarah could only laugh. She was way beyond child-bearing age and thought this news was a joke. The Lord's reaction was to inquire *why* the aged woman reacted in such a manner. "Sarah, why did you laugh? What caused you to laugh at this news directly from Me?" When God called the older woman of faith on her chuckle, she did what humans have done since Adam and Eve. She lied! Why would a woman of such great faith doubt the Lord's ability to do whatever He wanted? (Though I have no doubt I would have reacted the same and made jokes about it for the rest of my life.)

Moses led the new nation of Israel out of Egypt as far as the shore of the Red Sea, which left them trapped between the Egyptian army and the deep blue sea. They immediately began to whine at Moses and blame him for their present plight. The wimpy nation carried on so much that Moses challenged the bedraggled, formerly enslaved people to wait on the Lord. It appears he wasn't sure what to do either, so Moses began calling out to God for direction. God took notice of this freedom fighter and asked, "Why are you just standing there? Get on with it. March your people into the sea, and you will witness my power." Moses obeyed, and the rest is history.

WHY ARE YOU JUST STANDING THERE? GET ON WITH IT.

Jesus often asked his audience why they were doing certain things counter to faith. He said, "Why do you worry about clothes? Why do you look at the speck of sawdust in someone's eye while you have a log in your own? Why are you so afraid? Why did you doubt? Why do you ask me what is good?" And even to Jesus's Father, the Savior inquired from the cross, "Why have you forsaken me?"

Doing the right things for the wrong reasons is not acceptable to God. The designer of truth expects his followers to constantly evaluate their motives for their actions to detect if their movements are rooted in faith, truth, and most importantly love.

DOING THE RIGHT THINGS FOR THE WRONG REASONS IS NOT ACCEPTABLE TO GOD.

As leaders, we too should often implore followers to ask themselves the "why" questions.

As I write this chapter, the Worldwide Hillsong Church movement is greatly distressed. Several leaders of large, thriving congregations have confessed extramarital affairs and other unethical or immoral practices resulting in their resignation or dismissal. Then came the bombshell that has rocked the entire international movement; the worldwide originator and leader of Hillsong has also admitted to misdeeds, including inappropriate relations with females resulting first in his supposed Sabbath and weeks later his resignation. Hillsong congregations are fleeing the once powerful organization.

The first question to such news is *why*? Many followers who were close to these influential leaders revealed that some were power and pleasure hungry, and the illness went to the very top of the organization. Somewhere along the line, powerful men stopped asking why they were building this empire and did what they performed best: strictly adhering to a process that attracted ever increasing adherents through Grammy-level music productions and TED talk-style teaching. But many devotees discovered what happened on Sunday was not indicative of their leadership conduct for the remainder of the week. *Why?* God wants to know and expects leaders to answer forthrightly and honestly.

On the other hand, the more positive side of the motivation fence is the consideration of appealing to followers' senses of *why*.

People with deep convictions about their actions will work harder and more intelligently than those who work for a paycheck. Intrinsic motivation rooted in profound moral and ethical principles convinces followers to give their best, not because of a great speech, masterful plan, or even trust in the leader but sprouting from personal convictions. A good leader understands how to tap into convictions they hold in common with their followers and bring those deeply held beliefs to bear to solve a problem.

Nehma understood that the "wall" issue was more than a physical structure. It represented the security, pride, and integrity of the Israeli people, so he addressed the issue through their children. Any decent parent deeply desires that their children possess these characteristics and benefits. Children's security and safety are significant considerations for any parent, not to mention spousal well-being.

The bodyguard did not recruit and encourage workers with beautiful drawings of a restored wall. He did not discuss the wall's majesty and how marvelous each gate into the city would become. No, he understood there were more profound, more motivational reasons for this project. This undertaking would also symbolize the community's trust and belief in God. In essence Nehemiah inquired, "How do you think God feels about this mess? Does the condition of this city, His city, evoke pride and pleasure in his children?" Ultimately the bodyguard led them to the conclusion: Why would you *not* want to rebuild this wall?

Keeping the "why" question at the forefront of any program or project is a fundamental responsibility of a leader.

Food for Thought

Why do you lead? What motivates you?

Is it for your organization to get bigger, stronger, or more well-known in your circle? Will success get you that much desired raise in salary? Do you deeply desire recognition among your peers? Do you admittedly just enjoy more control over more people? Is your leadership truly "faith-based"?

What is the "why" for members and supporters of your organization? How often do you remind your team why they exist?

Read John 21:15-23. This was the famous moving scene when Jesus conducted a healing and purposeful counseling session with Peter while the other Apostles observed. Jesus had a job for Peter, but Peter had already severely blown it once, so the impulsive overachiever needed a gut check. How did Jesus orchestrate the "why" with the "what" in this conversation?

Bodyguard Tactic Forty

STEP UP!

"Leaders must lead!"

Leaders face problems thrust upon them by events beyond their control.

Nearly every organization has a specific mission and vision, "the main thing" of their existence. For most Christian organizations, Jesus Christ has already determined their purpose. Both individually and in the community, followers of Christ are expected to share the Good News of God's love with every people group on earth. These are the marching orders for all Christians.

However, keeping the main thing the main thing in real-life practice has its challenges. For instance, in the past few years, the world has experienced the onslaught of COVID-19, which has changed a myriad of otherwise normal activities. Churches, businesses, and various organizations were forced to stop meeting in person and learn other ways of communicating with one another. Community outreach came to a halt. The volume of issues presented by this radical shift will be studied for generations. For churches, it is difficult to maintain and encourage the spreading of the Gospel without the advantage of in-person gatherings.

The pandemic forced leaders at every level to pivot from their mission to simply figure out how to maintain and suffer loss. In other words, the main thing was placed on a shelf for an extended period while leaders tried to decipher new methods and practices just to stay afloat.

In America, a diverse nation, another critical issue was thrust upon the entire nation. A police officer, in full view of phone cameras, senselessly murdered George Floyd. Once again, our country's fundamental flaw was vividly on screen for all to see. This tragedy was followed by others of similar nature, which exacerbated the problem and caused outrage among millions of American citizens. Once again, race wars addressed by our country's worst conflict—the Civil War—floated to the top of our society's collective consciousness. For a short time, even COVID would take a back seat.

Now the nation faced two titanic issues. Leaders must deal with the pandemic *and* address race issues in their organizations.

I was unexpectedly blessed to retire in the early months of the pandemic, and I often tell people that I started a new chapter at the perfect time!

Leaders find themselves in a no-win situation when catastrophic events occur. No matter their decisions, many people will vehemently disagree and often exit. It's a classic "damned if you do, damned if you don't" situation. The added pressure of the "tyranny of the urgent" kicks in, and mission statements vanish in the hurricane of conditions beyond their control. The main thing simply cannot be the main thing right now becomes their silent plea.

When these unexpected weather conditions prevail, "a leader's gotta lead!"

My friend Greg Nettle leads a large organization called Stadia. Stadia's mission is to see to it that every child can access a healthy church and hear about the love of God through Jesus. Stadia aggressively pursues its noble motto, "We won't stop until every child has a church."

However, since the organization's goal is national and international, the issue of racial awareness, appreciation, and reconciliation is of considerable importance. Unlike most countries, the racial problems run deep in the U.S. They have not been reconciled since enslaved people were forcibly removed from their families and homes in Africa and brought to America to provide cheap labor for White business owners. Unfortunately, human prejudice runs deep and is a formidable foe, and some White Americans mistakenly believe their race is superior to others'. This view justified the enslavement and ill-treatment of African Americans and other races. Unfortunately for all Americans, this interpretation of various races is counterproductive, immoral, unjust, unethical, and challenging to overcome.

When racial equality and appreciation once again rose to a top priority in this country, many people reconsidered their views. They made meaningful and fruitful improvements in their thinking and actions. Meanwhile, many systemic injustices persist and are yet to be addressed. Our Bill of Rights and Constitution guarantee legal racial equality, but legality is a far cry from hearts endeared to others by genuine love and respect.

A LEADER'S GOTTA LEAD!

My friend Greg was now presented with a problem. "How can I address this critical issue in our multi-cultural, international organization while at the same time staying on point with our mission?" Quality leaders cannot simply ignore issues that are not their primary focus while their followers flounder in a sea of uncertainty about a new problem at their doorstep. During this period, Greg has done an admirable job of maintaining the direct mission of Stadia while addressing issues that are not going away and should be addressed. In short, he has stepped up and led during one of the most challenging times in the organization's history. He applied himself to learn and grow while leading his organization to do the same, and Stadia will come out the better for his leadership efforts. Meanwhile, Stadia continues to plant churches nationally and internationally, and the goal of every child having church access remains.

For better or worse, a leader must lead, and many constituents will jump ship in challenging situations. Jesus often experienced this phenomenon throughout his ministry, right up to the time his betrayer kissed him on the cheek in the Garden of Gethsemane.

It would have been easy for Nehma to buckle under pressure from opponents both outside and inside his community, but he would not be deterred from his mission. Meanwhile, he addressed each challenge that threatened their success head on. Neither Sanballat, his cronies, nor Nehma's own entitled people would prevent him from completing his mission. When inevitable negative issues reared their ugly heads, Nehma led because a leader's gotta lead!

Food for Thought

The two titanic issues experienced during the past few years forced leaders of most organizations to pivot numerous times. Can you think of a leader who you believe handled the crises well? What did they do that made their operation continue to thrive? What attributes of their character helped make them successful?

On the other hand, can you identify a leader who did not do an excellent job of handling these world-changing catastrophes? Where and why did they fall short?

How would you rate yourself as a leader through challenging circumstances? How could you improve?

Read 1 Samuel 13. When Israel and its army were in crisis mode because of the forthcoming Philistine invasion, King Saul made some foolish decisions in reaction.

Bodyguard Tactic Forty-One

Keep The Main Thing The Main Thing

"Leaders must stay focused."

My father designed glass-forming machinery. There was something profoundly appealing about the miracle of melting sand, pouring it into a mold, and seeing it come out the other side a Coke bottle. There were few glass-forming machinery companies during my father's life, and since he was one of the best in the world, he was well-known in the industry. You might still have some glass products in your cabinets produced on one of my father's machines from companies like Anchor Hocking, CorningWare, Brockway Glass, or Ball canning jars.

The continuous motion press was the fastest bottle-making device in the industry. Much of this machine and its predecessor, the Lynch 44, were designed in my garage. Dad overtook about half the garage to make himself a drafting office, in which he had many volumes of drafting books on shelves, all manner of drawing tools, a large drafting table, and a bright-white light that hung on a moving, retractable arm. When Dad was working late into the night, the scene reminded me of a mad scientist at work. The CMP took about five years to develop and required one key ingredient—focus.

This machinery designer's success was rooted in the discipline of concentrating most of his efforts upon a singular goal for an extended time. Dad had only completed the ninth grade in school, but he later attended an engineering school and slowly rose through his industry ranks to become his company's chief engineer. This position required him to keep an entire department on point for long, tedious projects.

The picture of my father, wearing a white shirt, tie, and large horn-rimmed bifocals, mechanical pencil and electric eraser in hand, hunching over a colossal table, wholly immersed in another world, is indelibly etched upon my brain. I learned that my favorite inventor could stay focused and maintain his attention on one project for several reasons.

Dad had a sense of calling to invent and create things that formerly did not exist, especially pertaining to glass. When he conversed about glass, his eyes lit up, and when he sat down at the table with several colleagues gathered around him, ideas flowed from his lips like a flood. He could also be angered by those he perceived to stand between him and his objective. My sister, who also worked in the same office for a time, laughingly recalls Dad's expletives exploding across the entire office and into the manufacturing department. Leaders discover they focus when the project is their holy grail, so they do not allow people or circumstances to divert their attention.

Much of Dad's work in our garage was done after 9:00 p.m. Though he worked on the project at the office as chief engineer, he was responsible for all the projects being engineered by his company. Though all this management was necessary, it distracted him from his pet project, the CMP machine. His other responsibilities forced him to create a time and place where he could zero in on his most important work, which turned out to be our garage. Influential leaders learn how to limit distractions both for themselves and their team. This feat often requires that one find a place to sequester from outside influences.

LEADERS MUST LIMIT DISTRACTIONS FOR THEMSELVES AND THEIR FOLLOWERS.

The leader's team must filter a constant barrage of pseudo-crises, new ideas, changes in direction, and loss of interest to give adequate attention to the prime purpose and goal. People can be like sheep; they tend to wander off. A good shepherd maintains close enough watch to notice when a team or individual is distracted, and they are ready to respond with sound guidance.

Our friend Nehma experienced an onslaught of distractions on many fronts. Listen to his story:

When word came to Sanballat, Tobiah, Geshem the Arab and the rest of our enemies that I had rebuilt the wall and not a gap was left in it—though up to that time, I had not set the doors in the gates—Sanballat and Geshem sent me this message: "Come, let us meet together in one of the villages on the plain of Ono."

But they were scheming to harm me; so I sent messengers to them with this reply: "I am carrying on a great project and cannot go down. Why should the work stop while I leave it and go down to you?" Four times they sent me the same message, and each time I gave them the same answer. (Nehemiah 6:1-4 NIV)

This plot was only one of many attempted distractions Nehma experienced. His famous line, "I am carrying on a great project and cannot go down," should be every leader's mantra for two reasons. If you are not doing a "great" work, when will you start? Secondly, as Jim Collins wrote in his famous book, *Good to Great*, there is a natural conflict between good and great. Nehma only performed tasks to feed his mission; the rest would have to wait.

> ## I'M CARRYING ON A GREAT PROJECT AND CANNOT COME DOWN.

In our world, focus itself is a challenging endeavor. For instance, I regularly view couples at a restaurant table who spend the entire meal watching a lifeless screen while the object of their love sits across the table doing the same. Why not just eat alone? Most folks live hectic lives, and when they get a few moments alone to dine out together it would seem helpful to stay on point: the point being their partner rather than Facebook friends. Go figure. Perhaps many relationships suffer due to partners losing focus on their mates.

A leader must learn to focus at home, work, and play.

Food for Thought

As you read this short chapter, was it hard to stay focused? When you pray, is it hard to give God your full attention? Do you, like me, sometimes take a mental trip to the Caribbean and back several times during your discussion? A constantly cluttered mind simply creates more clutter.

What is your present leadership focus? How well do you stay on point? What is distracting you?

What ways do you use to keep your team focused? Are your methods working?

Are there members of your team presently who are out of focus or off point?

In 2 Samuel 11, David provides a classic example of the dangers of losing focus on his mission. David was home. Where was the king supposed to be? What would have motivated the otherwise godly man to take this course of action? Note the domino effect of David's loss of focus.

Bodyguard Tactic Forty-Two

TROUBLE WITHIN

"Internal intrigue is often the most discouraging kind of opposition. Leaders must address it with patience, wisdom, and appropriate sternness."

It was the most despicable letter I had ever received from a member of my church and the result of months of complaining and gossip emanating from a small group gathering led by a mentor. A fairly new church member of this group accused me of lying, mishandling church funds, and taking the worship service format in a direction church members did not like. The accusations made in the letter were not as inflammatory as the vile language used to assault my character.

For several months, the leader of this group had allowed and ultimately encouraged this kind of activity during weekly group gatherings until the church's elders had to intervene and meet with the group. The church leaders listened quietly to their complaints and returned to the next board meeting with a report of their conversation. The leaders addressed and evaluated each charge, determining whether the allegations were unfounded or not in alignment with the direction of the church. These decisions were then relayed to the group. Within a month, the entire small group left the church and filtered into several other churches in the area but not without causing more problems on their way out.

We were deeply saddened to see this prominent member of our congregation allow such divisiveness. Their discussions and misinformation prompted the youngest member and novice Christian to vent his anger in my direction. Small groups can be a great blessing or a wretched curse. By the way, my friend and I remained friends through it all, and a few years later I had the privilege of speaking at his memorial service. His brief misdirected actions did not define his character or nullify a life of faithful service. He remains one of my most influential mentors for life.

A small group leader must keep the group on point. I am reminded of a method used by my son-in-law for this purpose. During the first meeting, he pulls out a pile of plastic dog poop. As he explains the ground rules for the gatherings, he holds up the poop, which gets a great laugh. Then comes the punch line: "We are not putting up with any bull crap, gossip, or complaining in this group, and if one of us heads down that road I will be throwing this pile of poop at you." Christopher's doggie do-do is the stuff of legend at his church. One does not expect those on their team to exhibit this behavior, but internal strife and political posturing are frequent in any organization. It is easy to become discouraged and distracted or even consider quitting when it happens.

A church has a predetermined mission set forth by Jesus in the Great Commandments and the Great Commission. Also, every church has a written and often unwritten set of values. The group may describe its values using different verbiage, but trust and mutual support are always necessary to keep the organization on point. When the ranks transgress these values, leaders are distracted from the mission while attempting to "put out brush fires" caused by gossip, complaining, and infighting.

Internal strife is like a snowball rolling downhill, and its practice quickly multiplies and rolls faster into a ball large enough to bring down a house. If internal intrigue and infighting are left unchecked, causing the loss of focus on the mission, even large organizations and corporations will fall behind.

INTERNAL STRIFE IS LIKE A SNOWBALL ROLLING DOWNHILL.

Nehma was no stranger to this phenomenon. At one point, the city's poorer citizens came complaining to their new governor that they were suffering and starving because the wealthy were exploiting them for personal gain. Many had relinquished their property and were required to sell their children into slavery to pay the king's taxes. The rich were getting richer on the backs of the poor. To make matters worse, they charged exorbitant interest from their own people.

Nehma explains his reaction to this strife:

When I heard their outcry and these charges, I was very angry. I pondered them in my mind and then accused the nobles and officials. I told them, "You are charging your own people interest!" So I called together a large meeting to deal with them and said: "As far as possible, we have bought back our fellow Jews who were sold to the Gentiles. Now you are selling your own people, only for them to be sold back to us!" They kept quiet, because they could find nothing to say.

So I continued, "What you are doing is not right. Shouldn't you walk in the fear of our God to avoid the reproach of our Gentile enemies? I and my brothers and my men are also lending the people money and grain. But let us stop charging interest! Give back to them immediately their fields, vineyards, olive groves and houses, and also the interest you are charging them—one percent of the money, grain, new wine and olive oil."

"We will give it back," they said. "And we will not demand anything more from them. We will do as you say."

Then I summoned the priests and made the nobles and officials take an oath to do what they had promised. I also shook out the folds of my robe and said, "In this way may God shake out of their house and possessions anyone who does not keep this promise. So may such a person be shaken out and emptied!" (Nehemiah 5:6-13 NIV)

Notice the progression of Nehma's solution to the problem.

* Anger: Like most leaders, he was ticked off when they learn of unnecessary divisiveness.

* Restraint: The wise leader did not act on his anger too quickly, which would have made matters worse.

* Get to the Source: The nobles and officials of Jerusalem were instigating this issue, so that is where his first discussion about the matter began.

* Address Everyone Involved: Nehma called a meeting of all the offenders.

* Stick to the Facts: This was a severe infraction, so Nehma addressed it as such with evidence and in no uncertain terms.

* Appeal to the Sense of Pride, Morality, and Ethics: He chastised them by comparing them to Gentiles whom they disliked, yet they could not deny they acted in the same manner. He followed with a simple convicting statement, "What you are doing is not right." Finally, he brought God into the matter, reminding them of what the Divine Judge thought of what they were doing.

* He Offered a Plan to Rectify the Offense: They must pay back and give back what they had extorted.

* Solicited Commitment: He made them present a public confession that they understood the charges and promised to keep their word. This step provided accountability for each of them.

As President Lincoln prophetically stated about the divided nation by quoting Jesus, "A house divided cannot stand." Internal unrest must be addressed decisively and with wisdom.

Food for Thought

Are there presently pods of unrest in your organization? How are you handling it?

How do you handle anger when division strikes? Do you have a person(s) to safely vent your frustrations? If not, find some!

Are you good at keeping to the known facts, or do you allow emotion to make you exaggerate or state evidence that you cannot verify? How can you do better?

Read James 4:13. According to James, what is often the root cause of conflict? Interestingly, most of the letters in the New Testament were written to address and resolve internal conflict.

Bodyguard Tactic Forty-Three

WATCH YOURSELF

"Leadership affords many fringe benefits, but it is not always wise to accept what is rightfully allotted."

Though General Robert E. Lee chose the wrong side for whom to fight during the Civil War, he was still a highly respected leader on both sides. His soldiers revered him because he turned down many of the perks of his position, including choosing to undergo the hardships of camp life with his troops rather than a local home, as was the practice of many men in his position. His troops were endeared to a leader who chose to make sacrifices along with his soldiers.

Simon Sinek wrote an outstanding book, *Leaders Eat Last*, describing a common Marine Corps practice. When the soldiers are in the mess hall lined up to eat, senior officers always place themselves behind enlisted men. Officers are keenly aware that success on the battlefield depends upon those they are leading, and this gesture is a sign of respect. Good leaders make sacrifices for the team. The Corps rule is "officers eat last."

Leaders have stayed longer, worked harder, studied more diligently, and accepted more responsibility than their followers. As such, when they achieve success and status, the temptation to take advantage of the fringe benefits of their position is ever present. "I deserve it" can become a subtle and sometimes not-so-hidden frame of mind. People who give in to this temptation accept perks when they should be turned down or at least delayed.

Followers carefully observe their leader's behavior to notice if the position has "gone to their head" so that the boss no longer identifies with the troops. When followers sense that their leader does not have their best interests in mind, they lose trust in the leadership structure imperative for organizational health. People will not go to bat for someone they do not trust.

John Maxwell is a successful leadership writer, student, trainer, and practitioner of leadership principles. Maxwell believes that a leader must move from the *perks* of leadership to the *price* of leadership. Those who quest for the personal benefits of leading rather than serving people often shipwreck their journey and hurt their organization.

As the lead pastor of a growing church with a large campus, I had many responsibilities and the need and opportunity to delegate many duties. During the early years of this ministry, I determined that I would never become so "big" that I was unwilling to do menial tasks such as picking up trash or helping to mow the acres of grass in our community park.

Our congregation chose to serve the community by offering an outstanding Easter egg event each Easter weekend. The Easter event was the largest attended event our church offered, drawing over 2,000 people on the Saturday morning before Easter. It was a massive undertaking that took months of preparation. We involved both the congregation and the community in stuffing over 40,000 plastic eggs for the hunt. Meanwhile, we offered entertainment in our multi-purpose auditorium, crafts, a petting zoo, and inflatable rides. Our entertainer returned Sunday morning to lead our children's services, drawing many "Egg-A-Rama" visitors to return for Easter services. The community appreciated this free service, and many started attending the church.

The entire process was exhausting for those in charge, including me. I considered Easter weekend one of the most arduous efforts every year, but it was well worth it. As the event winded down, we cleaned the building in preparation for Easter services. I could have easily walked away from the cleanup without questions from the staff or volunteers. Instead, I chose to stay and clean, usually sweeping the auditorium and hallways. Though it was tiring, I enjoyed staying until the end of the process.

I did not think much about it at the time, but church members and staff were watching me. One of my most honoring compliments through the years of my service was, "Pastor Don works like everyone else. I can't believe he is still here sweeping the floor." By doing what I felt was right, not claiming my "rights" as the senior leader, members and staff were endeared to my leadership. "Leaders eat last!"

I am not tooting my own horn but explaining something that came naturally to me. Don't ask people to do things you will not do, and don't accept every leadership perk just because you can.

Servant leadership was Nehma's chosen style. Nehma had just completed the unpleasant job of taking his nobles and officials to task over their unjust treatment of their subordinates and people experiencing poverty in the region. Now he turns his attention to explaining his unwillingness to accept the perks of being governor. He turned down his food and wine allotment, stopped charging taxes, and refused to acquire land from his subjects. He went above and beyond by feeding dozens and dozens of citizens at his personal table every day. No wonder he could get away with chastising unjust leaders when the entire community witnessed his willingness to forgo governor benefits and remain with his followers.

Interestingly, Nehma felt compelled to tell this part of his story. He deliberately demonstrated how servant leadership looked in action by contrasting the behavior of the nobles and officials with his own. His lifestyle *was* the lesson. Always accepting the perks of being at the top is foolish and counterproductive, so this wise manager made sure they knew he was different from what they usually witnessed.

Food for Thought

What impresses you about Nehma's leadership style? When do you think it is inappropriate for a leader to accept positional-related perks? When is it appropriate? Have you ever accepted a "gift" that you later regretted? (Note: I am not proposing that a leader should never accept a perk of the position, but that those decisions be made wisely and with discretion.)

Read Luke 20:45-47. Talk about accepting perks—check out this group of leaders.

Bodyguard Tactic Forty-Four

SERVANT LEADERSHIP REVISITED

"Leaders don't ask followers to do anything they would not do. The best leaders possess t he heart of a servant."

Though we touched on this subject in an earlier chapter, it bears more thought.

Servant leadership starts with desire and self-awareness. For most of us, especially if we are wired and gifted to lead, self-interest is a natural inclination. Looking out for number one relates to our need for survival but evolves well beyond that basic desire into the realm of putting oneself into the center of the universe. As flawed creatures, our inclinations, especially for leaders, can quickly deteriorate into self-indulgence.

Robert K. Greenleaf first coined the phrase "servant leadership" in his essays in 1970, though I think Jesus beat him to the draw about 2,000 years earlier. Servant leadership was not popular during this period of organizational development, and most companies used a top-down, authoritarian by-position approach to management. Greenleaf espoused that allegiance to a leader will be in direct proportion to the servant nature of the leader. Since then, a new leading method has taken an ever-increasing hold on organizational hierarchy.

Greenleaf explains that a natural servant is a person who sees leadership from the perspective of servanthood *first*. The interests and well-being of the followers drive this kind of leader, and service to others is the mooring from which organizational expeditions embark.

On the other hand, there is a person who follows the leader-first approach. Leadership self-interest is a typical approach to management in many organizations; it is authoritarian and staunchly adheres to pyramid systems of governance. Many churches practice this model, especially those led by a charismatic pastor or a staunchly hierarchical board of directors.

Servant leadership does not preclude the necessity for leaders to make decisions based on their authority, but the difference is motivation and implementation. The servant-leader sets aside personal preferences in favor of organizational and individual needs.

Servant leadership concerns itself with people over projects.

I was not what I considered an exemplary student throughout my educational career, which lasted sixteen years on undergraduate and graduate studies. Go figure, I love to learn. While working on my master's degree I was struggling both at the church I pastored and at home, so my schoolwork was also suffering more than normal. I was already famous for turning in papers *after* the due date, so much so that my close friend always jokingly asked if I went ahead and paid the late fees initially since I knew I would need extra time.

I knew I couldn't meet deadlines for one particular class and called my professor, who was a nationally well-known pastor and speaker, to explain my troubles. I fully expected to receive some chastisement and perhaps an ultimatum. Instead, through several phone conversations, I received encouragement and wisdom that got me through my travails and his classwork. My professor was an effective leader and was loved as a pastor and professor because *people* were always his priority. I'll never forget his kindness and example of quality leadership. He was a genuine servant leader.

There are many situations where the organization is so large that high-level leaders can't spend time with the lowest-level employees or volunteers. However, senior leaders can set an example of servant leadership by caring for employees through systems developed for that purpose.

Empathy is a key component of servant leadership and can be practiced at any level of an organization.

EMPATHY IS A KEY COMPONENT OF SERVANT LEADERSHIP.

Renowned psychologists Daniel Goleman and Paul Ekman identified three ingredients of empathy: cognitive, emotional, and compassionate. The psychologists define cognitive empathy as the ability to put oneself in someone else's shoes. It means you know or have a good idea of what someone else is feeling. You identify with their situation. When a CEO is required to "let people go" for the health of the organization, it should not be a pleasant experience because most people know what it's like to lose a job. Emotional empathy takes the feelings a step further from "knowing" to "physically" identifying with another person's sensations. For instance, when a friend describes the pain of having a tooth pulled, we might physically cringe even if we've never experienced a tooth removal. Compassionate empathy combines the other two ingredients, moving us to try to help the person if possible. The famous "Good Samaritan" is a display of the three kinds of empathy.

No matter how high up on the ladder one gets, they can practice empathy and help create an empathetic organizational culture. Numerous studies have shown that people are more productive when led with empathy.

When the church I pastored became too large for me to "know" everyone, it was not a pleasant experience. I enjoyed getting to know church members and hearing their stories with which I often identified. However, for the good of the church, I learned to exercise empathy in other ways. For instance, I wanted listeners to feel that I empathized with their situations in life and this positively affected my preaching style. It kept me from coming across as judgmental as if I were better than my listeners. Every person is different, but it behooves us to recognize that all of us experience common situations and feelings and react accordingly.

When Nehma recruited volunteers to rebuild the wall, he appealed to their personal well-being and that of their families. He approached them from this perspective because he made this effort for their and their children's sake. He was not manipulating or coercing them because of his position. He also knew that national pride was lacking, and the people felt humiliated and despondent, and the completion of this project meant more than the restoration of a wall. Nehma took on the headaches and sacrifices necessary to leave his comfy position in the king's court and serve his people through bold, servant leadership.

My friend Una Martone is the president and CEO of Leadership Harrisburg. She is an ardent proponent and practitioner of servant leadership. Una believes self-awareness is critical for servant leaders but not as common as one might think. Una provides some valuable guidance on this leadership issue:

There is a huge self-awareness gap in our society today. According to research conducted by The Eurich Group, nearly 95 percent of people believe that they are self-aware, but only 10-15 percent of people actually are. The research validates what I've witnessed throughout my career in leadership development. I've observed that many people focus on self-awareness only in terms of their strengths and weaknesses. They know who they are and so believe themselves to be self-aware. But they are missing the second and, perhaps, more important part of the equation. Self-awareness also includes an understanding of your impact on others. When you walk into a room are you bringing the energy UP or bringing it down? At its core, self-awareness includes things like using manners, smiling at people, being positive even in difficult situations, staying out of judgement, and a constant reflection on your actions, exchanges, and thoughts. Do your conversations center around you and your ideas or are you more curious about others? Do others seek you out because they know you'll listen, or do they seek coaching elsewhere? If you struggle with answering these questions on your own, engage with a trusted mentor and meet regularly to discuss your continued growth as a leader. Self-awareness is essential to servant leadership and the building block upon which all other servant leadership characteristics are stacked.

To embrace this model, one must repeatedly ask themselves some hard questions:

* Why am I motivated to lead?
* Why do I want to accomplish certain goals?

- What am I willing to do to get there?
- Do I sense an underlying need to control methodology details for my subordinates?
- Do I trust my followers?
- Do my *followers* trust me?
- What are my core values?
- How interested am I in controlling others' behavior?
- Do I genuinely care about fellow workers?
- Do I listen to people?
- Do I care about their opinions and respect their skills and passion?
- Do I ask good questions?
- Am I good at encouraging people around me?
- Do I feel better when I receive accolades or when someone who follows me gets the cheers?
- How do I want to be known?

My good friend and mentor, Jim, calls this your "hallway" reputation. A hallway reputation is what people say about you during casual conversations with other employees over lunch or during cocktail hour after work.

Food for Thought

How often and in what ways do you thank people who follow you? Do you have systems for showing appreciation? If you have a trusted colleague or follower, inquire about your hallway reputation. The term "know thyself" is a critical leadership trait.

On a scale of one to ten, what would you say is your "empathy" quotient? Can you identify situations in which you find it difficult to empathize?

Read Philippians 1:12-25. Consider the Apostle Paul's servant attitude. What are some of his character traits and actions that reveal his leadership approach?

Bodyguard Tactic Forty-Five

WHY WE DO WHAT WE DO

"Leadership is ultimately about people, not profit or projects."

Have you ever felt used by a leader? Have you experienced the sense that you were simply a means to an end that ultimately benefitted the one guiding the project? Being someone's tool is not a good feeling, and people do not like to be used. This fact is equally true for both for-profit and nonprofit institutions.

No matter the size of a company, it exists to meet some societal need, which means that the organization's ultimate purpose ends with real people. Companies also exist to provide employment, which again means people are a critical part of the success equation. Finally, companies exist to make a profit that benefits everyone. Jobs, services, and helpful products are the result of profits. However, when profits take precedence over people, many counterproductive and unpleasant situations emerge. High moral and ethical behavior declines, employee morale wanes, and product quality declines, as does the company.

Companies that provide reasonable wages, benefits, respect, and a healthy work environment win in the end. Employees who are respected, well-trained, and appreciated return the consideration with better products and services, which in turn provide quality products to customers. Good service and quality products produce loyal customers. In short, everyone wins.

Organizations depending upon volunteers will find it critical to pursue a people-first focus. When there is no paycheck waiting as a result of one's labor, volunteer satisfaction means the difference between success and failure. As such, it is helpful to remember *why* people volunteer for a team. Several reasons exist, and a wise leader regularly assesses how well they fulfill the volunteer's motivations. Here are a few.

ALWAYS REMEMBER WHY PEOPLE VOLUNTEER.

People voluntarily join an organization to fulfill a need for significance. Human beings need to sense that their lives matter. Unfortunately, one can fulfill this need not only positively or productively but also in a negative manner. For instance, some people put others down as a means to find significance. Others find constant complaining gives them a sense of self-worth since they feel they understand better than others what is wrong in the world. A leader must recognize that every function contributes to the organization's success and systematically work to make every person see, acknowledge, and enjoy their contribution. Leaders must make volunteers feel valued.

People volunteer because of some personal experience or tragedy. I volunteer with the United Cerebral Palsy organization in our area. I do so because I came to experience and understand that thousands in our region have disabilities. The afflicted and their families and friends share struggles well beyond the "normal" person. I have learned this fact firsthand in recent years since two of my daughters have children with special needs. Many volunteers for this organization do so because they have a child, parent, sibling, or friend grappling with physical or mental disabilities. UCP's motto alone gives me a reason to contribute time and money to this cause. *Every* person should experience "Life Without Limits." Quality leaders learn about volunteers' motivations and appreciate the deep connection between the volunteer service and the experience that motivated them to act.

My friend Janeen Latin is the president and CEO of UCP of Central Pennsylvania. She knows well the importance of meeting the needs of her clients, and equally as critical is the organization's ability to care for employees and volunteers. Janeen comments on the value of volunteer and employee care:

As a nonprofit human service organization, we rely on many people to fulfill our mission. One of our core culture principles is person focused. At UCP, we are person focused because we ensure that each person's interests and needs are the driving force behind our actions. This principle transcends not only the people we support, but also our employees and volunteers. We not only focus on the transactional relationship but understanding each person at a deeper level and understanding specifically why they do what they do. For employees this is accomplished through conversation and soliciting feedback through formal and informal channels and using that information to inform decisions. For volunteers this means connecting with each person on a personal level and understanding the reason they are selfless with their time so you can nurture the mutual relationship. As an organization, we believe that never wavering from the person-focused principle is a win-win.

> "WE BELIEVE THAT NEVER WAVERING FROM THE PERSON-FOCUSED PRINCIPLE IS A WIN-WIN."
> — JANEEN LATIN

Personal values inspire volunteers. Most people believe they are responsible for "giving back" or "passing on" their good fortune.

People volunteer motivated by guilt. Unfortunately, guilt is motivation to offer one's time and money for a cause. It is the responsibility of the leader to employ methods to move this person from a mindset of guilt to one of freedom and fulfillment.

Local churches are not profit-driven organizations, or at least they shouldn't be. A church, by nature and biblical charter, is a people-focused enterprise. However, churches can lose their focus in other ways. There are telltale signs that a congregation and its leaders are losing their people focus. Here are a few.

Undue emphasis on "numbers": There were a few times in my career as a pastor when I allowed my focus to shift to an unhealthy view of attendance statistics. I came through graduate school when the study of church growth was the rage. My master's degree focus was on church growth. The Bible teaches that the church should grow since growth is a sign that members and regular attendees possess a vital, enjoyable faith. People who love their God and their church naturally want to share those relationships with friends and family. If a church is healthy, it is a people movement that expands. However, like CEOs with profit motives, pastors can get off-kilter by worrying more about statistics than people. One national magazine produced a yearly report on the top one hundred fastest-growing and largest churches in America. Pastors, including myself, scrambled to see who made the "top one hundred" each year. I'm not sure God was so impressed. Whenever I allowed myself to become unduly concerned with our numbers, it was always a losing game that I regretted.

The multiplication of rules: Any organization needs rules and policies that entail what people, including staff members, can and cannot do. However, a wise leader keeps the number of rules to a minimum. Why? Rules, by nature, imply that "we do not trust you to do the right thing." For instance, a staff person might take advantage of a flexible schedule allowance and end up keeping no schedule, causing numerous problems. Rather than working with the individual personally, the leader might create a rule regulating all employees' schedules, which punishes other staff members for one colleague's mistake. The new policy subtly tells employees, "I don't trust you." When leaders multiply rules to keep people in line, they usually reveal insecurity or the need to control people, neither of which are healthy ways of leading.

Holding a "fortress" mentality: One of the responsibilities of church leaders is to maintain sound teaching in all areas of the church. But some pastors and church boards view themselves primarily as keepers of the kingdom. They see themselves as guards charged with warding off doctrinal threats. In their minds, the wolves of false teaching are always at the door. The result is an unhealthy emphasis on sound doctrine at the cost of caring for people. I've heard this called "bibliolatry." As Jesus taught, the scriptures were made *for* man. Man was not made for the scriptures. Overemphasis on "sound doctrine" often results with the church losing sight of its mission, or main thing, which is to seek out and love those who do not know Christ.

Throughout rebuilding the wall, Nehma repeatedly responded to community needs. When the builders were afraid of intimidating threats, he encouraged those who feared for their lives, and he provided solutions even while the project continued. When news came that people experiencing poverty in the community were being exploited, the compassionate leader slowed construction work to provide aid. He understood that well-cared-for workers give their best labor.

As important as the restoration project was to Nehma, the people were more critical, and he understood and responded well to the truth that God would be honored most by those who felt the Father's care and compassion. He must represent God to the community.

Food for Thought

In what ways are you directly investing in your employees or volunteers? What systems have you established toward this end? Are there individuals or a department devoted to employee and volunteer appreciation? If your organization depends upon voluntary donors, how do you consistently show appreciation for their sacrifice? Do you have a "care plan" for employees, volunteers, and donors?

As a leader, how do you view rulemaking? When confronted with an uncomfortable issue is your knee-jerk reaction to create new rule? Do you tend towards thinking that somehow more rules bring people closer to Jesus?

Read John 21:15-23. Jesus felt compelled to navigate the loss of confidence and purpose of one of His key players, Peter. How did the Teacher's focus on Peter support the mission that awaited him? What did observing this episode do for the other disciples watching the conversation?

Bodyguard Tactic Forty-Six

GIVE IT A REST!

"But while all this was going on, I was not in Jerusalem, for in the thirty-second year of Artaxerxes king of Babylon I had returned to the king." —Nehemiah 13:6

As you are reading this, your heart is beating about **4,800 times** per hour. That's a whopping **115,200 times** per day. Over the course of a year, your heart will beat about **42,048,000 times**! If you live to be **eighty** years old, your heart will have beaten approximately **3,363,840,000 times**. That should make you tired just reading about it. Your heart is indeed a workhorse. It never stops, and if it does, you won't be reading this anymore.

But, in fact, your heart does stop. It stops just as many times as it beats. For every beat there is a rest. And without the rest you would be dead in short order.

I became acutely aware of this in 2008 when my heart went into atrial fibrillation. AFib, as it is called, is a condition where certain cells in the heart muscle go rogue and start sending signals for the heart to beat when it should not. Before long, the upper chambers of the heart are beating so fast and so irregular that there is little rest and few, if any, full beats. This means that blood can coagulate in the heart and possibly be driven into the brain causing a stroke. An AFib heart needs some rest!

AFib sufferers often don't even know they have the condition. Other times a person becomes tired and feels a kind of quivering in the chest. Sometimes this silent killer is not noticed until it is too late. As hard as the heart works, it needs its rest to do its job correctly.

Like the normal heart, we may work long and hard, but there must be rest and rejuvenation on a regular basis. This is not something valued by American culture. People are judged by their ability to work and produce, not their ability to rest. We like the example of the Energizer Bunny that just keeps going and going and going. For most folks their ability to keep going and going is a badge of honor. After all, there is always so much to do, and I can do it all!

This is especially true of those in helping professions like ministry, and people in leadership roles. Pastors are driven to heal the never-ending flow of hurts in their flock and people expect them to be at their best every moment of every day. Leaders feel that they must stay ahead of their followers, and one does not stay ahead by resting. At least it seems. Many leaders feel guilty any time they are not working, and in fact, many never really leave work. Even on vacation they stay connected, believing that it will all fall apart without them. This demonstrates insecurity or arrogance, by the way.

I suppose if hearts could talk, they would feel the same way. "Man, that foot down there just keeps needing oxygen! It's relentless. It never stops. I need to beat faster and work harder." The truth is, no matter what the size, the flow of need in every organization never stops—ever. So, if you are leading, you better just keep going and going and going.

WE WERE NOT DESIGNED TO BE THE ENERGIZER BUNNY.

The problem is that humans were not designed to live in this manner. God made us in such a way that our work/rest cycles are absolutely necessary and the only way we stay healthy. If the human heart beats too much, for too long, the muscles stretch and become much less effective, and likely to wear out sooner than designed. The path of leadership, and especially pastoral and nonprofit leadership, is strewn with casualties of overworked and under-rested practitioners. Some buckle under the pressure, while others check out for good and do something else to make a living.

Many find other ways to establish false rest. False rest is when the leader turns to drinking too much, watching pornography, or parking themselves in front of a television for several hours a day. These practices release the "feel-good" hormone dopamine, which gives someone a temporary sense of euphoria. However, the feeling does not last and is addictive. What appears to be rest from high-pressure labor causes more stress in the long run. These and other similar unhealthy distractions are not rest. They are replacement. It is replacing one unhealthy practice with another. Perhaps that explains the workaholic problem as well.

Interestingly, Jesus seemed to find plenty of time for rest and we never sense that He felt overwhelmed by the needs of all those followers. He temporarily took leave of a successful ministry to recharge his batteries.

> ## JESUS FREQUENTLY TOOK TIME AWAY FROM A SUCCESSFUL MINISTRY TO REST.

How could He do this? How could time away be more important to Him than His actual ministry? Jesus's rest pattern was amazing considering that His job description was to save the world and show people how to live rich, full lives in the process. The line of people who needed His leadership stretched around the world. Yet, strangely enough, we sometimes saw the Miracle Worker walking away from a needy crowd, not toward them. He deliberately did not heal everyone. He frequently told His leaders-in-training to get away from the crowds. He never allowed other people to set His priorities or His schedule. There was always time for something other than work. I would say with tongue firmly in cheek, many leaders find themselves in much more demand than the Son of God. Meanwhile, they are desperately in need of rest and don't even know it.

Your brain needs to take a break! Different activities produce different kinds of brain waves. Activity, rest, daydreaming, and sleep all produce different waves, and our brains need to experience all four states regularly. During periods of rest, our minds chemically change, and this different state of mind replenishes our ability to focus, create, and process information it has recently experienced as well as integrate new information with other ideas.

One of my less-than-smart practices for many years was trying to work 24/7/365 and it took a toll on my well-being. I felt that I must always be on call and available to people in our church, and there was always so much work to get done. How could I take a break? Duh, the answer was simple—stop working! It is amazing how well the world continues to operate without your active contribution every minute.

Nehma was an ardent supporter of the command to take a day off (Sabbath) once a week. Did the bodyguard observe this practice simply because it was a law or was there another motivation? Nehma certainly believed the day off was to be dedicated to the Lord, but he was a wise leader and knew the value of this "rule" in the first place. Humans are not designed to work 24/7/365, and when they do, it is a recipe for burnout and physical exhaustion. Secondly, a mind and body that is never rested does not produce peak performance. Even professional athletes take rest every seven to ten days. If they do not, they are far more prone to injury, which will force them to rest far longer than they desire.

Nine years ago, my nephew and I took a forty-day sabbatical leave and walked the famed Camino Way across Spain. The journey gave us plenty of time to learn about the value of Sabbath rest and we may yet write a book on the subject together. Let me share a few of my nephew, Joseph's conclusions about the subject.

I define Sabbath as "giving life generative space." Ask the question, "In this moment, what gives life generative space?"

To help try to identify what kind of generative rest you need, break healthy rest into these categories.

Healthy rest includes these factors:

* Relaxation
* Recovery
* Reflection
* Rejuvenation
* Re-creation
* Resetting

Rest is an activity. When you see it this way, it allows you to focus on the activity you need at the time to recover Sabbath.

There are also unhealthy rest activities. Many fall into an undefined unhealthy rest, which doesn't give life generative space and can foster false hope for recovery.

There can be moments of Sabbath throughout your day. Recognize them and see them as rest.

Sabbath is the only "Christian discipline" God practices. It's a practice of letting life breathe deeply. It's an act of strength, not exhaustion. God doesn't practice it out of exhaustion. But, when ignored, we become exhausted because we haven't given life the needed generative space.

> **REST IS THE ONLY SPIRITUAL DISCIPLINE GOD PRACTICES.**

After work on the wall was completed and celebrated, Nehma returned to Persia. The journey home would allow him time to process his accomplishments without pressure and constant expectations of his followers. The bodyguard demonstrates the importance of not only taking weekly rest, but also extended periods as well.

Here are a few suggestions for working regular Sabbath rest into your schedule.

* **Stop the victim mentality.** "If I don't do this, nobody will." That statement is likely not true and exaggerated. Training people to take your place is one of the first maxims of quality leadership. Do not give in to the "tyranny of the unurgent."
* **Set boundaries and keep to them.** If you are leading a service organization, do not allow your clients 24/7 access to you, which sometimes means not giving out your phone

number. Explain your boundary and tell them who to contact when you are off.

* **Get over yourself.** The organization will get along just fine without you, and if it does not, something is wrong that needs to be addressed.

* **Curb your unhealthy desire to be needed.** Some leaders get such a rush of dopamine when the phone rings and they know it is someone needing help that it is addictive. We all want to be needed, but don't let that desire get out of hand and admit it when it has.

* **Discipline yourself to stop thinking about work when you are not working.** You will never actually rest until you let go of your daily responsibilities.

* **Don't be bullied by a workaholic boss.** I've known bosses who expect employees, or church boards that expect pastors, to answer all emails, text messages, and phone calls even on their days off and vacations. Your personal health and family come before work—period. Don't let someone else's unhealthy practices be forced upon you. Say, "No."

Food for Thought

Do you take regular days off each week? If not, why?

How do you rest and restore yourself on Sabbath days? Is it working?

Examine yourself based upon the six directives mentioned. Where are you weak and where are you strong? What will you do about your weaknesses?

What activities "fill your bucket," giving you a sense of rest?

Do you expect your followers to do the same practice, and do you provide them time off to do so?

Read Mark 6:31 and Luke 5:16. Do you believe Jesus's common practice was only for prayer? What did prayer in "lonely places" provide the Teacher? Do you think the Savior enjoyed other times of rest, even with his close friends? Consider Mary, Martha, and Lazarus.

Bodyguard Tactic Forty-Seven

A Lesson From Archery

"People will return to their old ways as soon as the pressure is off."

Have you ever strung a recurve bow? I enjoyed archery when I was young and became a proficient practitioner, and I often fished with my forty-pound recurve bow. Hitting a fish in the water is not easy, but I snagged a few through the years. One weighed thirty-two pounds, and that's no fish story!

Stringing a recurve bow can be tricky. You must place one loop of the bowstring on one end of the bow, then carefully bend the bow, often over your knee, and put the other loop on the other end. If you miss, you are liable to experience forty pounds of force smacking you in the head.

There are some interesting facts about archery. A bow is rather useless unless it is strung, and as soon as you let off the stringing pressure, the shooting device will always return to its original shape. The pressure created by bending the bow against its will gives it power. No tension, no force.

People are like archery bows. They can be taught, encouraged, and convinced to change their behavior, but it is a slow, sometimes arduous process. Until a new behavior is thoroughly instilled, they will return to their former behavior and way of thinking as soon as the pressure is off.

A few years ago, I lost about fifty pounds over several months. I accomplished this feat using four weight-loss aids. First, I started using an application on my smartphone that allowed me to track my calorie and nutrition intake. I found that recording what you consume is eye-opening. My favorite food is pizza, but I learned to "save up" calories if I wanted to consume it because those pies are packed with calories and carbohydrates. I also knew that I would be unable to stuff down entire pizzas twice a week and lose weight, and I learned to stop myself long before I finished a pie.

Secondly, I regularly exercised using a combination of weight training and cardio activity. This practice increased my health and helped burn extra calories.

Thirdly, I changed my eating habits in general. More protein, fewer carbs, more veggies, and fewer hamburger rolls were now part of my healthier regular diet.

Finally, I learned of a new medicine that sometimes helps one control urges to overeat. My doctor prescribed it, and I found it helpful.

For reasons unknown, I incrementally stopped adhering to my new system. What do you think happened? Yes, I gained back nearly every pound. As soon as I let up the pressure to change, I reverted to my former unhealthy ways. Now I am performing the process all over again!

Human brains are resistant to change. We make decisions based on neural pathways created over time. Say we grew up singing hymns in church, and we enjoyed this style of music. Singing the same genre of music week after week conditions our brains to feel comfortable with this music. The brain also subtly remembers this activity fondly, sees no good reason to take a chance on changing it, and believes the modification would be threatening. Our fight or flight response kicks in and people say, "I'm outta here," or, "It will be a cold day in hell when I sing those songs!" I guess most church members don't use that lingo, but that is what they mean, no matter how they say it.

To perceive a need to change music styles, one must be convinced that the new manner is more effective and can be just as enjoyable. To initiate this innovation, the leader must appeal to more profound convictions that supersede music preferences.

Many Christ-followers deeply desire to witness people who start attending church and eventually accept Jesus as their Savior and Lord. When someone far from God tells their story and enters the waters of baptism, most Christians consider it a special moment, and they are often willing to make sacrifices for the opportunity to witness such a life change. Drawing people to Jesus can even supersede their desire for the known.

However, our brains have already been hardwired for particular preferences, and it is a long process to rewire the system. Meanwhile, we learn that we can often have it both ways. We can still love hymns as much as ever while embracing music more suitable to new generations of seekers. But the leader must appreciate that to make the contemporary music style integral to the service, pressure must be applied for many weeks, months, or even years until the unknown becomes the new norm.

A wise leader discovers their followers' deepest motivations and repeatedly appeals to those principles as a rationale for change and improvement. This is a long process that must be addressed many times from numerous angles. Otherwise, people drift toward the familiar, even if it is harmful. If they discover that people do not know or understand foundational principles, change must start there.

Nehma returned to serve his boss back in Persia for about twelve years but then returned to Jerusalem. The bodyguard quickly learned that building a wall does not equal changing hearts and ways of living. His friend Eli was an associate of Tobias and allowed this crook to use temple storerooms as self-storage units. Meanwhile, offerings that were supposed to be directed to the Levites serving in the temple had ceased, so the temple keepers had to return to their own property to survive.

Then the governor learned that many were dishonoring the Sabbath by working and selling goods in Jerusalem. Nehma quickly nixed this practice and scorned them for this infraction of God's law. Finally, their leader learned that many were intermarrying with foreign pagan women and men, and their children could not even speak their native language, Hebrew. He cursed this group and beat some of them until they swore to discontinue this practice as instructed by God's law.

When the cat's away, the mice will play!

When you've patiently and artfully initiated a significant change in your organization, here are some suggestions for making it stick.

* **Over-Communicate**: If you've done it correctly, you have already communicated and over-communicated the need and the new solution. Most experts suggest at least ten touch points of quality conveyance, but I contend that you cannot over-communicate every aspect and rationale for

A Lesson From Archery

what you consider improvement. The temptation is to back off after one feels the goal has been implemented. Not good. Studies show that it takes at least a year to turn a ship, and 75 percent of all attempts fail.

* **Count the Cost**: Do your best to determine beforehand if the cost to your organization will be worth the loss associated with change. It is helpful not to get in the middle of a costly initiative only to discover that the payoff is not worth the price. This means keeping your personal interests and preferences at bay. Is this idea about *you* or the organization and its purpose? Will it really propel our mission and goals?

* **Do the Tough Thing**: Continually determine and be willing to engage naysayers or questioners in honest conversations. Emails, announcements, and marketing pieces will not keep some folks on board. Pay the price of tough talks. You usually learn something from every discussion and can include the new revelation in upcoming communications. If one person has the nerve to approach you, there are probably many more with the same concerns. If you are unwilling to talk with them, they will not be ready to stay on board.

* **Celebrate Often**: Celebrate every tiny victory related to the change, primarily through human stories. One good story is worth a hundred informational announcements.

* **Plan Ahead**: Plan how you will celebrate milestones.

* **Admit Your Mistakes**: Be open and honest about failures. Many leaders stumble, trying to cover up a wrong turn. People offer grace when leaders are open and honest but condemnation when they are caught covering or lying about a failure.

* **Expect Setbacks**: Often three steps forward and two steps back will be the pattern of progress.

* **Persevere!** Most lasting changes take longer than planned.
* **If It's Not Worth the Struggle, Don't Take the Risk.**
* **Don't Give Up!** No matter how well you plan and implement, sometimes your plan will fall flat. Perhaps you discover midstream that your idea was not so good after all! There will always be another opportunity. Don't give up.
* **Keep Your Pride in Check**: Don't let pride get the best of you. It is good to celebrate success, but keep it in perspective. Good leaders change organizations every day, and you are one leader in a long parade of leadership success stories.

Food for Thought

Can you identify changes in your life that did not stick? Why did they fade?

What motivated you to make a change? What was the process of change? If you made some improvements that endured, what process made the decision become a permanent part of your life? How can your self-evaluation teach you about leading change in your organization? Where have you failed in implementing change, and why? What would you do differently?

Read Nehemiah 13. In Nehemiah's absence, many Israelites and citizens of Jerusalem returned to their former ways. Why? Did Nehemiah fail in the matter of securing reforms? If so, why? If backsliding was inevitable, why? If you were Nehemiah, would you consider yourself a failure as a leader?

Bodyguard Tactic Forty-Eight

Tackling The Change Monster

*"Change is a slow-moving boat headed upstream.
A good leader is a change agent."*

"And no one after drinking old wine wants the new, for they say, 'The old is better.'" This is Jesus's thoughts on change as recorded in Luke 5:39 NIV.

It is not easy to turn a ship around, and it takes a lot of space; the larger the ship, the more complex it is—and the longer it takes—to rotate. On average, it takes from five to twenty minutes to turn a merchant vessel 180 degrees, and the turning radius is usually three to five times the ship's length.

It took about five years to complete the badly needed change. I arrived at my new ministry in 1982, excited and ready to implement new ideas, particularly the worship service methods in the little church on Good Hope Road. Capital Area was only about five years old when I arrived, but it might as well have been a hundred. The pioneers of the congregation were locked into most of their traditions and methods. Worship services were an hour and fifteen minutes of boredom. The music was dull and old-fashioned, weekly communion meditations were often like mini-sermons before the sermon, and the atmosphere lacked joy and enthusiasm. I would never have invited an unchurched friend to be our guest, which was embarrassing to my wife and me.

I was fresh out of college and didn't know much about leading a church, though I had served in management before going to college. In my naïve ignorance, I simply started changing things. The first Sunday I preached, I got on stage with a guitar, and to everyone's surprise I proceeded to belt out a semi-rock and roll gospel song. I had no idea this instrument was taboo unless you were attending church camp. Wait until they saw the drums on stage!

Kindly the congregation gave me a pass thinking, *Oh, he's young and inexperienced, and he will catch on to how we do things around here.* I did catch on, which made me more determined to change how they did things around there. We started singing contemporary choruses of the time, and the guitar became a fixture on stage most weeks. Every week I fielded complaints, some not very benevolent. Still, I persisted because I believed this improvement was backed by solid theology, and it was more than a personal preference issue.

Ever so slowly, our services morphed and grew. New people attended regularly, and the church was growing. By the time five or so years had elapsed, there was usually a keyboard, bass, two electric guitars, and drums on stage. I preached many sermons about worship and researched and wrote a white paper mapping out the new philosophy, fielding questions, and addressing common objections to praise and worship's updated "contemporary" style.

Progress was so slow and arduous that it felt like I had been hammering this anvil an entire lifetime. Well, the change worked and didn't work.

PROGRESS IS OFTEN SLOW AND ARDUOUS.

Most people loved the new style and invited their friends to join us. However, about thirty-five church pioneers had all they could take, so they left the church to start a new one. The new venture lasted only a few months. I was sad that the situation came to that conclusion but plenty happy to have those folks off my back.

Churches are like ships, even small congregations, and it is challenging to convince invested members that change is necessary and beneficial. Understanding this phenomenon makes change management a delicate balance of art and science. Nonprofit and for-profit organizations are no different since they too are comprised of human beings, and people generally don't like change because it makes them uneasy and insecure. Change also subtly implies that they are doing something wrong, which nobody wants to be told.

These factors mean patience is a supreme virtue for leaders who want to implement new methods and strategies. At the same time, like Nehma, patience should not allow one to stray from the truth and to call it out when people do stray.

After the wall was complete, Nehma called everyone together and had Ezra read the Law in their presence. The words they had probably not heard in years, perhaps ever, caused great consternation and sadness. However, Nehma quickly squelched this response and urged the community to rejoice and party. Finally, he dedicated the wall with much pomp and circumstance, and then he called upon the nation to make oaths of support for the commands and teachings of the Law.

The lists of oaths were long and required changes in many members' thoughts and behaviors. Community leaders and the assembly gave their words, which turned out to be worthless. The Israelites did not genuinely change their thinking and, thus, their behavior.

Nehma headed back to meet with Artaxerxes and give him an update. It was also common for governors and officials to come before the monarch and reaffirm their allegiance.

He may have returned to Jerusalem after only about a year, but when he did he found the community sliding back down a slippery slope to where they were the first time the bodyguard arrived. It is indeed challenging to teach old dogs new tricks.

Once again, the governor applied pressure for lasting reforms, but it's doubtful they endured. There were most likely numerous people who sincerely changed, but another large group returned to their old sinful ways as soon as the pressure was removed. Such is the nature of the change process. There is always a broad spectrum of adaptation to new ways, ranging from serious dedication to lip service to outright rejection. A leader must be prepared to address all three groups.

Here are some suggestions for initiating and implementing lasting change in an organization:

* **Raise Awareness.** People become so accustomed and comfortable with their environment that they see no need to try to change it. Whenever I was looking to make a significant change in our organization, I started throwing out thought-provoking ideas about two years ahead of my expected implementation. I often floated a possible change in a board meeting while calculating various acceptance lev-

els. If I could not convince the church leaders of the need to change, it would be unlikely others would get on board. It is vital to revisit the idea from different angles using facts and figures and a tug at their heartstrings. I also spread this information to key leaders throughout the congregation; by the time I made weighty proposals, the possible endeavor was not "new" news. Most people don't like surprises.

* **Do Your Homework.** Many people need more than the presentation of strong "feelings"; they need factual information that explains the need and possible solutions. "I feel like God is leading us to do this" does not hold water with many followers. They may think, *Well, he didn't tell me that, and I'm not feeling it.*

* **Communicate Through Concentric Rings of Influencers.** When embarking upon an improvement that requires change, start with the smallest group of leaders with large circles of influence in the organization. For me, this meant starting with three or four trusted advisors, then staff members, then the elder board, then influential people, then the ministry and small group facilitator teams, and finally the entire congregation.

* Here is an important observation. A local church is one of the few organizations where the senior leader can speak to all the troops weekly. If the change agent presents new material three weeks in a row, they will likely reach eighty to ninety percent of the organization. New ideas and awareness-raising can happen during sermons, announcements, video presentations, and social media. Information can be introduced subtly over time, slowly revealing a need and proposing possible solutions.

* **Communicate Often and in Various Formats.** It is difficult to over-communicate during this process. Most people must hear something ten to twelve times before the information is understood and supported. Many new programs and initiatives fail because of the lack of communication. Impart knowledge considering different personality types who receive ideas in various manners. There are five generally recognized adopter categories, and each one can be approached appropriately to their willingness to embrace new ideas.

    * Innovators   2.5%
    * Early Adopters   13.5%
    * Early Majority   34%
    * Late Majority   34%
    * Laggards   16%

It is helpful to remember that what you are presenting to a new audience is something you've been thinking about and researching for a long time. Cut them some slack—it's new news to them.

Technology has created numerous venues to disseminate information. Use them all to your advantage.

* **Seriously Consider Generational Approaches to Adopting New Ideas.** Millennials receive information differently from Gen-Xers and Gen-Zers, etc. Smart leaders communicate appropriately.

* **Be Open and Honest.** Openly admit when you've made a mistake. Take responsibility.

* **Offer Opportunities for Communal Conversation and Fishing for New Ideas.** It is next to impossible to think of every angle when implementing a newfangled idea. Be

humble enough to court and recognize valuable input to your vision.

* **Recognize and Reward Those Willing to Take a Chance on Something Novel.** People like to be recognized in big and small ways and will work harder when cited appropriately.

* **Use Favorable Terms to Replace the Word "Change" Whenever Possible.** Usually, a change is an intended *improvement*, so use constructive language to explain the new idea rather than an often negatively perceived word like change. One of my good friends and mentors, Jim Czupil, wisely once explained to me, "Don, stop calling it change. Call it an improvement or upgrade. People don't like to change, but they do want improvement."

Food For Thought

How patient are you? Do you get angry and frustrated when people are not open to your new ideas? What are the concentric circles of influence in your organization? What category of adopter are you? Have you developed a plan for recognizing and rewarding quality thinking and labor?

Read Nehemiah 2:11 and all of chapter three. Can you identify the rings of influence Nehma utilized to complete this project?

Bodyguard Tactic Forty-Nine

Making It Last

"Leaders must create systems that ensure growth."

A few years ago, we decided to change the name of our church. Rebranding a name for a local congregation is a delicate undertaking. I had been tossing this idea out in different circles for well over a year and finally decided to pull the trigger. Our name, Capital Area Christian Church, was outdated and now inaccurate since we had a campus that was not in the capital area. I was also planning to retire sometime soon and determined that I could leave this as a gift for my successor since it was a significant hurdle with which he would not have to concern himself. I felt the new senior leader would have plenty to keep him busy without this project.

The elder board discussed the improvement several times over the past few years, and I sensed they would be ready to make an affirmative decision so that I could get the ball rolling. We hired a branding company to lead us through the process, which was expensive but well worth the expenditure. Fortunately, this company was also designing an expansive addition to our facilities, so they already knew the church in depth. Meanwhile, I ramped up marketing for the upcoming news with the entire congregation.

Our branding company brought together my staff and three other key leaders, one a board member, and held hours of workshop sessions, helping us clearly define our identity, hopes, and dreams. They told us the name should reflect the personality of our church. After brainstorming and researching church names, we narrowed the field to six possibilities. We carefully examined and discussed each option and then began to vote, narrowing names to three. We extensively discussed each one and finally arrived at the new moniker, Vibrant - A Christian Church.

We then began discussing a logo and all the associated branding materials until we arrived at a new logo, color scheme, and any necessary marketing materials. The fruit of our labor was a branding book that determined and defined the parameters for all printed and online materials, indoor and outdoor signage, and a strategy to ensure proper use of the new materials.

Meanwhile, I discussed the process and product with a staff person from a large church in our area. I proudly showed her the brand products, for which I received encouragement and affirmation. However, she explained that her church went through the same process several years earlier, and she told me they also possessed a detailed brand book, but no one ever used it! No system was ever developed to ensure its implementation.

Follow-up systems count! Fortunately, we had indeed devised and implemented a strategy to ensure the brand's use across the board for all church departments, with a staff member responsible for monitoring and reporting success or failure back to the team. I've been gone from Vibrant for three years now, and they appear to still be using the brand book, so I've got that going for me.

Long-term planning to maintain lasting change might be the process's most overlooked component. Why? Because it is boring. All the fun stuff is over, so it's time to move on to something else. If leaders do not plan long-term implementation and monitoring for a new initiative, it is likely to fall flat, and leaders often won't even know it.

In my article, "Why Your Life Sucks and What You Can Do About It," I state, "Every vision must be equipped to become a reality" (donmarkhamilton.com). I have failed enough to become intimately familiar with the validity of this principle.

So what are the vital components of the ongoing growth of new endeavors? Here are a few.

* **Determine a detailed marketing strategy** to introduce the new program or product. Suppose yours is a for-profit company, and you are implementing something you want to become part of the culture. In that case, this strategy must extend to baseline employees and those higher up the food chain, especially if those are the workers who represent your company to the public. How will this idea be introduced at every necessary level, and by whom? Who will monitor, be responsible for, and regularly report on progress and failures? How will we determine our success?

* **Develop an atmosphere of open discussion about wins, losses, and solutions.** Those responsible must implement a method to receive genuine feedback on progress. What will this method be, and how high will the process go in the organization? Where does the buck stop on this initiative?

* **Provide ongoing training,** which helps employees and volunteers understand how the improvement applies to their jobs and how to make it part of their routines. Consistent employee and volunteer development shows concern for their enjoyment of their jobs and improves performance. One-and-done training is almost useless.

* **Determine what success looks like** and allow the picture to morph as leaders learn more about how well the new idea works. Nearly all new endeavors need to be tweaked, but the "how" only comes after people put it into practice. A leader unwilling to listen and learn is likely to fail.

* **Reward success.** As part of the long-term implementation strategy, determine ways followers can be recognized for quality work.

* **Find champions of the change and tell their story.** Story is more potent than statistics. The average person could give a rip about statistics, but one success story goes a long way in encouraging and promoting the virtues of a new program.

* **Be willing to face the reality that every new proposition does not turn out as planned.** Humility allows leaders to know how and when it is time to abandon a "brilliant" idea. You have just learned one way not to succeed in a particular area of company life, and only people who often fail ultimately succeed.

When Nehma returned from his visit with the king, he discovered that whatever long-term reform strategies he had employed did not work. People had already returned to their previous behaviors, and community leadership was ill-equipped to uphold the oaths the community had taken in Nehma's presence—and far from wholehearted in doing so. As they say, "Talk is cheap!" It is a potent lesson that a fifty-two-day project and a week of rejoicing accompanied by new commitments was not long enough to produce lasting thought and behavioral changes. Old habits die hard. If you want to institute significant, lasting change, expect to be in it for the long haul. Plan the entire process well and stick to it.

Food for Thought

What do you want to change in your church, company, or nonprofit? Have you thoroughly employed strategies such as those discussed and covered your bases? Where have you failed? What would you do differently? Where have you been successful?

Read Nehemiah 13. Where did the community fail, and what part, if any, did Nehemiah have in it? What could he have done more effectively?

Bodyguard Tactic Fifty

Close The Loop

"Wise leaders follow up."

It is worth a little more thought about the process of follow-up.

You've worked hard to make your worship service uplifting, inspiring, and relevant. Throughout the process, your first-time guest count has increased. Your follow-up team even came up with an easier attendance registration that increased the percentage of first-time guests willing to let you know they attended your service and offered an easy way to make further inquiries about your church.

However, your dismal second-time attendance rate did not budge. People were not giving your church a second chance. Why? After further inquiry, you discovered that your team did not close the loop. Though there was a reasonable follow-up strategy, after some investigation you learned the system had never been implemented. Guests were not receiving any kind of welcome or thanks for attending, though they permitted you to send them by completing your attendance registration. Even worse, several guests requested more information about your church or a phone call, but they did not receive either.

By this point, several people in your community did not return to your church and told their friends about their bad experiences, resulting in a missed opportunity for even more people to try out your church. Even worse, some requested information about baptism, which they did not receive. There are now seekers in the community who ventured a visit and were moved to inquire about this next step of faith but were rejected by being ignored.

We all have felt the sting of putting ourselves out there only to be ignored or rejected. Like developing systems to secure lasting change, creating effective ways to ensure people receive assistance and aftercare is an endeavor's dull side. Even when follow-up systems exist, they are useless if not implemented, which is often the case. This, too, is not the fun part of the process.

> **WE HAVE ALL FELT THE STING OF PUTTING OURSELVES OUT THERE ONLY TO BE IGNORED OR REJECTED.**

Leadership expert John Maxwell explains the importance of this practice. He compares the need for quality follow-through to a proper golf swing. One of the most challenging aspects of a good golf shot depends heavily on how well the player swings through all the way to the end. If the swing does not include the entire radius, the ball does not travel as far or accurately. Yet many golfers fail because they stop short of completing the swing.

During my thirty-eight-year church ministry, I conducted six capital fundraising campaigns. Carrying out a successful fundraising is a three-to-five-month process of utilizing various marketing strategies to inform, encourage, and challenge church members to make donations above and beyond their regular giving practices. For the pastor, the process is labor-intensive and leaves one worn out at the conclusion.

The campaign team builds excitement through small group gatherings and public announcements using various forms of media, mailings, and social media platforms. The entire process culminates with a banquet similar to a pep rally where attendees make multi-year financial commitments toward the campaign. The campaign banquet is usually very exciting. The project is finally complete, and the team can take a break. Not!

The real work now begins! A separate team must develop and implement a long-term follow-through communication strategy for two or three years, leading to another celebration upon completion. At this point, many campaigns fall short because maintaining this extended follow-up program is not exciting. Over the coming years, communication and information will slow to a trickle. Sometimes donations follow suit, and an opportunity that cannot be reclaimed is missed.

I've also learned this lesson as a writer. Books typically take one to two years to be completed, and that is before the publishing process begins. Writing 70,000 words is not easy. I have worked on this book for about twenty months, and I am nearing the completion of the first draft, which will be reviewed and edited many times. I also write a weekly blog that has lasted 124 weeks to date, along with other articles for publication.

I have learned firsthand the definition of writer's block and fatigue. Staring at a blank page each morning is haunting. There have been weeks where I neglected to keep adding pages to my work throughout the process. My nephew, a successful author, has assisted and encouraged me throughout this challenge. I'll never forget one discussion during one of my dry times, which ended with him making a simple statement: "Don, a writer's gotta write!" Who knows how many thousands of books lie on a shelf unfinished? How many articles are only half-written and stored away deeply inside someone's computer memory? If you want to write a book, you've got to follow through over the long haul.

How many unfinished projects gather dust in someone's garage or basement? How many songs still need a chorus three years later? How many company initiatives lie dormant? After two years pass, how many remodeling jobs are still waiting for completion? How many college degrees still need nine more credits completed for the student to walk across the stage for a diploma?

Fifty-two days had passed, and a brand-new wall now surrounded Jerusalem! A party was thrown, a dedication conducted, and the Law was read aloud to the community. For now, Nehemiah's job was over, so he packed up and headed back to Persia to meet with his boss to bring him the news.

Life was much easier for the builder in Persia. He lived in a beautiful home, enjoyed choice food, and had a much less stressful job. Case closed—goal attained!

But the wise leader never intended to put this chapter behind him and return to his old life. He intended to return to Zion from the start to see how his reforms had changed the community. A year or so later, he again came before the king, asking for permission to return to Jerusalem. The king agreed and sent him on his way.

The governor arrived back in the Holy City to find what he likely suspected would occur in his absence. The people abandoned a long list of reforms, and even a pagan used rooms in the temple for storage. So, the astute leader sets to work putting things right. If any of his excellent work would last, follow-up was critical, and he implemented it well.

Food for Thought

Are there projects or endeavors on which you have neglected to close the loop? How could that have been avoided? Why do leaders frequently fail to appropriately follow up? Can you identify programs in your organization that were left to flounder? Why did the neglect happen?

Do you designate and empower specific long-term follow-up teams as part of the initial strategic plan?

Read John 14:15 and John 14:25-27. Relatively speaking, Jesus spent a short time imparting His teaching and way of life to His followers, yet his organization is still fruitful over 2,000 years later. In what ways did the Teacher ensure follow-up?

Bodyguard Tactic Fifty-One

Movin' On

"Leaders recognize there is a time to move on, hand over the reins, or retire."

When is it time to move on?

There are numerous reasons it might be the right time to move into a new position, but one thing is clear. We will sooner or later turn the page to the next chapter of our lives. Sometimes we leave a job too quickly, while others show that we have stayed too long. Either way, it is usually a tough decision. Going in a new direction is scary because we are sailing into uncharted waters. We can only determine if we have made the right decision by venturing into the unknown.

I retired from a thirty-eight-year pastorate on the last day of May 2020. The need for me to move on became apparent only after many months of grueling responsibility, not the least of which was my wife's twenty-two-month illness and ultimate death. Our church also went through other significant deaths and a rash of spousal cancer among my leaders. One of our elders died in a horrific car crash. A good friend committed suicide, and several close relatives of my staff members also passed. We also changed the name of our church, designed a significant addition to our building, and conducted a capital campaign to raise funds for construction. All this while planning for my successor.

The following year after my wife's death, I slowly realized that I was mentally and physically exhausted, and I had lost most vision for the organization's future. I spoke with trusted advisors and listened to their advice about retirement. Then I decided it was time. It was a good decision! I am now enjoying a new season of life as a blogger, speaker, and writer.

I have a young friend in his thirties who was the general manager of a successful hotel in the area. His hotel has won several awards under his leadership, and for a few years, he thoroughly enjoyed his work. Then COVID-19 hit and changed everything. The hotel employs several individuals who are not career-oriented; they just need a job. However, under his guidance, most performed their job well and helped make the hotel successful.

During the pandemic, many workers at this level quit their employment, and thousands fled the workforce, leaving many small businesses struggling to stay open. He now found himself chronically short-staffed. Employee deficit equates to the G.M. performing nearly every job in the hotel, often working all day and night to maintain the high-quality level he desires.

What was once a rewarding career turned into a nightmare, and there was no end in sight. The situation sapped the joy and fulfillment from the job, and he was chronically exhausted from overwork while losing precious time with his new bride. Joshua concluded that it was time to move on and even change paths completely, which he wisely did.

Nehma completed his mission to rebuild the wall and revive the community. He developed systems to ensure the improvements endured and installed the right people in the right places. The twinge of retirement increased daily as he reflected on his legacy and called upon God to favor him for his faithfulness and hard work.

The aging leader's final season was not pleasurable. The reforms he engineered on his first trip to Jerusalem vanished quickly, and on this trip, his work mainly involved rebuking many segments of the community, including the leadership. Unfortunately, little did he know that this cycle would repeat itself many times in the coming years.

Nehma was not responsible for future generations and was not accountable for the people's actions after his tenure was complete. He was only answerable to his own leadership and calling. Now the aging bodyguard knew it was time to call it quits.

Leaders must accurately and honestly evaluate their environment regularly and be willing to face change when necessary. Whether it is to a new job, career, or retirement, the wise act is to move on to another season of life.

Food for Thought

How does this chapter affect you? Do you see yourself in any of these scenarios? Is it time to determine a new direction, or are you still fulfilled, passionate, and fruitful where you are?

Read Nehemiah 13 and reflect on Nehma's final chapter in Jerusalem.

Bodyguard Tactic Fifty-Two

Looking Back and Moving Forward

"Remember me with favor, my God."

How do you want to be remembered?

I was a Boy Scout when I was young, and it is one of my favorite memories from early adolescence. I rose to the Eagle Scout rank and became a member of the Order of the Arrow. I developed my first leadership chops and learned many valuable lessons through this organization. Some have accompanied me through life.

We often camped out for the weekend at various locations in our state. As you can imagine, thirty or forty adolescent boys can make a massive mess in short order, and trash would often accumulate at Boy Scout campsites. To my Scout leader, this was unacceptable, so he remedied the situation. After breaking camp and removing the tents, cooking equipment, and other necessary items, the entire troop lined up across the campsite area. We then walked purposely through the grounds, picking up trash or anything else that did not belong there. Mr. Friend, our troop leader, taught us a valuable life lesson. He said, "Always leave your campsite, or any other place for that matter, better than you found it."

ALWAYS LEAVE SOMETHING BETTER THAN YOU FOUND IT.

I've carried that principle through nearly every endeavor I've experienced. I try to leave the situation better than I found it. I am confident the wise Scoutmaster is fondly remembered by many men who now practice lessons taught at a campsite.

We make our mark on every position we occupy. We remember what we believe was our contribution and lasting signature and can reminisce with a sense of satisfaction, or perhaps not so much. Most of us will labor at one or two positions where we honestly conclude that we did not give our best, but we hope to review our entire careers and sense we have contributed.

We should derive personal pleasure from our accomplishments, but we also want to leave a quality legacy with our work associates. We should leave a place of employment better than we found it. Sometimes the last chapter of a job leaves a bad taste in our mouths, which is why we go, but an occupation or career should be evaluated in its entirety, not just the last few months.

We will positively affect many lives without knowing it. I received a note today from an old friend. Several years ago, I met he and his wife during a period of great turmoil and strife. They would have likely gone separate ways if they had stayed on the same trajectory. No one gets married believing they will end up divorced, and the journey to that decision is usually miserable. He thanked me for making such a difference in his life as I had enabled the couple to work out their problems and stay together. He told me I had significantly impacted his life and said he could never thank me enough. I had no idea of my positive influence on his life.

WE WILL POSITIVELY AFFECT MANY LIVES WITHOUT KNOWING IT.

If we keep people first and treat them with respect, compassion, and kindness, we will be successful no matter what we do. Our fond legacy is sealed in the memories of many souls.

In 444 B.C., one man responded to a need, a tragedy, by taking chances, working hard, and deliberately improving thousands of lives. We still learn from this person 2,500 years later. Nehemiah, the bodyguard, teaches us many keen life and leadership lessons, even from the grave. If one could learn and come near to the quality of the person with whom we have journeyed, we will have done well.

We must learn a final lesson from the bodyguard. His motivation came from a higher source than King Artaxerxes or the people of Jerusalem. In this man's mind, his life and legacy were all about serving his God, for he knew that the most critical judgment of his life would come from the Almighty, who granted him his life.

I propose this is a noble reason to become the best leader possible. Leaders are self-motivated, but if there does not exist a deeper, more solid foundation, we are liable to find ourselves ultimately way off course. Quality leadership comes from a deeper place than self; it comes from God.

Nehma brilliantly displays his deepest desire when he closes his chronicle by imploring his Maker: "Remember me with favor, my God."

The Creator's affirmation is the most meaningful recognition we could ever receive, and God granted his wish.

It has been good to travel this journey with you, and I hope you have benefited. With the help of God, keep becoming the most exemplary leader you can be. Many lives depend upon you and your determination.

Food for Thought

What legacy have you already left behind? What legacy are you leaving? What do you want people to say at your funeral? Read and remember Nehemiah 13:31.

Don Mark enjoys sharing his experience and wisdom with any group or organization that might benefit. If you would like to book Don for speaking, consulting, or teaching, he can be reached at **www.donmarkhamilton.com** or **donmarkhamilton@gmail.com**. Don also writes a weekly inspirational blog at donmarkhamilton.com if you are looking for inspiration and practical advice about issues we all face in life.

END

Printed in the USA
CPSIA information can be obtained
at www.ICGtesting.com
CBHW021218101124
17197CB00019B/83